Anzhelika Solovyeva

Technology in Russian Strategic Culture
From the Nineteenth Century to the Present Day

CHARLES UNIVERSITY
KAROLINUM PRESS 2024

KAROLINUM PRESS
Karolinum Press is a publishing department of Charles University
Ovocný trh 560/5, 116 36 Prague 1, Czech Republic
www.karolinum.cz
© Anzhelika Solovyeva, 2024
Set and printed in the Czech Republic by Karolinum Press
Layout by Jan Šerých
First edition

This research was supported by the Cooperatio Program at Charles University,
research area Political Science (POLS). The monograph has been published
with the support of the Faculty of Social Sciences, Charles University.

A catalogue record for this book is available from the National Library
of the Czech Republic.

ISBN 978-80-246-5663-2
ISBN 978-80-246-5681-6 (pdf)

https://doi.org/10.14712/9788024656816

The original manuscript was reviewed by Martin Solik, University of Ostrava,
Faculty of Science, Department of Human Geography and Regional
Development; and Marcin Kaczmarski, University of Glasgow, Security
Studies at the School of Social and Political Sciences.

Table of Contents

Acknowledgements	7
List of Abbreviations	8
List of Figures	9
Introduction	11

1. Military Technology in Russian Strategic Thinking	17
1.1 Technology as an Added Value to the Nation's Military Power	18
1.2 Technology as a Component of Defence Capability	20
1.3 Technology as a Political Artefact	21
1.4 Technology as a Highly Constrained Domain	22
1.5 Technology as a Source of Asymmetry	23
1.6 Technology as a Subject of Diplomacy	24
1.7 Concluding Remarks	25

2. Russia's Strategic Cultural Approach to Military-Technological Innovation: An Analytical Framework	27
2.1 Recurring Patterns and Strategic Culture	28
2.2 Triangular Conceptualization of Russia's Strategic Cultural Approach to Military-Technological Innovation	33
2.3 Russia's Organizational Culture: Developmental State Models	41
2.4 Putting the Process in Motion: Conflict Dynamics	43
2.5 Research Methodology	45
2.6 Concluding Remarks	48

3. Rifled Breech-Loading Weapons	49
3.1 The Crimean War as a Major Turning Point	50
3.2 The Quest for Symmetry and Emulative Tendencies	51
3.3 Beyond Technology: Preserving Russia's Asymmetric Advantage	62
3.4 Russia's Diplomatic Response: The Hague Conference of 1899	65
3.5 Synthesis of the Approach: A Range of Asymmetric Reactions	72

4. Nuclear Weapons and Delivery Vehicles   76
4.1 Asymmetric Response to the World's First Atomic Bombings   77
4.2 Forced into the Revolution in Military Affairs   79
4.3 The Circle Closes: The Role of the USSR
in Nuclear Arms Control   98
4.4 Synthesis of the Approach: Two Seemingly Incompatible Paths   103

5. Precision-Guided Conventional Weapons   108
5.1 Conceptualization of Revolutionary Potential   109
5.2 Going (A)symmetric: Failed Ambitions of the USSR   113
5.3 The Gulf War as a Major Turning Point   117
5.4 Asymmetric Assurance: The Nuclear Escalation Ladder   120
5.5 Seeking Symmetry: Embarking on the Revolution
in Military Affairs   123
5.6 Twisted (A)symmetries   138
5.7 Synthesis of the Approach: Ambitions for Symmetry
and Asymmetric Engagement   144

6. Conclusion   149
6.1 Synthesis and Outline of the Russian Strategic
Cultural Approach to Military-Technological Innovation   151
6.1.1 Reactive Innovation   152
6.1.2 Punctuated Innovation   155
6.1.3 Compensatory Innovation   157
6.1.4 Reluctant Innovation   158
6.1.5 Steered Innovation   161
6.1.6 Symbolic Innovation   162
6.1.7 Manpower-Balanced Innovation   165
6.2 Asymmetric Balancing and Further Contributions   167

Summary   171
List of References   172
List of Interviews   197

Acknowledgements

This book is a revised version of my dissertation project. It would not have been possible without all the immense support and encouragement that I received from my dissertation supervisor, Prof. Nik Hynek, his keen guidance, challenging insights, as well as the opportunities he has provided throughout my PhD studies. I am also deeply grateful to Prof. Graeme P. Herd, Dr Nikolai Sokov, Prof. Simon Miles, Dr Stephen Blank, Mr Samuel Bendett, Prof. Iver B. Neumann, Prof. Mark Galeotti, Dr Dmitry Gorenburg, Prof. Vasily A. Veselov, and Dr Scott Keefer[1] for taking the time to speak with me, and sincerely appreciate their insightful comments on different aspects of this research. I owe a special debt to Prof. Simon Miles for drawing my attention to the East View Global Press Archives, and to the Charles University Central Library for helping me access archival documents otherwise unavailable to the general public. Furthermore, this manuscript would have been poorer without the constructive feedback of two dissertation opponents, Prof. Vít Střitecký and Prof. Jan Eichler, and two independent reviewers invited by Karolinum, whose valuable contributions I gratefully acknowledge, too. On a more personal note, I am endlessly grateful to my family for their long-standing support and enduring with great patience my absence on many occasions I would have otherwise shared with them. Last, but certainly not least, this research was supported by the Cooperatio Program at Charles University, research area Political Science (POLS).

---

1   Contributors are listed in accordance with the *List of Interviews*.

List of Abbreviations

A2/AD – anti-access/area denial
ABM – anti-ballistic missile
AI – artificial intelligence
ASAT – anti-satellite weapon
C4ISR – command, control, communications, computers, intelligence, surveillance, and reconnaissance
CIS – Commonwealth of Independent States
CPSU – Communist Party of the Soviet Union
GDP – gross domestic product
ICBM – intercontinental ballistic missile
INF – intermediate-range nuclear forces
ISR – intelligence, surveillance, and reconnaissance
IT-RMA – information technology revolution in military affairs
MAD – mutually assured destruction
MIRV – multiple independently targetable re-entry vehicle
MTR – military-technical revolution
PLSS – Precision Location Strike System
R&D – research and development
RMA – revolution in military affairs
SALT – Strategic Arms Limitation Talks
SDI – Strategic Defense Initiative
SLBM – submarine-launched ballistic missile
UAV – unmanned aerial vehicle
UNAEC – United Nations Atomic Energy Commission

List of Figures

Fig. 1 The strategic cultural approach
to military-technological innovation in Russia   41

Fig. 2 Conflict matrix from the Russian perspective   44

Fig. 3 The approach to military-technological innovation
in Imperial Russia   75

Fig. 4 The approach to military-technological innovation
in the Soviet Union   107

Fig. 5 The approach to military-technological innovation
in post-Soviet Russia   147

Fig. 6 Conflict spectra spurring military-technological
innovation in Russia   156

Introduction

*[I]t is dangerous to transfer the features of your strategic culture
to the opposite side and look at [the opponent's strategic culture]
through the prism of your strategic culture.*
Ivanov (2007: 88)

This book poses the following question: *To what extent there has been a distinct culture of military-technological innovation in Russia?* To exhaustively answer it, the findings from three case studies are employed: the introduction of rifled breech-loading weapons in the nineteenth century, the invention of nuclear weapons in the twentieth century, and the development of precision-guided weapons in the twenty-first century (particularly in Russia as they were developed much earlier in the US). The significance of this research lies in connecting what would traditionally be studied separately, in understanding the interplay between symmetry and asymmetry in Russian military strategy and doctrine, and in tracing the historical roots of Russian military thought and its contemporary conceptual and practical manifestations. As will be demonstrated, modern history related to the construction of warfare technology in Russian military thinking begins with the end of the Napoleonic Wars, and not World War II, as often assumed.

There is plenty of literature on Russian strategic culture, technology, and military doctrine. However, the existing knowledge on Russia's strategic cultural approach to military-technological innovation is fragmented and incomplete. Considerations of the role of military technology are rarely and marginally, if at all, integrated into the discussion on Russian strategic culture. At the same time, there is a rich body of knowledge on Russia's military technology, military doctrine, and military reform. However, in spite of successful efforts to accommodate these findings into Russia's broader strategic and cultural context, there are limitations in the previous studies: their focus has often been limited either to a particular time period, a particular strategic (typically bilateral) context, or a particular kind of technology (either nuclear or conventional). One study is of particular note: Adamsky (2010), one of the key researchers on the subject of Russia's culture of war and military thought, produced a seminal work comparing and contrasting the American, the Russian, and the Israeli cultural approaches to the so-called IT-RMA. Similarly to this book, although in a very different way, he conceptualized this analysis in terms of the relationship between strategic culture and RMA. However, the limitations of this otherwise great contribution to the field for fully grasping the Russian strategic cultural approach to technology are its timeframe, its narrow technological focus, and its comparative lens which means the author's full attention was not devoted to the analysis of Russia. Generally speaking, the gap has been in the inability to link research results across different time periods and across different kinds of technology in the Russian context.

This book seeks to strike a balance between these different approaches and, therefore, its contribution is manifold. First, it focuses on and comprehensively delineates a particular element of Russia's otherwise multi-faceted strategic culture: its strategic cultural approach to military-technological innovation. Second, this study takes a *longue durée* perspective. Not only does it make the most effective analysis of historical patterns of cultural reproduction possible, but the incorporation of nineteenth-century data also allows for stepping outside the traditional boundaries of technology competition in the bilateral relationships between the US and the USSR, NATO and the Warsaw Pact, or the US and post-Soviet Russia. Third, the analysis presented takes a balanced approach to military technology in the Russian context. Both conventional and nuclear capabilities are put under the microscope, providing a nuanced and complex understanding of the Russian cultural approach to military-technological innovation. Fourth, this book relies extensively on primary data obtained from Russian archives. The main archival source is the military-theoretical journal of the War Ministry of the Russian Empire, then the Ministry of Defence of the USSR, and later the Ministry of Defence of the Russian Federation. It was published as *Voennyi Sbornik* ('Military Collection') between 1858–1917 and as *Voennaya*

Mysl' ('Military Thought') from 1937. For this reason, the key objective of this book is defined as tracing the history and culture of predominantly *military* thinking in relation to warfare technologies in Russia. The value added of this research is the author's ability to read and analytically comprehend all the materials in their original language, especially considering the difference between nineteenth-century and modern spellings and vocabularies which may be a barrier for a non-native speaker. Systematic reference to archival records allows the author to complement, refine, and even challenge the existing empirical knowledge. Western sources are brought on board contextually in order to fill data gaps, provide critical insights, and balance opinions where necessary because the goal here is to reconstruct the *inter-subjective* Russian (and Soviet) understanding of related matters. Last, but not least, the author has conducted a series of expert interviews, which represents a distinct contribution. Here the idea was to triangulate the method of documentary research. The pool of interviewees comprised mainly European and American experts for that purpose.

The structure and content of this book is as follows. **Chapter 1** presents a structured literature review which is used as the basis for developing a specific set of arguments. One caveat is important: though inspired by the existing scholarship, these arguments are not derived directly from it. They are also informed by results from the author's previous analysis so this is where the contribution of this book begins. The goal is to build initial empirical knowledge about the relationship between Russia's strategic culture and its approach to military-technological innovation. Six arguments are eventually put forward. They cover a broad range of issues related to Russia's strategic cultural approach to military-technological innovation, including its understanding of the relationship between technology and spirituality, the main rationales behind this kind of innovation, the logical order of steps in the process of military-technological innovation, and the general purpose of arms control and disarmament.

Chapter 2 partially builds on the discussion presented in Chapter 1 but goes significantly beyond: it bridges the available empirical knowledge with theoretical knowledge on military-technological innovation and related processes. Its goal is to theorize the Russian way of innovation in the military-technological realm. In doing so, it takes on board – and links together in a coherent framework – the notion of strategic culture; the concept of RMAs and the popular assumption that responses to them can be symmetric, emulative, or asymmetric; and the logic of arms control and disarmament. This discussion focuses, inter alia, on some of the key differences and similarities between Russian and Western theorizations of the same, which is seen as an important side contribution of this book. What is eventually offered and graphically nuanced is a triangular conceptualization of Russia's strategic cultural approach to military-technological innovation (Fig. 1). One of its key contributions is to theorize the relationship between strategic culture and military-technological innovation. Another side contribution is in linking the concepts of strategic culture and RMA with the term 'developmental state' and showing how one's culture of military industrialization shapes the organizational process of military-technological innovation. Conflict dynamics are theorized as the trigger for every round of military-technological innovation. The latter two insights are turned into arguments, complementing those put forward in Chapter 1.

This conceptual framework will serve as the basis for the empirical analysis of the hundred and fifty-year history of military-technological innovation in Russia and will help to capture Russia's permanent oscillation between different possible ways of responding to Western innovation. Even though this model serves a particular purpose in this book, its relevance goes beyond the specific cases examined here and this is where its general theoretical contribution lies: since it theorizes the options available for a technological laggard in responding to military-technological innovation elsewhere, it is applicable in a much wider set of cases. It goes without saying that the same model can be readily applied to study different processes of military-technological innovation in Russia not covered in this study such as its approach to the current AI-RMA.

The following chapters use the sets of criteria and theoretical assumptions developed in the first two chapters to inquire into the dynamics of military-technological innovation in Russia over the last hundred and fifty years.

Chapter 3 focuses on nineteenth-century developments, in particular Russia's military-technological revolution of the second half of the nineteenth century: the introduction of rifled and breech-loading weapons. It begins by drawing attention to the decisive role of the Crimean War (1853–1856). Then the discussion proceeds to elucidate Russia's multi-faceted reaction to the technological advantage enjoyed by other European powers. Besides embarking on its own, albeit limited, re-armament programme, Russia sought to bypass or offset the others' competitive advantage by putting greater emphasis on the fighting spirit of the Russian soldier and actively engaging in disarmament diplomacy under the banner of humanitarian disarmament. The key findings are graphically synthesized (Fig. 3).

Chapter 4 concentrates on the nuclear revolution of the mid- to late-twentieth century. It opens with a discussion of the Soviets' controversial reaction to the atomic bombings of Hiroshima and Nagasaki. On the one hand, Soviet political leaders and military experts denied the revolutionary potential of nuclear weapons, at least at the discursive level. On the other hand, the Soviet Union started its own atomic bomb project not long after. Attention then shifts to the co-existence of two opposing tendencies throughout the whole studied period: advocacy activities in the matter of nuclear arms control, non-proliferation, and disarmament; and the simultaneous quest for the development of capabilities comparable to that of the US. The chapter similarly concludes with a graphic representation of the key points (Fig. 4).

Chapter 5 is devoted to the study of the revolution in warfare brought about by precision guidance technologies in the late twentieth to early twenty-first century. The chapter begins with a discussion of Soviet writings on the radical modernization of conventional weapons in the US in the 1970s–1980s. The Soviet immediate response to these developments reflected two seemingly incompatible ambitions which ultimately failed: catching up on the one hand; and removing the threat of war, ending the arms race, and taking steps towards real disarmament on the other. After a careful consideration of these issues, the discussion proceeds to the analysis of the key formative events for post-Soviet Russia: the Gulf War (1990–1991), the 1998 bombing of Iraq (code-named Operation Desert Fox), the NATO air strikes in Yugoslavia (1999), the Chechen Wars (mainly the phase starting in 1999), and the Russo-Georgian War (2008). Only when contextual nuances are discussed and explained does attention shift to Russia's real efforts to catch up with the West, as well as its asymmetric countermeasures in the realms of technology and operational art. Although this chapter does not focus extensively on the ongoing armed conflict in Ukraine, some preliminary findings associated with it are integrated into the discussion for a better understanding of the issues tackled in this book. The associated results are presented and discussed with graphical illustrations (Fig. 5). One of the key running themes in this chapter is the relationship – in particular that of mutual substitution – between conventional and nuclear weapons.

The concluding section of this book summarizes the findings and, whenever appropriate and possible, reflects upon them from a 2022 perspective. In particular, it presents the analysis and synthesis of the key similarities and recurring patterns across the three studied cases. This is where the central research question of whether and to what extent there has been a distinct culture of Russia's military-technological innovation is addressed. It is for this reason that the concluding section focuses primarily on cultural continuity rather than change or, in other words, the degree to which it is possible to call it a strategic cultural approach in a long-term historical perspective. The *seven facets* of Russia's strategic cultural approach to military-technological innovation are eventually distinguished and comprehensively defined in this section.

1. Military Technology in Russian Strategic Thinking

This chapter synthesizes and structures the existing knowledge on the relationship between strategic culture and military-technological innovation in Russia. In doing so, it maps out a framework that draws together two bodies of literature: the literature on Russian (including Soviet)[2] strategic culture, with a particular focus on its technological dimension, and the literature on military-technological innovation in Russia (including the Soviet Union). It shows that the available knowledge on the Russian cultural approach to military-technological innovation is fragmented and incomplete. Furthermore, the existing literature often refers to different periods of Russian history with little insight into or understanding of the historicity of military-technological innovation in Rus-

---

[2] At the risk of oversimplification, the words 'Russia' or 'Russian' are used consistently throughout this text as if they represented a homogeneous construct. It may seem odd, knowing that, historically, Russia is a multi-national and multi-ethnic country, and especially knowing that the USSR is part of the analysis, but there is a reason to it. At a very basic level, what matters is the difference between the Russian words *russkiy* and *rossiyanin*, a difference which the English word 'Russian' cannot capture. The former stands for ethnic Russians; the latter captures all citizens belonging to the Russian state, regardless of their nationality, language, or religion. The Russian passport is a tool of homogenization and even possible expansion as evident, for instance, in the issuing of Russian passports to Ukrainians living in Russian-held territories in eastern Ukraine. The role of a homogenizing device in the Soviet Union was performed by communist ideology. In either case, cultural homogenization under the leadership of the Russian state has been a persistent feature throughout all of Russian history. This is why it is safe, at least in the context of this research, to move back and forth in history and analyse the 'Russian' cultural approach, sometimes even referring to 'Soviet' as 'Russian'. It is also why the authors of military publications cited here as representative of the 'Russian' perspective are not necessarily ethnic Russians. Their representativeness is judged by the fact of their publications being featured in the country's main military journal.

sia. The ultimate goal is not to engage in explicit theory testing. Rather, it is to take assumptions derived from prior scholarship as a point of departure, regardless of the time period covered, and refine them, where appropriate, to make sure they are consistent with the actual *longue durée* process of military-technological innovation in Russia.

Six specific arguments are offered, and empirical data are subsequently used to demonstrate their validity from the *longue durée* perspective. Taking such a perspective is particularly important. The question of continuity and change in the Russian culture of strategic thought has been extensively discussed in the literature and many scholars agree that Russia has a strategic culture that is relatively unchanging and enduring. Ermarth (2006: 4) argued that the 'continuity' of Russian strategic culture is 'truly striking' (Ermarth 2006: 4). Eitelhuber (2009: 1) also concluded that Russian strategic culture is 'fairly stable'. Covington (2016: 39) similarly noted that Russia's 'traditional' culture of strategic thought has a 'deeply rooted nature'. Discussing the Russian art of strategy, including the available technological tools, Adamsky (2018: 35) also drew attention to the 'remarkable historical continuity' of Russian strategic culture. However, there has not been an absolute consensus on this issue. Baev (2020: 21) recently recorded that Russian strategic culture is 'evolving remarkably fast'. Most importantly, there has been limited attention paid to the role and relative importance of rapidly changing technology. Tracing this over three different time periods, the current study aims to remedy this gap.

1.1 Technology as an Added Value to the Nation's Military Power

Two (not necessarily conflicting) strands of argument about the general role of technology in Russian strategic culture have been particularly well represented in the existing scholarship. On the one hand, Russia has never been viewed as techno-centric. Adamsky (2010: 56) argued that there is a strong belief in Russia that 'battles are won by men ... not by machines'. He (2010: 43, 56) also explained that emphasis has rather been placed on spiritual power and psychological factors such as the endurance, patience, self-restraint, bravery, and moral fortitude of the Russian soldier. Blank (Interview no. 4) generally agreed that Russia has been in 'a unique spiritual centre'. This is, at least in part, because Russia has always been rich in its sheer quantity of military manpower, as clarified by Ermarth (2006: 5). Becker (1993: 28) also characterized Russia's strategic-military approach as 'manpower-intensive'. Thus, through the lens of Russian strategic culture, weapons have traditionally been viewed as 'mass multipliers', rather than as means of fighting better with fewer numbers (Ermarth 2006: 5; Adamsky 2010: 44). One caveat is needed, however. In making this particular argument, Ermarth (2006: 5) referred to industrial age weapons. Miles (Interview no. 3) rightly remarked, however, that it is not only Russian strategic thinkers who have been driven by the spirituality of war. For example, he mentioned that the fighting spirit of the French soldier was a popular narrative in France during both World War I and World War II.

In contrast, Blank (Interview no. 4) stressed that the above has been a 'major' but not a 'dominant' trend. Russia's emphasis on fighting spirit and morale, he explained, does not mean its preference for – or even satisfaction with – inferior technology, especially now when manpower is no longer abundant and when Russia has seen what high-tech weapons can do in warfare. Bendett (Interview no. 5) made basically the same argument, saying that 'spirit alone is not enough'. Russia recognizes, in his view, that it is 'locked in an unending technological race' with its potential adversaries, now mainly the US and NATO. He spotted that, particularly in recent years, Russia has stressed the need to develop new and modernized high-tech military systems for its Armed Forces. Gorenburg (Interview no. 8) agreed that the argument of Russia rejecting the significance of technology in favour of traditional spiritual values is 'more of a stereotype than reality'. Adamsky (2010: 44) acknowledged that Soviet military leaders were similarly 'convinced' of the importance of technology for modern warfare.

Both perspectives hold true as they are not mutually exclusive. The dilemma of spirituality *versus* technology has always been a matter of degree in Russia. However, there has not yet been a systematic analysis that would trace the change in the relationship between the quality of combat manpower and technology in Russian military thinking over the last hundred and fifty years. This study extends and contributes to the current academic debate in the following direction. Preliminary findings related to the ongoing armed conflict in Ukraine are also taken into consideration.

Argument 1: Technology has been an emerging factor in Russian military thinking but a more traditional manpower-centred approach to warfare has endured to this day.

1.2 Technology as a Component of Defence Capability

Another popular narrative about Russian strategic culture in the existing literature is that of *defensive militarization*. The history of Russia testifies to the fact that it 'must be constantly prepared to defend', according to Tolshmyakov and Orlova (2020: 35). They reminded us that, in the thirteenth to nineteenth centuries, the state of peace was rather an 'exception' for Russia, while war was 'a cruel rule'. To be more precise, in the seventeenth century, Russia fought for 48 years, and in the eighteenth century for 56 years. Russia was also at the 'epicentre' of almost all major military events of the twentieth century, including both world wars. Also referring to Russia's place in the course of history, Ilnitsky (2021: 20) called it 'a warrior country' (страна-воин). Eitelhuber (2009: 8) characterized Russian strategic culture as 'militaristic'; Ermarth (2006: 3), as 'highly militarized'. Becker (1993: 38) called attention to the fact that the population would sacrifice for the state, calling it the '[m]ilitarization of society'. All of this is true in no small part because Russia lacks natural, easily defendable geographical borders which, on the one hand often invited external attack and, on the other hand facilitated expansionist ambitions driven by the desire to keep the enemy as far away as possible (Eitelhuber 2009: 8; Becker 1993: 27). The latter was called 'defensive aggressiveness' by Kotkin (2016) and 'defensive expansionistic propensity' by Becker (1993: 27). It should not be forgotten that, in addition to external security considerations, Russia also has a long history of internal conflicts (Eitelhuber 2009: 5). Such existential conditions created a solid basis for military power to play the 'state-forming role' in Russia (Ilnitsky 2021: 20).

However, as also comes across very clearly from the above discussion, it would be a mistake to characterize Russia's militarization (including, inevitably, in the technological domain) as purely defensive. Blank (Interview no. 4) suggested viewing it through the prism of the offence-defence relationship. 'When they say "defensive", don't buy it so quickly,' he added. Covington (2016: 13–14) expressed virtually the same idea. Explaining that an effective strategic defence always depends on offensive actions, he stressed that Russia sees 'no contradiction' between pre-emptive tactical offence and being defensive. Therefore, the term 'defence' in Russian military thinking is largely about defending the expected political aims, rather than about the actual conduct of operations (Kofman et al. 2021: 14). Depicting Russia's cultural approach to military-technological innovation as 'defensive' may be misleading because it is not about defensive technologies only. Herd (Interview no. 1) suggested an alternative, equally suitable, term to characterize Russia's general approach: 'reactive'. Indeed, this term may be more suitable as it is more neutral with respect to technology and, at the same time, is in line with the Russian perspective. What proves the latter is one of the statements by the Chief of the General Staff of the Soviet Armed Forces (1977–1984), Nikolai V. Ogarkov. In his book *History Teaches Vigilance*, he (1985: 77) characterized Soviet military doctrine as defensive-reactive, stressing 'the principle of *reactive* [emphasis added], that is, defensive, actions.' In this book, however, 'reactive' is not understood as synonymous with 'defensive'. It is treated as part of the broader context of Russia's geographical and geopolitical imagination, as well as the respective political aims.

Argument 2: Russia's military-technological innovation has, as a rule, been a reaction to Western innovation (for further details, see Argument 8).

1.3 Technology as a Political Artefact

The next major assumption underlying the existing scholarship is that Russia's grand strategy, including its technological dimension, relies upon the self-image of a *great power*. It was Peter the Great, as Eitelhuber (2009: 7) found, that set Russia on this path at the beginning of the eighteenth century. Ever since, Russia has tried to be recognized by the major world powers as their 'equal' (Neumann 2008: 128). The role of a junior partner or any kind of subordination have generally been 'inconceivable' (Igumnova 2011: 257). However, Neumann (2008: 128) legitimately argued that Russia's great power status could only be understood from a narrow realist perspective, that is, its ability to project power, particularly military power. In his view (Interview no. 6) this is where, unlike in many other areas, Russia could compete with the West. Becker (1993: 38) similarly noted that Russia has sought international prestige and great power status via military means. Unsurprisingly, then, military parades have been used as a means of producing a powerful visual image of Russia's military power at home and abroad (McDermott 2009: 7).

Technology plays no small part in this. According to Baev (2020: 7), Russia's claims to great power status have been underpinned primarily by its large nuclear arsenal, as further testified to by Russia's poor military performance during its invasion of Ukraine in 2022. Eitelhuber

(2009: 7) mentioned, however, citing A. Pushkov, that nuclear *and* conventional weapons are both important elements in Russia's pretensions to greatness. Going broader, he (2009: 7–8) even identified Russia's 'high potential' in the fields of science and technology as a factor 'adding' to its great power status. Therefore, lagging behind the technological frontier could challenge the image of Russia as a great power, and Neumann (Interview no. 6) generally agreed that Russia's military-technological innovation has often coincided with the perceived loss of great power status.

Argument 3: Military-technological innovation in Russia has, to a large extent, been driven by elite aspirations to restore Russia's historical great power status.

1.4 Technology as a Highly Constrained Domain

One more principal observation about the process of military-technological innovation in Russia can be obtained from the available literature. Russia has typically given very little space to exploratory experimentation. For example, Evangelista (1988) drew contrasts between the Soviet 'top-down' and the US 'bottom-up' approaches to innovation. Zysk (2021a: 545) also characterized Russia's traditional innovation model as 'state-driven, top-down'. Snyder (1994: 182–183) developed this idea further, explaining that, for latecomers like Russia, it would usually be the state that, substituting for missing entrepreneurial ability and private capital, would take the lead in mobilizing economic resources for innovation. Adamsky (2010: 45–46) also recorded that practice would usually be driven by theory, meaning weapons would usually be matched directly to practical needs in Russia. He went on to clarify that doctrines and operational concepts would, as a rule, be formulated first, and appropriate force structures would subsequently be designed. Other experts similarly stressed that Russia's military doctrine has typically been 'informed' by military science (Kofman et al. 2021: 6). Therefore there is little room for manoeuver as far as Russia's military-technological innovation is concerned.

Argument 4: Russia's military-technological innovation has been steered by military science and the government (for further details, see Argument 7).

1.5 Technology as a Source of Asymmetry

Another popular belief is that Russia, usually being the side playing catch-up in its arms race with the West, has tended towards asymmetric responses. For example, Kotkin (2016) underlined that the experience of relative military and industrial 'backwardness' has often led Russia to 'catch up'. Galeotti (Interview no. 7) generally agreed that 'pretty much throughout its history ... Russia has faced the problem of the fact that it will be dealing with more technologically advanced antagonists.' In this sense, he distinguished between the Western approach ('how do we exploit our specific technological edge?') and the Russian approach ('how do we find a way of countering the rival's technological edge?'). Herd (Interview no. 1) especially stressed that, from the Russian perspective, it is important to grasp 'the role of technology *as held by adversaries* [emphasis added]'. Unsurprisingly, then, the Soviets (and hence Russians) would often prefer, according to Adamsky (2010: 46), to respond by exploiting adversaries' weaknesses and opposing them with their own strengths. He made particularly clear that they could take indirect action not only in the technological realm but also at the level of concepts and operational creativity. Galeotti (Interview no. 7) agreed that Russia has generally exploited both 'technological and tactical asymmetry'. Covington (2016: 5) similarly spotted that the Russian understanding of 'asymmetry' was not only about its military posture but also about its strategy and actual practices. Elsewhere, Adamsky (2018: 49) additionally highlighted that Russia's 'indirect-asymmetrical' actions could possibly go beyond the military domain and involve non-military measures. Most importantly, he traced the Russian quest for asymmetry to the Tsarist and Soviet traditions. What is important to note is that the narrative of Russia's asymmetric approach is not reducible to the way in which the West *views* Russia. In fact, it quite accurately captures what Russia actually *thinks*. Even the term 'asymmetric response' (асимметричный ответ) has penetrated the Russian professional discourse (Kokoshin 2009: 49).

However, Russia's usual starting position as a technological laggard and its persistent tendency to catch up does not necessarily mean going *asymmetric*. This catching-up process has two different dimensions, one of which is underestimated in the existing literature. Besides asymmetric measures – which, in addition to the aforesaid, also include diplomatic measures, as discussed below – Russia has been in a permanent quest for *symmetry* vis-à-vis the West. Gareev (2008) highlighted that Russia has often, especially in the past, resorted to 'straightforward', i.e. symmetrical, actions while responding to each round of the arms race with the West. Kokoshin (2009: 49) cited him as 'rightly' drawing attention to this general historical tendency. Therefore, what is generally known as Russia's 'asymmetric approach' does not fully capture the direction of its military-technological innovation. Gorenburg (Interview no. 8) also rightfully remarked that, in reality, '"asymmetry" is one of those words that you are never quite sure what it means.' Chapter 5 most clearly demonstrates that the boundaries between Russia's asymmetric and symmetric responses are blurred. Covington (2016: 22) suggested an alternative term to characterize Russia's asymmetric approach – a 'compensatory approach'. This term is more accurate from a broader perspective because, even though Covington (2016) did not fully develop this idea, it is more neutral and captures Russia's asymmetric *and* symmetric measures taken to catch up with the West.

Argument 5: Russia's military-technological innovation has been driven by the need to compensate for the technological gap between itself and the adversary (symmetrically) to the extent possible, and for the latter's technological advantage (asymmetrically).

1.6 Technology as a Subject of Diplomacy

The last major finding is that Russia has often utilized arms control and disarmament as perhaps the fastest means of overcoming its technological backwardness. In doing so, Russia has pursued two objectives, according to the best available knowledge today: closing the technological gap between itself and the adversary for both strategic and status-related considerations, and relieving immediate pressure on its own military budget. For example, Ermarth (2006: 9) noted that Russia would typically use arms control negotiations and the surrounding propaganda 'to constrain the US and its allies from exploiting their superior technology.' Shoumikhin (2009: 142, 150) similarly recorded that Russia would generally treat arms control and disarmament negotiations as a means of 'slowing down, if not reversing' US technological progress, and eventually as a venue for 'equalizing' their strategic potential. Brooks (2020: 90) also added that bilateral arms control would usually symbolize the equality and respect that Russia expected and believed it deserved.

Blank (Interview no. 4) agreed that the question of Russia's 'status' – its desire to be treated as an 'equal' – was a significant driver behind Russia's fascination with arms control and disarmament. He further argued, however, that Russia would also be strongly motivated by the need to relieve pressure on its own military budget because it could not afford to 'throw money' into military buildup on par with the US. Herd (Interview no. 1) generally concurred that, besides 'instrumentalizing' arms control, Russia has also seen it as 'status-enhancing' in the sense of being in the same 'room' with technologically leading states.

The above arguments relate primarily to the bilateral context of the Cold War and, to an extent, the post-Cold War period. The literature on nineteenth-century disarmament captures another important aspect: Russia's original interest in humanitarian disarmament. For example, Keefer (2014: 450) described the Russian disarmament initiative of 1868 (discussed in detail in Chapter 3) as 'as much a reaction to the revolutionary changes in technology as *a truly humanitarian gesture* [emphasis added].' It was a rather unique moment in Russian history. Ever since Russia's arguments in favour of arms control and disarmament have often contained explicit appeals to morals, values, or ethics, as illustrated below. Yet much of it can be dismissed as propaganda as the language of human suffering would always make a strong case for arms control and disarmament negotiations, even if real motives were different. Nevertheless, there is evidence of other rare moments when Russia seemingly acted in the interest of reducing the role of weapons in global politics, even if always for a combination of reasons.

Argument 6: Russia has used arms control and disarmament as a means of equalizing its position vis-a-vis the most technologically advanced states (strategic and symbolic reasons), relieving immediate pressure on its military budget (economic reasons), and, to a much lesser extent historically, reducing the role of weapons in global politics (humanitarian, or what appear to be principled reasons).

1.7 Concluding Remarks

The six arguments put forward in this chapter characterize the Russian strategic cultural approach to military-technological innovation. Derived from the existing literature, the interviews conducted by the author, and the author's own knowledge of the problematic, they will underlie the following empirical analysis. However, before turning to the empirics, it is important to theorize the relationship between strategic culture and military-technological innovation. The overarching goal of doing so is to create a solid basis upon which the raw empirical data can be organized before it can be used for any kind of argumentation. This is the subject of Chapter 2. Most importantly, it is where the last two arguments guiding the empirical focus of this book are put forward.

2. Russia's Strategic Cultural Approach to Military-Technological Innovation: An Analytical Framework

This chapter outlines the theoretical and methodological framework of this research. In terms of the theoretical perspective adopted, it defines military-technological innovation for the purposes of this study and, most importantly, theorizes its relationship with strategic culture within a given context. Since its primary objective is to conceptualize the Russian strategic cultural approach to military-technological innovation, the theoretical framework presented below partially builds on the discussion of Russia's strategic culture presented in Chapter 1. It is useful to recall that the previous chapter put forward six empirical arguments. The last two arguments are derived from the theoretical discussion and, therefore, presented in this chapter.

The structure of this chapter is as follows. It opens with the introduction of the concept of strategic culture, as understood by Western and Russian theorists. What follows is a nuanced theorization of the relationship between military-technological innovation and strategic culture and a triangular conceptualization of Russia's strategic cultural approach to military-technological innovation. The focus is on the options available to a technological laggard in an accelerating arms race scenario. What is particularly important is that, whenever possible, this multi-faceted conceptualization relies on Russian (and Soviet) understandings of related concepts and terms. This allows the author to bring the theoretical framework of this study, aimed at understanding certain aspects of Russian culture, even closer to grasping the Russian way of thinking. The chapter closes with a detailed elaboration of the methodology of this research. Particular attention is drawn to the fact that the analysis presented here relies extensively on primary data collected from Russian and Soviet archives, as well as expert interviews.

2.1 Recurring Patterns and Strategic Culture

Military-technological innovation and related processes do not occur in a vacuum. They are situated, contextualized. One of the ways to theorize the impact of culture on strategic national choices, especially the views of a given country towards the role and efficacy of the use of military force, as contained in the existing literature, is the concept of *strategic culture*. The availability and reliability of military equipment, as well as attitudes towards the application of military technology constitute an important part of it. For example, Adamsky (2010: 5) comprehensively demonstrated through the examples of the US, the USSR, and Israel that one's strategic culture provides the decisive context for its RMAs.

There have been three generations of strategic culture theorization. The difference between them lies primarily in the role they assign to strategic culture. For the first generation, originally focused on explaining why the US and the USSR thought differently about their nuclear arsenals, strategic culture is a deeply rooted and semi-permanent context for – and therefore inseparable from – one's strategic behaviour (Snyder 1977: v; Gray 1999: 62). Gray (1981a: 22) particularly defined strategic culture as 'referring to modes of *thought and action* [emphasis added] with respect to force'. In contrast, the third generation views one's strategic ideas as separable from its behaviour patterns and assesses, in a methodologically sound way, the relative impact of the former on the latter in different situations (e.g. Johnston 1995a; 1995b). The second generation, drawing on the scholarship of post-structuralists and post-Marxists, stands out most prominently. It takes a critical perspective and defines strategic culture in terms of discursive manipulation and constant (re)interpretations of a country's strategic culture by its elites (e.g. Klein 1988; 1989).

It is particularly the first generation that provides a conceptual framework for the empirical analysis undertaken in the subsequent chapters, and there are two major reasons for this. First, their assumptions match the historical realities of Russia. The previous chapter contained the idea, borrowed from the existing literature, that Russian strategic culture is relatively enduring. Gray (1999: 56), one of the pioneers of the first generation of strategic culture theorization, also characterized Russian society as 'high-context'.

Second, the Russian understanding of the term 'strategic culture' resembles what has generally been argued by scholars of the first generation of the strategic culture school in the West. This discussion should begin by noting that Russian scholars often referred to the first generation of literature on strategic culture in their own studies (Ivanov 2007: 97; Oganisyan 2017: 47). There have also been similarities at the level of more specific theoretical assumptions. First of all, the Russian perspective suggests that strategic culture is 'an attribute not only of the armed forces or even the state machine, but of the entire people as a whole' (Bartosh 2020: 9). Fedorov (2002: 8) concurred that strategic culture 'captures the perceptions of the elite and society'. This is because, as Rykhtik (2003: 204) explained, the government and the governing bodies of the armed forces 'always act in a certain [shared] value system of coordinates' while making decisions concerning national security and foreign policy. This is very much in line with how first-generation theorists defined the keepers or bearers of strategic culture. For example, Gray (1981b: 62) viewed strategic culture, which he alternatively addressed as a national style in strategy, as always belonging to 'a particular nation'. However, Mikhailyonok (2012: 132) clarified that the formation and implementation of the national will, as well as the assumption of immediate responsibility are still 'concentrated in a small decision-making apparatus.' That said, this book will not inquire into possible disagreements within Russian strategic culture, even though different sub-cultures may sometimes exist alongside one dominant national culture, as acknowledged by Gray (1981b: 57–58). The focus will be on Russia's dominant strategic culture, supposedly shared by most members of society and represented primarily by the broader political-military circle.

Another similarity lies in the very definition of strategic culture, and particularly in the understanding that one's strategic culture is inherently inseparable from one's behaviour. For example, Mikhalev and Zvoshchik (2018: 54) called Gray's definition of strategic culture – 'an appeal to the ways of *thinking and acting* [emphasis added] in dealing with issues of the use of force, rooted in national historical experience' (rephrased by the authors) – the 'classic definition'. A. A. Kokoshin defined strategic culture in similar terms, drawing attention not only to the indivisible connection between strategic thought and strategic behaviour but once again to the fact that strategic culture is a eventually property of a whole nation:

> Strategic culture ... is expressed in the special character of the behaviour of the armed forces inherent in a given country and its people, and in the ways in which military force is used. Strategic culture is a set of stereotypes of sustainable behaviour of the relevant subject in the large-scale

use of military force in terms of its political tasks and military goals, including in the preparation, adoption and implementation of strategic decisions (cited in Bartosh 2020: 9).

Therefore, Russia's strategic cultural traits will be tracked in the following chapters both at the level of discourse and practice, particularly at the level of political-military discourses and practices. Arguing that culture cannot be seen as separate from behaviour, same as people's minds cannot be seen as separate from their bodies, Gray (1999: 53, 55) suggested using the term 'style'. Viewed in this perspective, the focus of this book is the Russian style of military-technological innovation.

The next point of agreement is that Russian theorists, same as first-generation scholars in the West, have recognized that strategic culture is always deeply rooted within a particular context. For example, Mikhailyonok (2012: 132) defined strategic culture as 'a concentrated expression of national historical experience and national identity.' Being more precise in this regard, Ivanov (2007: 87) argued that strategic culture is 'a reflection of both the military-strategic experience and the social and cultural-historical development of the state.' Bartosh (2020: 16) similarly argued that each state's strategic behaviour is affected by 'its own historical baggage of accumulated experience, beliefs, cultural influences, geographical and resource constraints.' According to him, (2020: 17–18) inputs into one's strategic culture include the following factors:

- *territorial and geographical factors* (the spatial and territorial position of the country, the availability and accessibility of natural resources, the country's access to the oceans, etc.);
- *political factors* (the country's political regime and form of government, the degree of effectiveness of the political system, the nature of the party system and the presence or absence of political pluralism, the country's place in the system of international relations, the degree of state involvement in international conflicts and the nature of these conflicts, the presence or absence of acute political conflicts within the country, etc.);
- *military-strategic factors* (the level of combat capability and combat readiness of the country's armed forces, the level of development of the military-industrial complex and its ability to provide the armed forces with military equipment and weapons, the effectiveness of the system of military personnel training, the country's participation in military-political alliances and the nature of its international

military-technical cooperation, the presence of historical experience of participation in wars, the readiness and ability of the armed forces to participate in peacekeeping operations or in the fight against international terrorism, etc.);

- *economic factors* (the level of economic sovereignty, the level of development of the country's industrial base and productive forces, the nature and type of economic social relations, mobilization capabilities of the country and reserves of strategic resources, the standards of living, etc.);
- *environmental factors* (the level of environmental pollution, the availability and implementation of environmentally friendly technological processes in production, the degree of depletion of natural resources, the degree of use of resource-saving technologies, the availability and security of the storage of weapons of mass destruction, as well as the methods and reliability of disposal of radioactive, poisonous, flammable, and other wastes, etc.);
- *ethnic factors* (the level of homogeneity and national consolidation of the country, the presence and nature of internal inter-ethnic conflicts, the position of ethnic diasporas abroad and the nature of relations with them, the types of national self-determination in a multinational country, etc.);
- *demographic factors* (population size and dynamics, the educational and cultural level of the population, mobilization capabilities of the country in terms of human resources, etc.);
- *religious factors* (the main religions and confessions and their place and role in the country's political system, the presence or absence of internal conflicts on inter-religious grounds, religious components of international conflicts involving the country, etc.);
- *other factors* (the general level of public consciousness and culture, the degree of religiosity, the degree of ideological unity, the nature of military doctrine, the level of development of military thought, the professionalism of the political and military leadership, the competence of civil servants, the effectiveness of the structural organization of the state apparatus, national-historical traditions, national-psychological characteristics of the country's population, etc.).

Milaeva and Siushkin (2012: 19) identified the following indicators of the development of each particular state shaping its strategic culture: its geopolitical position, economic and defence potential, political structures, legal and political culture, historical experience of resolving foreign policy conflicts, level of involvement in the processes of globalization, as well as the adopted normative documents that determine its security strategy, and the scientific and educational potential of the society.

However, the purpose of listing all these contributing factors is not to analyse the roots of Russian strategic culture, but it is important for at least one reason: it shows that, from the Russian perspective, context-specific factors and historical experiences of all kinds 'weigh heavily' (precisely as Gray (1981b: 2) argued) on the formation of one's strategic culture. In making his argument, Gray (1981a: 22) similarly insisted that strategic culture 'flows from geopolitical, historical, economic, and other unique influences.' Another representative of the first generation in the West, Jones (1990: 37), distinguished the following elements that constitute one's national, including strategic, culture: the nature and geography of the state, its social-economic and governmental-administrative system, as well as military-administrative institutions, the pattern of political-military interaction (possibly integration), the definition of security and national goals established by the state's political and military leadership and the style of diplomacy and military strategy developed for the achievement of those goals, the ethnic culture of its founding people and their history, as well as the available technological base.

Since it may be difficult, if not impossible, to escape such a wide range of influences, strategic culture is a pervasive and relatively inflexible source of strategic behaviour, as viewed by the first generation of Western – and many Russian – theorists. This is precisely what the first generation of theorization has been criticized for by advocates of the third generation: 'If "strategic culture" is said to be the product of nearly all relevant explanatory variables, then there is little conceptual space for a non-strategic culture explanation of strategic choice' (Johnston 1995b: 37).

Indeed, if first-generation assumptions are taken seriously, it may be difficult to establish reliable causalities between all these sorts of influences and strategic behaviour. This is exactly why Gray (1999: 62 and 68) suggested viewing strategic culture as a 'context', whose effects 'will be more or less strongly stamped upon strategic behaviour of all kinds.' Taking the same approach, this research does not trace the sources of Russian strategic culture and does not seek to find a causal relationship between Russia's strategic culture and approach to military-technological innovation. Instead, it focuses on the identification of – supposedly – relatively stable and recurring features of Russia's strategic cultural approach to military-technological innovation.

Strategic culture should be viewed as the ever-present constitutive context for one's strategic behaviour 'relevant to the threat or use of force for political purposes' (Gray 1999: 50). It is certainly a broad category and Russia's strategic cultural approach to military-technological innovation should be viewed as one of its facets or dimensions, which requires further theoretical elaboration (Fig. 1). Since there is a paucity of studies examining the Russian style of military-technological innovation, the information presented in the previous chapter is insufficient and taken only as a starting point. Then the goal is to trace over an extended period of time and define Russia's strategic cultural approach to military-technological innovation, as expressed in recurring discourses and practices and manifesting itself more or less strongly at every critical moment. Therefore, the goal is reversed: it is not to put Russian RMAs into the country's broader and thoroughly researched strategic cultural context, but to identify, initially relying on the fragmented and incomplete data available, whether and to what extent there has been a distinct culture, or style of military-technological innovation in Russia.

2.2 Triangular Conceptualization of Russia's Strategic Cultural Approach to Military-Technological Innovation

In this section, a triangular conceptualization of Russia's strategic cultural approach to military-technological innovation is developed and presented. Probably the most widely used concept to address military-technological innovation is the RMA. It is a highly contested concept, with many different approaches to theorizing it and, as a result, many different approaches to viewing the history of RMAs (Hynek and Solovyeva 2022: 9–14). The debate over the role of technology in military innovation has been one of the key dimensions of the RMA debate. It is generally accepted that technology plays an important role in facilitating RMAs (van Creveld 1991: 32; Toffler and Toffler 1993: 31–34; Rogers 2000: 30; Murray and Knox 2001a: 12; Cohen 2004: 399; Adamsky 2010: 1). However, there has been no consensus on the degree of technological impact. At one extreme are scholars such as Krepinevich (1994). He conceptualized technology as a *necessary* condition for every RMA. At the other extreme are those who treated technology as a *relatively insignificant* factor (Murray 1997) and believed it *rarely* plays a decisive role (Murray and Knox 2001b: 180). Other contributions fall in between these two extremes. For example, some scholars assume that technology *usually* (e.g. Fitzsimonds and van Tol 1994: 25), *normally* (e.g. Morgan 2000: 134), or *often* (e.g. Sloan 2002: 25) drives change in military affairs. More sceptical scholars insist that it *sometimes* and *not always* makes a big difference (Hundley 1999: 14; Horowitz 2010: 22).

Two major approaches eventually stand out as the leading sources of theorization. Not only do they differ with respect to the role of technology, but they also assign different weights to different factors in the overall composition of change. One body of literature takes technology seriously and theorizes the requisites of change. Despite differences in formulation, their proposed set of indicators basically includes technological innovation, changes in operational concepts and doctrines, as well as corresponding organizational adaptations (Krepinevich 1994; Fitzsimonds and van Tol 1994: 25–29; Hundley 1999: 14–22, 33; Morgan 2000: 135–138).

The other body of literature theorizes more flexible sets of indicators, maintaining that technology can, but does not necessarily have to be, the main driving force. Although it helps them to get closer to reality and better capture the variety of military revolutions, there has been no agreement on the precise nature and composition of change. For example, Rogers (2000: 22–24) analysed *revolutions in military affairs* as changes in how war is fought, including technical, tactical, and strategic innovations. However, he argued that such revolutions can in certain, but not all, cases have extremely wide-ranging social, economic, and political implications. Whenever it is the case, he used another term: *military revolutions*. Murray and Knox (2001a: 6–12) focused on *military revolutions* recasting the entirety of society, the state, and the system of military organization. However, they acknowledged the existence of less profound transformations that either accompanied or followed such revolutions. They studied them as *revolutions in military affairs*, and each as a complex mix of tactical, organizational, doctrinal, and technological innovations. These two approaches are similar in terms of viewing military revolutions as much broader structural changes compared to RMAs, but they apparently differ in how they theorize the relationship between these two terms and phenomena.

To find a way through these differences for the purposes of this study, it is important to consider the Russian perspective. Russian or, to be more specific, Soviet writings on military-technological innovation are discussed mainly in the context of the so-called IT-RMA and often traced back to the late 1970s (Adamsky 2010: 3–4). However, such a narrow empirical focus may create a false impression that that was precisely the time and context when the Soviets started to conceptualize revolutions in warfare. That is not the case. Soviet military experts already used the terms RMA and MTR in the late 1960s and early 1970s. Both terms were applied, sometimes interchangeably, to conceptualize the emergence of nuclear weapons and new means of their delivery (Nikitin and Baranov 1968: 5, 14; Vishnevsky and Golomb 1970: 63; Vasiliev 1974: 90). One important caveat here is that this finding challenges another popular belief that US experts, mainly analysts in the Pentagon's Office of Net Assessment led by Andrew Marshall, 'broadened' the Soviet-sourced concept of MTR to RMA (Gray 2006: 23), or used the concept of RMA 'alternatively' to what the Soviets originally offered (Satterfield 2010: 262).

Even though Soviet military experts characterized the nuclear revolution as both an RMA and an MTR, there is a principal difference between these two terms. According to the Western literature, the concept of RMA puts greater emphasis on doctrinal and organizational aspects of military transformation, while that of MTR rests on the primacy of technology (Fitzsimonds and van Tol 1994: 26; Thompson 2011: 85). Military analysts in the USSR were aware of this difference but it was their choice to focus on technology-led RMAs, i.e. MTRs. Evidence available in the archive of *Voennaya Mysl'*, the military-theoretical journal of the Ministry of Defence of the Soviet Union (later the Russian Federation), clearly testifies to this. For example, Vasiliev (1974: 90) conceptualized the difference between RMAs and MTRs almost along the same lines as Western experts would later follow to distinguish between the two:

'Revolution in military affairs' rightly began to denote the deepest revolution in the military sphere, which is conditioned primarily by the massive introduction of nuclear warheads into the armed forces and new means of delivering them to targets located anywhere in the world – various types of missiles and electronic control systems of new weapons and troops. In recent years, this phenomenon is more often called the 'military-technical revolution,' thereby emphasizing that the fundamental basis and essence of the ongoing changes are nothing other than qualitative changes in military equipment, and primarily weapons.

Therefore, every single MTR could, from the Soviet perspective, be alternatively called an RMA. That said, this book gives preference to the more commonly used term of RMA. But since it focuses on three technology-led RMAs in Russia, as explained in the following section, the original Soviet logic of MTRs is applicable. It means that each of these RMAs will be studied as consisting primarily, yet not exclusively, in the use of innovative technologies.

However, Soviet military experts also realized that military-technological innovation could not be explained solely in terms of technology. Every revolution would, according to them, begin with fundamental changes in military equipment and weapons, but would also involve changes in the methods and forms of warfare, as linked to the development of new principles and military strategies, as well as in the organization of armed forces, their training, and education (Vishnevsky and Golomb 1970: 63; Korobeinikov, Shabaev, and Sokolov 1967: 44; Povaliy 1967: 72–73; 1973: 65). This clearly shows the Soviet conceptualization of change is much closer to the technology-centred approach within the existing – mainly Western – literature on RMAs, introduced above. Even Ogarkov, one of the key Soviet theorists in the matter of RMAs (in particular, MTRs) and Chief of the Soviet General Staff, as mentioned above, was cited (Sloan 2002: 26) as saying that a revolution of this kind would consist of 'new technologies [being mentioned first], evolving military systems, operational innovation and organizational adaptation.' The following indicators, inspired by the existing Soviet and Western literature, will serve as gauges for dissecting each of the studied RMAs: fundamental changes in military equipment and weapons (*technological innovation*), changes in operational principles and military strategies reflecting and contributing to the changing character of warfare (*conceptual innovation*), and changes in the organization of armed forces, their training, and education (*organizational adaptation*). One caveat is that a change of this magnitude will be tracked over an extended period in each of the case studies. It takes time for a revolution to manifest fully. Povaliy (1967: 72–73) explained (using the term 'RMA') that it can span 'a fairly long period'. Nikitin and Baranov (1968: 14) also noted (using the term 'MTR') that it is 'not only the result, but also the process.'

It is fair to highlight that, in the Soviet understanding, such changes would not necessarily be restricted to the military domain. For example, according to Vasiliev (1974: 90), a revolution of this kind (he used the term 'MTR') can go 'far beyond the purely military sphere' and have a 'direct or indirect' impact on politics, economics, ideology, diplomacy, science, morality, etc. The very idea that RMAs may potentially have far-reaching implications brings the Soviet conceptualization a bit closer to the approach taken by Rogers (2000: 22–24) and Knox and Murray (2001a: 6–12), as introduced above. It means that the Soviet approach would, from today's perspective, occupy the middle ground between the two previously discussed approaches to theorizing RMAs in the West. However, the relationship between military and non-military (social, political, economic, etc.) change goes beyond the scope of this book.

Korobeinikov, Shabaev, and Sokolov (1967: 44) came up with an additional indicator of change which was 'a qualitatively new approach to the problem of man-technology.' Zheltikov and Polyakov (1966: 53) recorded the same kind of change, arguing that an RMA '*necessarily* [emphasis added] emphasizes the relevance of the question of the role of technology and man in modern warfare.' These assumptions testify to a rather unique approach to understanding RMAs in the USSR. Given the significance of this particular aspect to Soviet military experts, shifts in the relative importance of technology versus the human element will be seriously considered as yet another necessary component of each of the three studied RMAs.

In addition to the aforementioned, there is one more theoretical consideration, and it relates directly to the conditions under which RMAs can be exploited. For example, Vasiliev (1974: 91) captured it well, citing one of the publications by Voenizdat (a Russian abbreviation for Военное Издательство, meaning 'Military Publication'), the publishing house of the Soviet Ministry of Defence. In particular, he drew attention to 'the dependence of the methods of armed struggle on economic conditions'. That said, economic conditions of possibility – both constraints and facilitating conditions – will be considered in each of the studied cases of RMAs.

However, the above is still not enough to fully grasp the process of military-technological innovation. The fact that military innovations, including new technologies, do not diffuse across states and their militaries in the same way or at the same time needs to be taken into serious consideration (Krause 1992: 206; Goldman and Andres 1999: 80–81, 122–124; Horowitz 2010: 18–19, 25, 41–55). This is what clearly tells us that exploiting an RMA does not necessarily mean taking the lead. Revolutionary breakthroughs in one or a group of countries may generate *symmetric*, sometimes even *emulative*, or *asymmetric* responses from other countries (Hashim 1998: 432). The former basically implies that the catching-up side itself embarks on an RMA. As discussed in the previous chapter, Russia (including the Soviet Union) has often lagged behind and aspired to catch up to the West in the exploitation of RMAs. Therefore, this theoretical consideration is of particular importance and the following chapters testify to its relevance for understanding military-technological innovation in Russia. Nevertheless, the previous chapter also indicated that Russia has often responded asymmetrically to Western RMAs. It is why this theoretical perspective is integrated too. Responding in an asymmetric way means the deployment of different technologies or the development of alternative ways of fighting to offset or bypass the leader's competitive advantage (Hashim 1998: 432). Such asymmetric responses, often involving low-cost technologies or other relatively inexpensive and low-tech countermeasures, can 'selectively mitigate' the key advantages of the opponent's RMA (Raska 2016: 14–15). Raska (2016: 67) also drew attention to the possibility of creating 'reverse asymmetry', i.e. creatively exploiting qualitative superiority in order to compensate for one's own quantitative inferiority (or vice versa). In fact, and as the following chapters will show, Russia has sometimes clearly prioritized, though primarily as discourse, quality over quantity both in terms of weapons and their operators due to the lack of financial resources to keep pace with the magnitude of Western RMAs. The same term may be applied in situations where one's objective is to eliminate the leader's initial competitive advantage by surpassing its originally superior capabilities (possibly in both qualitative and quantitative terms). It will then most accurately characterize the Soviet approach to the nuclear arms race with the US.

However, besides technological and operational asymmetric means to undermine or circumvent the opponent's military-technological superiority, there is one more asymmetric tool that is available to technologically inferior parties – *arms control and disarmament diplomacy*. At the very basic level, arms control is a way of limiting arms competition, while disarmament is typically about reversing it (Goldblat: 2002: 3). In other words, the former implies restraint on the number, character, development, or use of certain armaments, while the latter means their reduction or abolition (Bull 1961: 3–4). Even though arms control and disarmament are not the same, they are closely interconnected. What is especially important is that disarmament advocacy may be part of a state's arms control policy in the form of what Larsen (2002: 3) called 'a means-to-an-end approach'. This perspective captures, for example, some aspects of the Soviet thinking in relation to nuclear weapons, as demonstrated in Chapter 4. The form of arms control agreements may vary – from treaties, conventions, and protocols to joint or simultaneous statements and common understandings (Goldblat: 2002: 3). At the same time, arms control may be viewed as a process, involving not only bilateral or multilateral, but also unilateral steps (Larsen 2002: 3). Unilateral restraint efforts are no less important because if one state announces that it is not going to proceed with the development or deployment of a new kind of weapon, the other side may, in turn, exercise reciprocal restraint (Scoville 1976: 172). The unilateral Soviet pledge not to use nuclear weapons first, made in 1982, is an example of a failed initiative since the US refused to reciprocate.

Different motivations, and often their combination, drive arms control and disarmament initiatives. At the very basic level, arms control addresses the negative effects of a security dilemma, under which evidence of a new military programme by one state requires other states to respond and prevent it from achieving superiority (Larsen 2002: 2). Schelling and Halperin (1961/1985: 3) distinguished the following key motives for entering into arms control negotiations: reducing the costs of preparing for war, reducing the likelihood of war, and reducing the scope and violence if war occurs. Larsen (2002: 8) drew attention to the critical role of technology in all of this, arguing that restraining certain types of technology is often practically 'synonymous' with reducing the risk of war. Roger (1978/1979: 94) agreed that arms control agreements can 'minimize the economic costs of the arms race by restricting the areas of military competition.' No doubt technologically inferior states would typically be more interested in arms control and disarmament negotiations. Since the failure to adopt revolutionary military technologies may lead one to military defeats, it would usually be in one's best interest to forestall armed conflicts. The following chapters illustrate that all of this is relevant to Russia, in line with the sixth argument put forward in Chapter 1. Not only have arms races often been a heavy burden for its economy, but it has also always been the catching-up side in its arms race with the West. It is for these reasons, inter alia, that Russia has often been at the forefront of arms control and disarmament negotiations, as will be shown.

Arms control initiatives may also have a symbolic meaning. The role of symbolism in this regard is twofold. On the one hand, such proposals or agreements may be used mainly as political or diplomatic 'signals' rather than sincere moves towards arms limitation (Morgan 2012: 18). The Soviet no-first-use pledge, referred to above and put into context in Chapter 4, can be regarded as such because it would be hard to believe, even then, that the Soviet Union would not strike first against an impeding nuclear attack by the US or NATO. On the other hand, even though this argument originally relates to the bilateral relations in the Cold War context, arms control agreements may be a credible signal that the contracting parties regard one another as 'equals' (Brooks 2020: 85). Indeed, reversing or slowing down the momentum of the adversary's technological superiority and, most importantly, creating at least an impression of approximate technological equality has often been yet another motive for Russia (including the Soviet Union) to advocate for arms control and disarmament. Perhaps the only moment when this objective was fully achieved in practice, however, was during the Cold War, as will be discussed in detail in Chapter 4.

One important fact should not be missed. What has often prompted the development of arms control and disarmament treaties is humanitarian concern (Borrie 2006: 9). It has usually been the role of non-state actors to promote the humanitarian cause but, whatever their real motives (possibly genuinely humanitarian, at least to an extent), states have often framed their motivation for entering arms control negotiations in terms of ethics and humanitarian principles (Hynek and Solovyeva 2020). Russia was at the origin of this tradition, as will be shown in Chapter 3, and has continued to capitalize on this, repeatedly resorting to the discourse of human suffering, as will be illustrated in Chapters 4 and 5.

What complements the discussion presented in the previous section, the first generation of strategic culture theorization is applicable for analysing RMAs as well as approaches to arms control and disarmament, and its founders immediately realized the relevance of strategic culture for understanding these processes. Discussing how decision-makers in different countries approach issues posed by technological change, Snyder (1977: 9) noted that '[p]reexisting strategic notions can strongly influence doctrinal and organizational adaptations to new technologies.' These three possible vectors of influence – new technologies and doctrinal and organizational adaptations – reiterate the basic definition of an RMA. It means that RMAs can well be studied through the prism of strategic culture. Putting together the features of American strategic culture, Gray (1981a: 44) also drew attention to the possibility of studying national approaches to arms control (and, by extension, disarmament) through the lenses of strategic culture.

In view of the above, Russia's strategic cultural approach to military-technological innovation can be represented by a triangle, itself constituting only one dimension of the country's otherwise multi-faceted strategic culture (Fig. 1). The angles depict the three most common responses by Russia to RMAs originating principally in the West. One of them, located at the very top and visualizing the highest level of ambition, captures Russia's permanent quest for symmetry, including

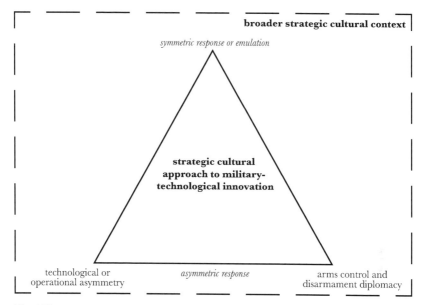

Fig. 1 The strategic cultural approach to military-technological innovation in Russia. The author's own figure.

by emulation. The other ones illustrate the two possible options for an asymmetric response: in the realm of technology or operational art, and in that of diplomacy. The former is an alternative path of innovation to military equipment or military art, or even an opportunity to reinforce one's own existing comparative advantages, while the latter is a way to restrain or reverse another's military-technological innovation, if only for a limited time. Three options are not mutually exclusive. As the following chapters will show, there always exists a kind of oscillation in Russia between different possible ways of responding to Western innovation.

2.3 Russia's Organizational Culture: Developmental State Models

What well deserves a separate discussion is the developmental state mindset of the Russian leadership. As argued and systematically illustrated in this book, it constitutes an attribute of the Russian strategic cultural approach to military-technological innovation. In particular,

Moscow's developmental state mindset will be traced at the level of organizational adaptation, which constitutes an integral part of every RMA, as previously discussed. Moreover, taking politico-economic aspects of this process into consideration is important because, as stressed by Blank (Interview no. 4), to reform the military in a fundamental way – in Russian history – means to reform the entire state and, most importantly, put the state economy on a sound basis. From the very beginning, Russia has drawn inspiration from European and East Asian developmental states, especially Germany and Japan, in their models of economic growth and industrialization. However, there are two possible gaps associated with the application of this term to Russia. First, Weiss (2000: 23) rightly noted that the term 'developmental state' has almost become synonymous with 'the state in East Asia'. Second, even if applied to Russia, it has usually been applied to contemporary Russia (e.g. Dutkiewicz 2011; Bluhm and Varga 2020; Szakonyi 2020). This book goes beyond the existing literature. It systematically applies the concept to the Russian state, taking a *longue durée* perspective and demonstrating its enduring relevance to nineteenth- to twenty-first-century Russia. It also offers a more nuanced conceptualization of this long history of the developmental state mindset of the leadership in Moscow. However, the goal is not to inquire into Moscow's developmental state mindset in broader politico-economic terms. Instead, this book concentrates on the impact of this general mindset on military-technological innovation in Russia. This is a reasonable choice. Tracing the three hundred-year history of Russian modernization, Belykh and Mau (2020: 41) drew attention to the fact that Russia has traditionally prioritized modernization in the military sphere and in industries associated with it.

The key attributes of what international political economy scholars call a 'developmental state' are as follows: (1) the existence of an elite state bureaucracy that chooses the industries to be developed, identifies the best means of rapidly developing those chosen industries, and supervises competition in the designated strategic sectors; (2) a political system in which this bureaucracy is given sufficient scope to take initiative and operate effectively; and (3) the perfection of market-conforming methods of state intervention in the economy (Johnson 1999: 38–39). The key driving factor for one's developmental state mindset is one's strategic objective of enhancing the productive powers of the nation and ultimately closing the 'technology gap' between oneself and the industrialized countries (Weiss 2000: 23). This is why the developmental state model has proved particularly useful for late-developing countries (Law 2009: 257).

The term 'developmental state', according to Johnson (1999: 32), was originally intended to go beyond the contrast between the American and Soviet economies. Positioned between these two opposites, it came to be viewed as 'the plan-rational capitalist developmental state [model], conjoining private ownership with state guidance' (Woo-Cumings 1999: 2). In regards to this, it is important to highlight that the original term was not just a 'developmental state', but a *capitalist* [emphasis added] developmental state', thus clearly indicating the direction in which it would typically strive (Johnson 1999: 32). This concept is best applicable, although with some modifications, to post-Soviet Russia. To be more precise, this book will discuss the shortcomings of Russian capitalism and propose to address Russia as a *quasi-capitalist* developmental state instead. Going further, this book suggests two complementary concepts which will help to grasp the nineteenth and the twentieth-century dynamics respectively: a *proto*-developmental state and a *command* developmental state. The former will serve to capture the characteristics of Imperial Russia as an imperfect developmental state. The latter will be applied to grasp the highly centralized and strictly planned developmental approach of the USSR. It will be shown that characterizing the Soviets' approach to military-technological innovation as an outgrowth or bare continuation of their 'command economy', in broader terms, fails to capture the complexity of respective processes. Russian scholars argue that the Asian experience cannot be easily absorbed by Russia (Alexandrov 2007) but they find it useful (Krasilshchikov 2003: 40; Ramazanov 2008: 71; Zevin 2008: 157–158). This book shows in the example of the Russian approach to military-technological innovation that Russia has a long history of developmental tendencies but it has never fully matched the original Asian 'developmental state' experience, as actively studied in the West.

Argument 7: The ways in which military-technological innovation has been steered by the government in Russia (see Argument 4) can be best conceptualized by the evolving developmental state mindset of the Russian leadership.

2.4 Putting the Process in Motion: Conflict Dynamics

Since Russia usually responds to arms sophistication, rather than proactively initiating it, as argued above, there must be a trigger for every round of its military-technological innovation. It is assumed here that conflict dynamics may well be such a trigger. The distinctions between different types of conflict that could hypothetically make a difference in this regard yield four dimensions that are important to consider: whether it is a violent or non-violent conflict, and whether Russia is directly involved in it or not. This relationship may be visualized by a simple matrix with four quadrants (Fig. 2). According to one of the existing definitions based on the analysis of a large number of conflicts, a violent conflict is either a severe crisis or a war, and a non-violent conflict is a latent conflict or any crisis situation (Pfetsch and Rohloff 2000: XIII).

Therefore, the final key argument of this book is that conflicts within a defined range of intensity and relevance have typically spurred military-technological innovation in Russia. However, the objective is not only to prove the validity of the argument but also to discover which conflict dynamics in particular have historically had the strongest impact on Russia's decision to innovate.

Argument 8: The process of military-technological innovation in Russia has typically been spurred (for further details, see Argument 2) by certain conflict dynamics.

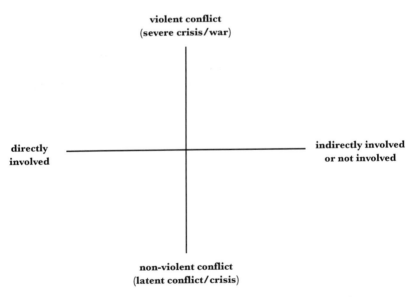

Fig. 2 Conflict matrix from the Russian perspective. The author's own figure, partially based on the typology by Pfetsch and Rohloff (2000: XIII).

2.5 Research Methodology

From the methodological perspective, this is a longitudinal analysis of Russian military-technological innovation. The key objective is the cross-time comparison within a single unit, i.e. the analysis is limited to one country – Russia. Time is used for increasing the number of cases (or sub-units) through periodization. Therefore, the same country in different time periods is treated as a set of distinct cases, and this becomes the basis for intra-case comparisons over time (della Porta 2008: 207, 217).

The history this study refers to covers three time periods. Before discussing the logic behind this, it is important to clarify that temporal variance is assessed not across consecutive periods but across different periods separated by certain intervals of time (della Porta 2008: 220). This periodization takes three dimensions into account: the central role of new technologies creating a major break with the past, the relative importance of changes, and their magnitude or scale. Three technology-led, equally significant, and truly major transformations in Russia's military-technological condition are identified, each pertaining to a different century: rifled and breech-loading weapons in the nineteenth century, nuclear weapons in the twentieth century, and precision-guided weapons in the twenty-first century. Even though the latter revolution began much earlier in the US as part of the IT-RMA and Soviet military theorists immediately realized its revolutionary potential, as discussed above, Russia embarked on it properly only in the twenty-first century. Further explanations concerning these particular choices are given in the introductory sections of the respective chapters. The conceptual model introduced above is used as a lens in the comparative analysis of these three cases, and subsequently as a means of grasping the Russian style of military-technological innovation.

The analysis builds primarily on the use of three types of data: archival data, data obtained directly from experts, and secondary sources. Therefore, in addition to secondary research, two primary data collection methods are used for the purposes of this study: archival research and expert interviews. Regarding the former, the main archival source of primary data is the main military-theoretical journal of the Ministry of Defence of the USSR (later the Russian Federation): *Voennaya Mysl'* ('Military Thought'). Since this study takes a *longue durée* perspective, it is important to note that this journal was originally founded under the name *Voennyi Sbornik* ('Military Collection'). It is why the analysis of nineteenth century dynamics presented in Chapter 3 refers to the latter, while the twentieth to twenty-first century developments presented in Chapters 4 and 5 cite the former. Other minor sources are used occasionally, among them: *Vestnik Evropy, Pravda, Russian Herald, Artillery Magazine, Military-Industrial Courier, Review of the Army and Navy, National Defence, Bulletin of Moscow University*, as well as publications by Politizdat (the central publishing house of political and historical-party literature in the USSR), Voenizdat (the publishing house of the Ministry of Defence of the USSR), and the Central Publishing and Printing Complex of Strategic Rocket Forces (Russian abbreviation 'ЦИПК РВСН'). As native language proficiency often enhances nuances not easily translatable, the author's ability to read these materials in their original language is seen as a crucial side contribution and simultaneously the minimum necessary condition for producing this work.

In addition to archival data, other primary data such as that obtained from official state documents, transcripts of speeches, and statements by representatives of the state are sometimes referred to as well. For the best possible understanding of the developments and processes of thinking in each specific period and throughout different periods in history, emphasis is placed on gathering and systematically interpreting period-specific contextual knowledge and original sources whenever possible. The intention is to reconstruct the history of how the same issues have been interpreted and approached in Russia over more than a hundred years. More recent scholarly interpretations of this history and various Western sources, all representing secondary sources in the context of this research, are used only occasionally. Their role is to fill data gaps, provide critical insights and balance opinions where deemed necessary, and capture the Western understanding of military-technological innovation in Russia.

Besides archival and other official documents supplemented with secondary sources to compensate for missing or incomplete records, expert interviews are also used for data collection. The interviewees were selected not only for their specialization, in one or another way related to Russian strategic culture, technology, and military doctrine, but also for their nationality and location. Out of the ten interviewees, at least one is a Russia-based scholar, at least one is a Russian scholar based in the West, at least one is a European scholar, and at least one is an American scholar. This enabled the representation of multiple perspectives, even if to a limited degree given the total number of interviewees. Thanks to the 'snowballing' technique, further interviewees were identified and invited based on recommendations from previous interviewees. To give the interviewees more opportunity to fully express themselves, interviews were semi-structured. Each interview consisted of a set of open-ended questions which, depending on the responses, were followed by more specific questions (Lamont and Boduszynski 2020: 105–106). All interviewees gave their voluntary consent to be cited in this work.

The principal method of data analysis in this book is discourse analysis, particularly interpretive structural discourse analysis. Unlike critical or other kinds of discourse analysis, this approach simply focuses on discourses that support particular social and organizational contexts. The relationship between individual texts (archival documents and other relevant documents, speeches, and statements which provide accounts of insiders' interpretations of the context) constituting wider discourses (inter-related sets of texts) and their broader social context are explored from the social constructivist perspective (Philips and Hardy 2002: 3–6, 23–24). This perspective suggests that meanings, and hence knowledge, are socially constructed, same as the social world. The relationship between these two processes is reflexive, or constitutive, meaning that 'the social construction of knowledge can itself affect the construction of social reality and vice versa' (Guzzini 2005: 496, 499). It is perhaps the most adequate method for analysing RMAs because RMAs themselves entail both discursive and material transformations, as discussed above, and the following chapters vividly illustrate that the stream of influence works both ways; the introduction of new technologies spurs discourses of transformation which, in turn, facilitate broader transformations in military thought and practice. This method is equally suitable for studying strategic culture because, at least from the perspective of first-generation scholars, the relationship between strategic ideas and strategic experience is mutually constitutive (Gray 1999: 54).

The nexus between Russian strategic culture and its experience with RMAs is also studied here as mutually constitutive, not causal, because the main question posed in this research does not begin with 'why' or 'how', but with 'what', in particular 'what has been the relationship between'. This is a typical question of constitutive theories, according to Wendt (1998: 104–105). The focus is on the factors and properties constituting the Russian cultural approach to military-technological innovation.

2.6 Concluding Remarks

This chapter introduced the theoretical and methodological framework of this book. In doing so, it relied extensively on a strand of theoretical literature produced in Russia (and the USSR). Not only did it take the Russian perspective seriously, as would generally be expected from the analysis presented here, but it also contributed to a better understanding of the similarities and differences between Russian and Western conceptions.

The key contribution of this chapter consisted in introducing and graphically representing a novel triangular model of Russia's strategic cultural approach to military-technological innovation (Fig. 1). Another side contribution was to theorize the triggers of military-technological innovation in Russia (Fig. 2). The presented model is tailored to the Russian context but its practical applicability goes beyond that. Generally speaking, it theorizes the options available to a technological laggard in an accelerating arms race scenario. It means the model can be used, even if refined accordingly, to inquire into other countries' responses to Western innovation, for example, that of China.

The following chapters will apply this model to three different periods in Russian history. In particular, the triangular conceptualization of military-technological innovation and related processes will help to capture Russia's oscillation between different possible ways of responding to Western innovation in each of the studied cases. Recurring discourses and practices will be traced over the last hundred and fifty years with the help of the concept of strategic culture. So, while the model of military-technological innovation will be applied separately in each of the three following chapters, with the findings eventually compared and contrasted, that of strategic culture will serve as an overarching framework applied across the entire period studied. To this end, it is the final chapter of this book that is dedicated to the discussion of the Russian strategic cultural approach to military technological innovation.

3. Rifled Breech-Loading Weapons

This chapter studies the introduction of rifled, and then also breech-loading weapons as the greatest military-technological innovation in Imperial Russia in the mid- to late-nineteenth century. Even though it was around the same time that the Navy was transitioning from sails to steam, the focus here is on terrestrial weapons systems. The reason for this is that Russia remained pre-eminently a land power in the second half of the nineteenth century, as dictated by its geography and long-standing tradition. Even the naval budget remained under 20 per cent of the budget for land forces between 1863–1894 (Pintner 1984: 243–244). If the focus were to be on the greatest innovation during this timeframe, technological changes in land warfare had a much more direct relevance to the Russian way of war and are, therefore, brought to the fore in this chapter.[3]

The chapter begins by considering the role of the Crimean War (1853–1856). It then proceeds to discuss Russia's respective responses in overcoming its technological inferiority vis-à-vis the West. Three consecutive sections are dedicated to the analysis of related aspects. The concluding section graphically illustrates the key findings (Fig. 3).

---

3   For the same reason, the analysis does not systematically engage with the Russo-Japanese War, which did otherwise have a major impact on Russian military thinking.

3.1 The Crimean War as a Major Turning Point

From Peter the Great's defeat of Charles XII at Poltava in 1709 to Alexander I's spectacular victories over Napoleon in 1812–1815, Russia emerged victorious in almost every conflict and proved itself as a major military power (Pintner 1984: 231). Neumann (2008: 138–139) accurately noted that its great power status was then 'institutionalized' at the Congress of Vienna in 1815 and that, from this very moment to the Crimean War, Russia was 'secure in its great powerhood.' Zaionchkovsky (1952: 44) particularly recorded that during the thirty years of the reign of Nicholas I, the state of Imperial Russia's army was depicted in all official reports 'in extremely high colours', while its combat power was 'invincible'. However, its defeat in the Crimean War made it increasing difficult for Russia to maintain its position vis-à-vis other major European powers (Pintner 1984: 231). Russia's great power status (Neumann 2008: 128) and the 'prestige' of tsarism in Europe were seriously undermined, and the country was left, to a considerable degree, in 'political isolation' (Zaionchkovsky 1952: 44). Russia's military was also exposed, especially its technological backwardness. At the time of Russia's successful military campaigns (1709–1856), military technology was not only relatively simple, generally characterized by low rates of fire, short range, and inaccuracy, but also 'static' (Pintner 1984: 232). Russia's military decline was associated with its inability to harness rapid technnological progress, which brought about the increase in the range, accuracy, and destructive capacity of all types of weapons, and particularly the introduction of rifles (Zaionchkovsky 1952: 44; Pintner 1984: 232). This sense of loss was one of the key drivers not only behind Russia's decision to innovate, but also behind its decision to take the lead in disarmament negotiations.

Zimmerman, whose article appeared in *Voennyi Sbornik*, an official magazine of the Russian War Ministry, expressed his concerns about Russia's defeat in the Crimean War. He drew attention to the fact that Russia had hitherto been 'considered, and not without reason, the *first* [emphasis added] military power in the world', and that it possessed 'enormous capacities for the war effort' (Zimmerman 1859: 380–381). Fedorov (1911: 37–38), however, admitted that 'quite rightly' the 'insufficiency' of Russia's weapons was considered to be one of the main reasons for its defeats. Zaionchkovsky (1952: 23) provided evidence in support of the fact that, by the beginning of the Crimean War, the Russian army was armed almost exclusively with smooth-bore guns, while Western

European armies were largely armed with rifled weapons. In addition, he (1952: 27) stressed that Russia also employed artillery weapons in insufficient numbers. According to him (1952: 28), no major changes occurred during the Crimean War, especially in artillery weapons. The Russian army received considerable quantities of rifled guns, he admitted (1952: 28), but it was only a slight increase in the overall percentage of rifled weapons. Fedorov (1911: 37) specifically highlighted, however, that even these weapons represented the first improvement in rifling technology, while Allied troops were armed with the most advanced rifled weapons.

The insignificant accuracy and range of smooth-bore weapons also implied, and Fedorov (1904: 111) considered it 'natural', that the Russian army did not take firearms training seriously. Alabin, a participant of the Crimean War, fairly and accurately summarized the state of war:

> Are we ready for war? To be honest, no, we are far from ready. ... Firstly, we are poorly armed. ... We have very few people who know how to shoot, since this art has never been properly studied. ... We are all obsessed ... exclusively with marching and the correct stretching of the toe (cited in Zaionchkovsky 1952: 38).

It is remarkable that, among other things, he brought attention to another structural problem of that time: the country's armed forces were largely perceived through a symbolic, rather than pragmatic, prism. This problem was similarly spotted by D. A. Miliutin, the future War Minister (1861–81): 'Everything is just great for parades, and just terrible for war' (cited in Panaeva 1986: 232). In one of the articles, published in *Voennyi Sbornik* in 1861, the author eventually concluded that the Crimean War 'was precisely one of such events for Russia which, producing major social shifts, directed them along other paths' (N. D. N. 1861a: 5). The discussion below demonstrates that there were significant implications of these conflict dynamics for the country's military.

3.2 The Quest for Symmetry and Emulative Tendencies

'The *armed world* [emphasis added], accompanied by massive military preparations ... constitutes the hallmark of the modern age' stressed Glinoetsky (1868: 59) in one of his articles published in *Voennyi Sbornik*.

Russia was concerned about its position in this new security environment. In one of the reports from the Main Artillery Directorate to the War Minister, the following statement appeared: 'Russia cannot ... and should not lag behind other major European powers in the thorough-going re-armament of its army, no matter how tangible the costs may be for the state' (cited in Fedorov 1911: 119). So, it was a matter of symbolic meaning as much as a practical concern for Russia.

Russia was, therefore, committed to respond to the current arms race symmetrically, itself embarking on the ongoing RMA. Leer (1861a: 35) emphasized the fact that newly emerging military technologies only assured a short-lived competitive advantage and implicitly called for their wider exploitation on the battlefield, and his original assumptions are very much in line with RMA theory today:

> It is known that the one who employs a new tool on the battlefield *first* [emphasis added] acquires enormous benefits. ... [R]ifled weapons brought significant advantages to the Allies in the Crimea as the other side [Russia] was armed with smooth-bore ones. At the same time, it is impossible not to notice that from the moment this technology was made common in all armies, its influence began to manifest itself on a much smaller scale.

Before proceeding to discuss the Russian RMA, it is important to consider the state of the country's political economy. This is because, as discussed in Chapter 2, every RMA depends on its contextual economic conditions in theory. Milioukov (1911: 7), describing the situation in general, concluded that it was 'impossible to increase both the country's defence spending and social policy spending at the same time.' According to him, it was the time for civilized mankind to 'think and finally make ... a *choice* [emphasis added]'. N. O. Sukhozanet, Russia's War Minister (1856–1861) preceding Miliutin, compromised on the need to strengthen the defence capability of the state and was primarily driven by the desire to reduce military spending as much as possible. Miliutin would subsequently characterize his policy as follows:

> [A]ll the measures taken by General Sukhozanet had the sole purpose of reducing military spending ... Continuing down this path, it was possible to bring the state to complete impotence, at a time when all other European powers were strengthening their armaments (cited in Zaionchkovsky 1952: 47).

Yet Miliutin himself faced a difficult choice when he took office: on the one hand, he had to strengthen the combat capability of Russia's armed forces, but on the other hand, he had to minimize the budget of the War Ministry (Zaionchkovsky 1952: 50–51).

Russia's major military modernization programme was, therefore, the product of a carefully balanced effort to catch up with the West, mainly driven by Miliutin as the new War Minister (1861–81). In his report to the War Ministry of 15 January 1862, Miliutin wrote, commenting particularly on the Crimean War:

> This war ... led us to the realization of the need for the most active measures to supply our troops with modern weapons. ... We must now frankly admit ... that the material condition of our artillery and military armaments lagged behind those of other European powers (cited in Zaionchkovsky 1952: 138).

Elsewhere he identified the key priorities in the realm of technology:

> In the present state of the art of war, *artillery technology* [emphasis added] has become extremely important. The perfection of weapons now gives a decisive advantage to the army which in this respect is ahead of the others. We are convinced of this truth by the bitter experience of the last war. Our troops, supplied with *rifled guns* [emphasis added] hastily converted from smooth-bore guns, and too late, had to suffer heavy losses and usually redeemed the imperfection of their weapons with their stamina (cited in Zaionchkovsky 1952: 56–57).

Concerning the role of artillery, Baumgarten (1887a: 73), whose articles on this subject appeared in *Voennyi Sbornik*, agreed that 'the improvement of firearms and the extensive development of military forces and military art ... bring artillery to the fore.'

The Russian RMA was a holistic change, eventually. Changes were simultaneously taking place at all possible levels from the introduction of new technologies and the conceptual realization of their revolutionary potential to various tactical and organizational adaptations. The re-armament process took place in two steps: the first consisted of the replacement of smooth-bore weapons with rifled, muzzle-loading ones and lasted approximately until 1866; the second, from 1866 onwards, was characterized by the introduction of rifled, breech-loading weapons. Russia was falling behind the others in implementing change, even at the latter stage, as captured, for example, by Miliutin: 'We barely finished the re-armament of our entire army with ... rifles, when the question of loading guns from behind ... was already raised in all states' (cited in Zaionchkovsky 1952: 139). This even more clearly illustrates the catch-up character of military-technological innovation in Russia.

Not only small arms but also artillery weapons underwent this transformation. Rifling technology was more or less systematically applied to the latter circa 1860. In 1866, it was decided that all batteries of field artillery, horse and foot, were to have rifled, breech-loading weapons (Zaionchkovsky 1952: 136–138, 158).

Particularly important is that there was a clear understanding of the necessity of this technological change. Russian military experts quickly recognized the undeniable advantages of both rifled weapons and breech-loading weapons. Leer (1861a: 36) foregrounded two major advantages of rifled weapons over smooth-bore ones: accuracy and greater range. He (1861a: 32) particularly emphasized that the accuracy of fire increased at least ten times, and the range five times. In relation to rifled artillery pieces, Baumgarten (1887b: 167) similarly highlighted 'their great reach and accuracy'.

Leer (1861a: 40–41) also captured the revolutionary potential of breech-loading weapons, particularly citing the Prussian army:

> There is no doubt that the Prussian example of arming the infantry with breech-loading guns should soon find followers in other European armies. The benefits of this technology are undoubted. ... We dare to say affirmatively that the first war in which Prussia will participate will show all the advantages of this weapon and force it to be introduced in other armies.

Observing the actual use of breech-loading weapons on the battlefield during the Franco-Prussian War (1870–1871), Zeddeler (1876: 62) also found that their fire, due to its expanding scope of damage, 'acquired a formidable, previously unknown force.' These two references point at another important aspect of the Russian cultural approach to military-technological innovation: closely observing others as a way of learning. Milioukov (1911: 42) similarly highlighted 'the terrible destructive effect' of such weapons. It is important to clarify that the increased destructiveness of these weapons was often linked to the speed at which they could be put to use, i.e. the ability to continuously fire, unlike with muzzle-loading weapons. Zeddeler (1876: 71) spotted that, with the latter, in part due to the relatively long reloading time, 'the troops suffered much less loss from fire', and that only with the introduction of the former did fire 'become of *paramount importance* [emphasis added]'. Leer (1861a: 40–41) agreed that the main benefit of breech-loading weapons was to 'save time'.

The immense impact of rapid fire was increasingly recognized also in relation to other revolutionary technologies accompanying the same revolution. One of the articles published in *Voennyi Sbornik* in 1870 noted that the Franco-Prussian War had clearly proved the military utility of rotary cannons. The author (N. L. 1870: 139) drew particular attention to their revolutionary potential, saying such weapons 'will be introduced into all armies, and, due to their properties, they will probably have a great influence on the course of battles.' The same author (1870: 150) still acknowledged that, despite the increasing speed of their fire, rotary cannons could not replace field artillery as they would only be effective at comparatively short range. To gain competitive advantage, Russia equipped almost all artillery brigades with rotary cannons by the beginning of 1874. However, it eventually appeared that these weapons could only provide limited advantages. Zaionchkovsky (1952: 161) argued that they did not live up to their purpose due to their insufficient range and clarified they were only the 'prototype' of rapid-fire artillery.

Von der Hoven (1883: 253), whose article also appeared in *Voennyi Sbornik*, also drew attention to the revolutionary potential of quick-firing, in particular magazine-equipped, guns for infantry and cavalry too: 'The facts of the adoption of such weapons in the armies of different states testify to the awareness of the benefits that these weapons can deliver to a soldier at certain moments of battle.' Russia fell behind its competitors in the adoption of this type of weapons as well. While foreign armies had experimented with this technology since the late 1870s and most Western European states proceeded with the re-armament of their armies in 1886, Russia lacked funding and had to adopt a slower, more careful, and patient approach. Mosin's rifle was finally put into service in 1891 and stayed in service for over fifty years (Zaionchkovsky 1973: 156, 158).

Besides the introduction of new technologies and the realization of their transformative impact, the transition from smooth-bore to rifled, especially breech-loading, weapons (and later also magazine-equipped guns) required other operational principles. This is exactly what RMA theory suggests as well, meaning that Russia's steps in this direction were clearly steps towards its full exploitation of the ongoing RMA. First of all, the primacy of fire made Russian military experts argue in favour of loose formation infantry tactics. Leer (1861b: 64) stressed that it was 'necessary to give *full advantage* [emphasis added] to loose formation.' Another author (D-N 1859: 79–80), whose article was featured in *Voennyi Sbornik*, spotted early on that the increase in the number of infantrymen armed with rifles would render loose formation of 'paramount importance'. Both experts highlighted that the deployment of the infantry in loose formation was not an altogether new principle but they concurred that its full potential would be realized and exploited only with the introduction of rifled weapons (D-N 1859: 79–80; Leer 1861a: 30). Zeddeler (1876: 64) emphasized the importance of fighting in loose formation for 'the reduction of losses'.

Another closely related conceptual innovation was that the surrounding terrain could be used 'as a weapon' in this new type of combat, as suggested by Faletsky (1890: 54–55) who made an interesting and important observation:

> At a time when, due to the imperfection of firearms, success was achieved exclusively by close (hand-to-hand) combat, the use of the terrain was ... limited to the construction of obstacles that made it difficult for the enemy to approach. The enormous progress of long-range weapons now makes it possible to use the terrain for the actual conduct of combat and ... precisely for the more favourable effects of weapons ...

The application of rifling technology to artillery weapons required just the opposite: concentration of fire instead of its dispersal. This trend is captured, for example, in the following statement by Baumgarten (1887b: 171):

> The negligible accuracy of smooth-bore weapons made it necessary to transfer the shooting almost entirely into the hands of the gunner. Each weapon fired in a more or less independent way ... The introduction of rifled weapons changed the conditions. The excellent accuracy of these weapons deprived gunners of their former independence and transferred battery fire in its entirety into the hands of the battery commander.

Elsewhere he (1890: 111) specified that the fragmentation of the battery would certainly contradict 'the basic properties of artillery'. According to him, the main properties of artillery fire would be most clearly expressed if it was 'concentrated' which, in turn, could be achieved only by increasing the number of participating weapons. He (1887b: 166) otherwise called this principle of artillery deployment 'artillery masses', and the desired effect 'concentrated artillery fire'. He (1887b: 163) clarified, however, that this tactical approach was not entirely new but only the introduction of rifled weapons paved the way for it to transition from the field of theory to the field of combat practice. Olshevsky (1890: 116–117) similarly concluded that fragmented parts of the battery were unable to successfully fight, especially if it was necessary to shoot at moving targets.

In addition to more sophisticated tactics, the development of military equipment entailed the adaptation of organization. On 20 July 1855, a special commission for military improvements was created, of which Miliutin himself was a member since February 1856. One of the key tasks assigned to this commission was the improvement of weapons (Zaionchkovsky 1952: 45–46). The system of combat training underwent a major transformation as well. Military experts of the day concurred that the need for peacetime military training had increased in importance. This change was precisely associated with the introduction of rifled weapons. Leer (1861a: 37; 1861c: 298) repeatedly highlighted that rifled weapons were more complex from a technological viewpoint and, therefore, taking full advantage of their range and precision was a 'special art'. It is remarkable that not only targeted shooting, but also gymnastics, loose formation training, and other types of physical and mental training were recognized as important elements of the training programme (Leer 1861c: 305). Vannovsky (1861: 445) went further and gave clear priority to quality over quantity by asking himself and the reader 'what benefit a randomly fired bullet will bring to the shooter when he cannot find the *cause* [emphasis added] of an unsuccessful shot.' According to him (1861: 447), shooters had to understand, inter alia, the impact of wind and sunlight, a partially charged magazine, raw powder, poorly cast bullets, and improper loading on the execution and accuracy of shots. He (1861: 448) even recommended that the training programme be divided into two parts: preparatory exercises first and then actual shooting. One caveat is important. The significance of training was recognized not only with respect to the infantry but also in relation against the use of artillery weapons. For example, Baumgarten (1890: 116) drew attention to 'the close dependence of the positive properties of artillery fire on the degree of perfection to which its discipline and technique are brought through thorough training of battery personnel and their commanding staff.'

In view of this difference in tactics, different qualities were eventually demanded of infantrymen and artillerymen. What was increasingly required of an infantryman, according to Leer (1861c: 310), was 'inventiveness and independence (the ability to act without supervisors)'. Referring specifically to the deployment of 'artillery masses', Baumgarten (1887a: 74) underlined that improvisation was 'unthinkable' and therefore unacceptable in relation to artillery weapons. 'In actual combat, we will use only what we thoroughly prepare and learn *in peacetime* [emphasis added]', he added.

All these ideas gradually translated into real organizational practices, as detailed below (Zaionchkovsky 1952: 182–184, 187). In 1862, a special committee for the organization and education of troops was created under the War Ministry. In 1863, the War Minister issued a special order on training recruits which required them, among other things, to practice loading guns, shooting, and fighting in loose formation. Emphasis was increasingly put on the meaningful assimilation by recruits of the knowledge they acquired because one of the key objectives set out in this document was that 'recruits understand well what practical purpose each technique or exercise serves.' New tactical principles were reflected in the new charter of the combat infantry service, developed in the period from 1855 to 1866. For example, this document laid stress on the importance of loose formation in the deployment of infantry. In one of the subsequent reports of the Committee for the Organization and Education of Troops, there was a clear call 'to give full preference to firing from loose formation' (Report 1879: 92). Also of great importance for the development of the new training system was the textbook by the Professor of the Military Academy, M. Dragomirov, published in 1866. It is particularly noteworthy that one of the instructions of 1869 paid special attention to exercises 'with the use of the terrain', i.e. the use of the surrounding terrain for cover and defeating the enemy. New combat charters of the foot and horse artillery services were published in 1859. However, these charters maintained, to a greater extent than others, their original 'parade' (плац-парадный) character which hampered the progress of implementation of new principles of practice-oriented training. For example, according to these regulations, the whole battery had to be 'charged simultaneously as one gun', which obviously had symbolic rather than practical value. The above was also discussed in great detail in Zaionchkovsky (1952: 183, 185, 200–201).

Furthermore, the number of projectiles available for artillery batteries was significantly reduced, mainly for cost reasons, in 1867 (Zaionchkovsky 1952: 201). In his article published in *Artillery Magazine*, the official magazine of the Artillery Department of the Russian Empire, Petrakov (1871: 483–484) came to the conclusion that the country's artillery received little training in part due to 'the limited supply of training ammunition'. In fact, there was also a deep distrust of technology which also hindered its more effective utilization. This issue will be addressed in more detail in the next section but it is important to note now for the following reason. Comparing the Russian approach to that of the Prussian army, Baumgarten (1888: 296) discovered that the latter was guided by principles which did not contradict 'the spirit of the weapon' and were not based on 'an unconditional denial of the material force of artillery fire'. On the contrary, Russia had, according to him, developed a mistrust of the material power of artillery fire. The following section illustrates that this has been a constraining factor to major changes in Russian military thought. Nevertheless, the guide to shooting from artillery pieces, compiled by V. Shklyarevich in 1874, was an important theoretical contribution to the development of rifle shooting techniques (Zaionchkovsky 1952: 202).

Organizational adaptations were not limited to the development and codification of new training techniques. First of all, the process of re-armament required building up the necessary infrastructure. The War Ministry considered it essential to reduce Russia's reliance on foreign imports. In one of his letters to the state controller Chevkin concerning the construction of a new arms factory, Miliutin wrote: 'You will be frightened by the huge figure of the estimated total expenditure, but this investment can hardly be avoided if we want Russia to be secure in terms of weapons in the future and be able to do without foreign orders' (cited in Zaionchkovsky 1952: 140). He particularly associated the development of Russia's domestic arms industry with the maintenance of its status: 'Russia is not Egypt ... to be limiting itself to buying guns abroad for the entire army' (cited in Fedorov 1911: 237). Significant steps were taken in the development of Russia's military industry such as the construction of steel plants in Obukhov and Perm, or the reconstruction of the arms factory in Tula (Zaionchkovsky 1952: 179).

There were even bottom-up initiatives. The Tula gunsmiths appealed to the government to provide them with an order for the manufacture of 25,000 guns in 1857:

> We ... would like to serve our fatherland ... to show that we have not lagged behind foreigners in weapons work and can work regularly and carefully ... and therefore we dare to convincingly ask for the gracious intercession of your imperial Highness to deliver us an order for weapons (cited in Zaionchkovsky 1952: 137).

However, these initiatives were constrained by the government, still preferring to order weapons abroad. There were two reasons for this: the 'inherent slavish commitment' of the tsarist government to all the foreign stuff (иностранщина) (Zaionchkovsky 1952: 137) and the underdevelopment of domestic arms production capability, which made foreign orders more attractive in terms of the balance between speed, quality, and price (Fedorov 1911: 120). Graf (1861: 394) spotted a similar problem in his article in *Voennyi Sbornik*: 'Our Tula guns, in the accuracy of shooting, cannot compete with ... French ones which are even much cheaper.'

The rudiments of a business model were visible too. For example, the Tula arms factory was handed over to 'rental-commercial management' (арендно-коммерческое управление). It was an important step after the abolition of forced labour but the new tenant, through their government connections, acquired the factory lease without competition as it was considered impossible to rent it to 'private speculators, and even more so to foreigners'. Loyalty was the 'supreme qualification' for appointment to key posts under tsarism (Pipes 1993: 444). Shortly after the transfer of the factory to rental-commercial management, in November 1865, the society of Tula gunsmiths turned to the War Ministry with a request to transfer it to their collective ownership on more favourable terms. However, their proposal was rejected (Zaionchkovsky 1952: 141–142). Taking a broader perspective, Owen (1985: 589) reflected on 'the complicated pattern of cooperation and conflict between *capitalism* [emphasis added] and the tsarist state'.

The above clearly illustrates that Imperial Russia had some characteristics of what could, from today's perspective, be termed a 'developmental state'. The tsarist regime clearly facilitated the conditions under which the tsar and his loyal bureaucrats would make final decisions about the distribution of funding and support between different industries and sectors of the economy, as also illustrated by the difficult 'guns vs butter' decisions in this chapter. The development of defence-industrial capabilities was closely coordinated from above, even if arms factories were formally under the so-called 'rental-commercial' deals. One of the key objectives was to reduce or close the gap between Russia and its technologically superior competitors, primarily in the military realm. At the same time, there was space – albeit very limited and highly conditioned – for private ownership and bottom-up initiatives. Competition for weapons orders from the government was also emerging, yet the tsar clearly favoured foreign entrepreneurs. From a more general perspective, the elites took an integrated approach to the country's modernization, proceeding almost simultaneously with the abolition of serfdom, judicial reforms, reforms of higher and secondary education, financial and economic reforms, as well as military reforms (Belykh and Mau 2020: 31–32). There was an increasing realization of the need to invest in a war-capable economy and society, rather than just an army, especially under the changing conditions of war, and Glinoetsky (1859: 750) drew attention to the principle that 'if you want to live in peace, [you must] have *all the means* [emphasis added] for waging war.' Imperial Russia can, therefore, be considered as an emerging, imperfect developmental state, or a *proto*-developmental state.

There is another aspect of the evolving organizational infrastructure that deserves note. It was not possible to take full advantage of new and improved weapons without establishing effective communication channels. Annenkov (1866: 350) wrote:

> The ability to *quickly concentrate* [emphasis added] significant masses of troops at each threatened point, or just before the start of the implementation of the planned campaign, is of great importance *especially for us, given the vast extent of the borders of our fatherland* [emphasis added].

Another author of *Voennyi Sbornik* spotted the same: 'Russia ... is in the most disadvantageous position of all the European states. The vast expanses of our territory ... destroy any possibility of rapidly mobilizing the army' (N. D. N. 1861b: 314). Maksheev (1890a: 31) went on to further argue that railroads were 'a new means of war'. In another part of the same article, he drew attention to the Franco-Prussian War, in particular the brilliant victories of the Prussians, as a perfect example of how the timely organization and effective utilization of military railroads could contribute to one's military might (Maksheev 1890b: 242). It is yet another demonstration of the significance of observations in the development of Russia's own understanding of – and approach to – military-technological innovations.

The 'military lines of communication' created by railroads were increasingly seen as useful for the timely occupation of defensive positions and sudden offensive operations; the reinforcement of weakly occupied points; the rapid transmission of orders, news, and all kinds of information; the departure of the sick, wounded, and prisoners; as well as for all kinds of supplies. Last but not least, a fully functional strategic railway network could significantly reduce costs for the maintenance and mobilization of the army. Not only would it allow for the replacement of Russia's permanent army, at least partially, with a system of reserves, but it would also make it possible to save considerable amounts of money that would otherwise be spent on a costly and lengthy process of mobilization (N. D. N. 1861b: 315, 320). Exploring the ways in which railways could truly contribute to military efforts, Annenkov (1866: 344–345) particularly recommended developing a reliable system of rules and training the army in boarding and unloading. Russia did make some progress towards the creation of an integrated network of railway lines in European Russia (*Voennyi Sbornik* 1863: 527). Before the spread of railways, in 1859, for example, it took more than five months to mobilize 67,000 reserve troops. In 1867, it was possible to mobilize 350,000 reserve troops in six weeks. In 1876, reserve troops could arrive at assembly points by the fifth day of mobilization, and the army would be complete in European Russia on the fifteenth day (Maksheev 1890a: 37).

What deserves attention in this regard is one of the statements by the Russian philosopher and theoretician A. K. Khomiakov. It relates primarily to Russia's position towards the development of military railways but captures the general Russian approach to military innovation, as also illustrated in the following chapters:

> When all other countries are crisscrossed by railroads and are able rapidly to concentrate and to shift their armed forces, Russia must necessarily be able to do the same. It is difficult, it is expensive, but, alas, inevitable. ... With regard to railroads, as in many other things, we are particularly fortunate; we did not have to expend energy on experiments and strain our imagination; *we can and shall reap the fruits of others' labor* [emphasis added] (cited in Wolfe 1967: 177).

3.3 Beyond Technology: Preserving Russia's Asymmetric Advantage

While the above was made to increase Russia's competitive edge and match the rapidly evolving military capabilities of other great powers, Russian military experts actively spoke out in favour of preserving Russia's traditional asymmetric advantage, spiritual power, even in the age of increasingly mechanized warfare. The general logic of pursuing an asymmetric response was captured by Leer (1894: 53–54): 'Striving to be strong where the enemy is weak – exposing [our] strong side and evading [our] weak one.'

Indeed, Russia used to put great emphasis on its spiritual power, meaning its operational and not necessarily technological edge, and this tradition has deep roots. 'The bullet is a fool; the bayonet is a fine chap,' as the famous Russian general A. Suvorov used to say. Many years later Fadeev (1867: 84) explicitly agreed with this statement: 'The Russian soldier is a hand-to-hand fighter, not a shooter; he becomes a shooter, like a cavalryman, only half way.' In fact, this way of thinking deeply penetrated the Russian army. Only with the introduction of more accurate, long-range rifled weapons did this view gradually begin to change (Fedorov 1904: 123). This discussion is important. One of the key indicators of every RMA, at least from the Russian perspective as discussed in Chapter 2, is a qualitatively new approach to the problem of man-technology. The studied revolution did indeed facilitate change in Russian military thought in response to the introduction of revolutionary technologies. Zeddeler (1876: 72) highlighted, for example, that fire could no longer be recognized as a mere prelude to the battle with bayonets; on the contrary, it acquired an 'independent and often decisive influence.'

However, in part due to a deep distrust of technology in Russian military circles, as discussed previously, a more careful approach was adopted. Von-Vocht (1890: 264) warned that gunfighting did not completely exclude hand-to-hand combat and the use of bayonets. The author (D. U. S. 1861: 62) of another article, also published in *Voennyi Sbornik*, similarly spotted that it was misleading to think that the bayonet had lost its former significance with the introduction of improved rifled weapons. The key point is that Russian military experts believed that fights with bayonets were relatively rare because whenever both sides converged, the moral impression made by the enemy's continuously advancing fire was 'so overwhelming' that one's own forces retreated before the collision (Von-Vocht 1890: 264). What was required of them at this 'most decisive moment', in order to bring the battle to 'its final point – to hand-to-hand clash', was a reserve of fearlessness and mental strength. The same author (Leer 1861d: 57) went on to argue as follows: 'If the moral element in an attacking unit is raised to this level, then, despite any appreciable strength of the enemy's fire, success will be on its side.' In other words, victory would always be on the side of the army 'that has *the best spirit* [emphasis added]' (D. U. S. 1861: 63). This clearly illustrates that there was a persistent belief in Russia that spiritual power could fully compensate for technological inferiority.

It is exactly where, according to Russian military experts, their country would always have a decisive advantage over its opponents. Zimmerman (1859: 389) captured the exceptional character of the Russian warrior in the following words: 'As for the *innate ability* [emphasis added] for military art, everyone will agree with me that the Russians will not yield to anyone in this.' Medem (1859: 430) particularly focused on the spirit of daring and courage inherent in horse artillery and came to this conclusion: 'Russian horse artillery has always possessed and still possesses these properties to such an excellent degree that no foreign horse artillery, in this respect, can compare with it.' He (1859: 422) even spotted a very interesting difference between the Russian approach and that of Western Europe. In the cases where it was necessary to hastily form several horse batteries, Western European armies would typically go for experienced gunners, while Russia would usually prioritize excellent riders.

So even at the time when effects from the adoption of new technologies were already apparent, Russia did not give up on its traditional advantage. For example, it is remarkable that, having to choose between intelligence and character, both being equally important, Leer (1863: 59) still gave preference to the latter. Elsewhere he (1861a: 37) elaborated on the role of technologies in this equation and arrived at the conclusion that the introduction of advanced weapons was demanded partly by their material merits and 'most of all' by their moral influence. It is because, according to him, 'nothing can be so harmful to success ... as the soldier's conviction that his weapon is worse than the enemy's.' Even training was seen in this light. Some degree of assurance that the soldier could accurately hit the enemy was seen as a source of his 'self-confidence', without which there could be no striving for victory (D. U. S. 1861: 63). Nor did technologies undermine the significance of spiritual power in field artillery, in the view of Russian military experts. Being aware of the acute need for better trained gunners in Russian horse artillery, Medem (1859: 411) still maintained that their special artillery duties were 'no less important and necessary than cavalry duties.' He (1859: 430) understood the latter, inter alia, as 'the production of movements and actions at a speed impossible for foot artillery, and *in a truly cavalry spirit, boldly, dashingly, even courageously* [emphasis added].' Moreover, there is another interesting fact that similarly demonstrates the primacy of morale in the Russian army. Being aware of the need to prioritize loose formations over close-order formations in the deployment of infantry, as explained previously, Leer (1861b: 65) expressed concerns over the possible decrease of the 'moral element' due to the increased degree of independence given to individual combatants and the subsequent lack of control over their performance.

3.4 Russia's Diplomatic Response: The Hague Conference of 1899

Despite all the progress achieved, Russia's technological backwardness was still apparent. Perhaps the best test of military power is war itself and what played an important role for Russia in this respect was the Russo-Turkish war (1877–1878). This war testified to the decline of Russia's military might. Despite the victorious outcome of the campaign, it revealed that Russia lagged behind in both small arms and artillery, and had major gaps in the training of troops (Zaionchkovsky 1973: 249). Russia lacked heavy and siege artillery, and in particular long-range artillery weapons. Baumgarten (1888: 296) confirmed virtually the same fact: 'Everyone is talking about the weak, even poor, performance of our artillery in the last campaign.' Zeddeler (1878: 72) in turn captured Russia's backwardness in firearms, as revealed by the Russo-Turkish war: 'The greater part of our army went to war with Krnka guns; the extent of their inferior quality compared to Turkish weapons was known.' Krnka guns were inferior to their Turkish counterparts at least in firing range. At the same time, the re-armament of the Russian army was not complete by the beginning of the war and, as a result, different divisions were often armed with different weapons (Zaionchkovsky 1952: 341–342). In one of his reports from the battlefield, General Skobelev noted that such differences impacted the logistics and subsequently the army's overall performance: 'The battle from eight o'clock in the morning to eight o'clock in the evening forced many units to deplete their cartridges ... and their timely resupply, due to the difference in weapons, was extremely difficult' (Collection 1903: 215). According to one of the participants, the Russo-Turkish war also revealed that Russia conceded to Turkey in the amount of available ammunition:

> It was noon. Artillery and rifle fire, which began in the morning, thundered without interruption. No separate shots could be heard, and everything has merged into one rumble, from which one could hardly hear a human word. One must be surprised what a mass of cartridges and shells the Turks managed to save up ... in order to *shoot so generously* [emphasis added] as they did (Ostapov 1890: 184).

One likely explanation for this imbalance was that the Russian army largely followed 'the principle of rare fire', driven by the need to save cartridges, as highlighted by Zeddeler (1878: 68). There was clearly a demand for increased military expenditure. However, the Russo-Turkish war had severe economic consequences for Russia (Belykh and Mau 2020: 33). In the meantime, the formation of military blocs facilitated the arms race, especially as Germany, Austria-Hungary, and Italy entered into a Tripartite Alliance against Russia in 1882 (Chernyavsky 2017: 30–31). Even though the Russian Navy is not the focus of this chapter, one of the reports of the Minister of Naval Forces captures the general spirit of that time. This report was submitted to Alexander III in 1884 and its significance is in highlighting the important symbolic value of further military modernization for Russia: 'Russia *cannot leave the Areopagus of the great powers* [emphasis added] and make them forget about itself.' In response, the Minister of Finance wrote: 'To walk further along the path of increasing expenses ... would mean ... walking to suicide' (both cited in Nefedov 2010: 376). Once again, it was a tension between Russia's expansionary ambitions on the one hand and limited material resources on the other.

The 1890s marked another turning point. The Krupp corporation created new rapid-fire cannons which could fire six rounds per minute. French designers almost kept up with the Germans, and the French gun of 1897 had an even higher rate of fire (Nefedov 2010: 375). Austria was also in the process of fitting its army out with new artillery. The question of re-equipping field artillery arose in Russia. However, Russia was feeling the increasing costs of armaments 'more painfully' than its principal enemies, Germany and Austria-Hungary (Best 1999: 622). Bloch (1898: 176–177) explicitly stated:

[I]n the current state of Russia, reducing the cost of preparing for war is no less, and perhaps even more necessary for her than for other European states. ... These forces are necessary for Russia to conduct a different struggle: not on the battlefield, but with its economic backwardness, poverty and ignorance of the people.

It is fair to say that Russia had a very clear appreciation of the situation and had no illusions. For example, the following was stated in the report of 1892: 'The War Ministry is fully aware that the financial situation of the empire does not allow us to compete in armaments with our Western neighbours' (cited in Nefedov 2010: 375). There was more clarity in the report of 1896:

> In the near future, the War Ministry will probably have a new, very extensive task, namely, to re-equip field artillery with quick-firing cannons. ... Our artillery will no doubt *have to follow the example of the artilleries of the Western armies* [emphasis added], in order not to yield to them in armament and in the effectiveness of fire; but the re-equipping of artillery will present us with great difficulties, both in terms of the significant amount of funds required, and especially due to the low productivity of our factories ... (cited in Zaionchkovsky 1973: 162–163).

Pintner (1984: 243) came up with a particularly important finding which tells us a great deal about Russia's investment priorities. Heavily relying on Russian (including primary) sources, he found no clear trend in the proportion of weapons expenses in Russia's total military budget for the whole studied period: it remained at roughly 12–13 per cent between 1870–1873, and only went up to 13–16 per cent between 1893–1897. Surprisingly, there was no upward trend despite the ongoing re-armament programme.

The impossibility of overcoming its military, and more importantly technological, backwardness motivated Russia's asymmetric response in the diplomatic realm, in particular, its disarmament efforts which culminated in the Hague Peace Conference of 1899. In one of the articles published in *Vestnik Evropy* (1898: 380–381), Russia's objective was presented as follows:

> The Imperial Government believes that the present time is very favourable for finding, through international discussion, the most effective means to ensure true and lasting peace for all peoples and, *above all* [emphasis added], for putting a limit on the ever-increasing development of modern armaments.

Another volume of *Vestnik Evropy* (1899a: 808–810) reprinted the message of Russia's Minister of Foreign Affairs to the representatives of foreign states in St Petersburg which circulated on 30 December 1898. This message contained the following disarmament-oriented propositions: maintenance of the current composition of land and sea armed forces, as well as military budgets for a certain period of time and exploring the means by which they can be reduced in the future; prohibition of putting into use any new firearms or explosives (including gunpowder) more powerful than that currently accepted in both rifle and gun projectiles; restrictions on the use of existing destructive explosive compositions; and prohibition of the use of projectiles from balloons or in any other similar way.

The desire to save on military spending was apparently one of the key motives for Russia to propose the convening of an international conference, according to Chernyavsky (2017: 30–31). He additionally highlighted that acting as the initiator of an international discussion of these issues was also a way for Russia to increase its 'international authority', and in particular the authority of Nicholas II. This is a very important point too as A. N. Kuropatkin, the Russian War Minister (1898–1904), attached great symbolic significance to Russia's peace and disarmament initiative:

> A step of historical importance has been made. ... *The profound respect of the people has been forever secured* [emphasis added] by the Autocrat who has taken upon himself to inform the world about the possibility of another world, other than the so-called armed world now destroying us (cited in Pustogarov 2000: 157).

The loss of Russia's military power was, therefore, being compensated for with the pursuit of global political leadership and a heightened sense of cultural and historical superiority. As regards the latter, Russia had long perceived itself as playing a special role in establishing a more rightful and reasonable international order, and saw this occasion as yet another opportunity to consolidate its prominent role. Martens (1900: 24–25), whose article appeared in *Vestnik Evropy*, reminded everyone of Catherine II, who proclaimed the basic principles of maritime neutrality in 1780; Paul I, who further developed the principles of armed neutrality in 1800; Alexander I, who raised the question of disarmament as early as 1816; and Alexander II, who called for an international military conference to ban explosive bullets weighing less than 400 grams in 1868 and called for the Brussels Conference in 1874. He concluded that he did not know 'any other civilized nation which would have made so many attempts for a peaceful resolution of pressing issues of international order and law.'

Regardless of any manifestations of self-interest – be they economic or purely cultural – Russia appealed to common values and principles in its quest for disarmament. Generally, it presented its initiative as altruistic. One of the articles published in *Vestnik Evropy* (1898: 380–381) highlighted 'the *philanthropic and generous* [emphasis added] intentions' of Russia. The same article (1898: 382) proposed that Russia was best suited to take the lead because, being the least in need of land and political acquisitions, it occupied a 'neutral position' vis-à-vis other great powers and even maintained a 'balance' between them due to its vast territory and population.

Russia was very active in convincing other countries that it was in their best interest to stop the arms race. It persistently portrayed war as inconceivable and, hence, war preparations as burdensome and meaningless. The most specific illustrative statement on this point is the following one by Slonimsky (1898: 781): 'A war between the great states of Europe already seems unthinkable, but the means for war are constantly accumulating, making one seem to forget the very purpose for which they are intended.' Milioukov (1911: 18) drew attention to the vicious circle in which every great power had found itself and likely without realizing:

> Industry, nourished by war, in turn begins to push for war and for a constant increase in military preparations. To suspend or at least reduce the spending would mean subjecting an entire branch of industry to a crisis, throwing an entire army of workers out onto the street.

He (1911: 44) concluded that the question of victory would always come down to the question of finances under the present conditions. Considering the costs of all wars fought in the nineteenth century, Bloch (1898: 181) found and reported that preparations for war and the wars themselves had turned out to be 'painful and ruinous for the European nations, regardless of whether they led to defeat or victory.'

Moral principles were also invoked in defence of the initiative. Slonimsky (1898: 783) associated war, under the current means and conditions of battle, with 'a *grandiose suicide of civilized humanity* [emphasis added], unthinkable even in a fit of madness.' Bloch (1898: 219) also appealed to 'the considerations of humanity', warning that a 'growing mass of suffering' was waiting for the victims of war. In his view, the possible destruction that could be achieved with new weapons technologies had gone 'far beyond the morally permissible'. One caveat is important here. Bloch was one of the key people behind the idea of convening the Hague Conference and had a strong influence on the Russian tsar (Best

1999: 622). His seminal study *The War of the Future in Its Technical, Economic and Political Relations* (abridged title: *Is War Now Impossible?*), originally written in Russian, was translated into English, French, and German and 'carried considerable weight' beyond Russia (Vagts 2000: 33). Most importantly, his work was made available to the First Commission, dealing with the issue of disarmament, during the Conference itself (*Vestnik Evropy* 1899b: 802). Martens (1900: 6–7) also expressed the hope for a less violent future that would be achieved by preventing war, including through arms limitations, or at least placing it 'in the narrowest framework from the perspective of *humanity* [emphasis added]'. These were the questions that, according to him, had long perplexed 'the best minds of the civilized world'. Many years later, Pustogarov (2000: 158) evaluated Martens' intentions as generally sincere, insisting that he considered the arms race to be incompatible with the establishment of a stable world and, therefore, always reacted to it negatively.

As a matter of fact, Russia's ethical reasoning for the Hague Conference cannot be considered separately from the Conference at St Petersburg summoned by Alexander II in 1868. The Declaration of St Petersburg, which came out of it, was the first formal agreement restricting the use of weapons in war (Higgins 1909/2010: 7). The initiative originated primarily in Miliutin's address to Gorchakov, the Minister of Foreign Affairs, on 4 May 1868. In this address, Miliutin differentiated between explosive bullets equipped with capsules, which would explode only upon hitting hard objects such as ammunition boxes, and newly invented explosive bullets without capsules, which would explode upon contact with soft objects such as human or animal bodies. The latter, according to him, would 'intensify human suffering, without any immediate benefit to military purposes.' As a result, he classified weapons of this sort as 'barbaric means'. On 9 May 1868, Gorchakov sent a message to Russia's embassies and missions abroad. He generally agreed with Miliutin and called on the states to 'harmonize the demands of war with the demands of humanity' (both cited in *Voennyi Sbornik* 1868: 37–38, 40). What matters most is that the Russian army already possessed both types of explosive bullets, gaining, at least for a time, significant military advantages. Miliutin confirmed this fact:

> The results *acquired through experience* [emphasis added] have shown that, from a technical point of view, the use of explosive bullets does not present any inconvenience, both for action against ammunition boxes, as well as against people and horses (cited in *Voennyi Sbornik* 1868: 38).

However, Russia was prepared to abandon the military utility of this type of bullet completely, if it was necessary for the prevention of humanitarian disasters, as Miliutin also made clear: 'the Russian War Ministry is *ready to completely abandon* [emphasis added] the use of explosive bullets, or at least limit themselves to the use of bullets with capsules' (cited in *Voennyi Sbornik* 1868: 39).

This demonstrates that Russia did not merely hide its strategic intentions behind noble discourse, but was sincere at St Petersburg and, hence, most likely also at The Hague. Veselov (Interview no. 9) clarified that Russia paid serious attention to the humanitarian consequences of war, especially as war itself was turning into mechanized slaughter, simply because Russia had to fight frequently and repeatedly experienced the horrors and devastation caused by war. He emphasized the fact that Miliutin himself experienced war firsthand and considered it to be his primary motivation in calling for a complete, or at least a partial, ban on explosive bullets. Keefer (Interview no. 10) generally confirmed that Russia's broader strategic interests coincided with the tsar's initial humanitarian concerns.

Therefore, the state of affairs before the Hague Conference was well captured in a statement by G. von Staal, the representative of Russia at the Conference (and eventually its chairman): 'We see that, among nations, there is a commonality of material and moral interests' (cited in Rybachenok 2005: 360–362). Milioukov (1911: 6) was a bit more sceptical:

> Obviously, it is not only the motives of abstract morality that make modern mankind think more and more about the ways of eliminating the armed world. A *more real* [emphasis added] reason for the rapidly growing interest in the issue is the huge increase in the burden of military armaments.

Russia's reaction to the results achieved at the Conference leaves no doubt that Russia's motives were mixed. Martens (1900: 14–15) regretfully admitted that the Conference 'did not resolve the issue of disarmament in the sense that many philanthropists around the world desired.' But he paid tribute to three declarations that were signed at the Conference: one prohibiting discharging shells and explosives from balloons; another banning the use of projectiles for the sole purpose of spreading poisonous gases; and the third prohibiting the use of expanding bullets, of which dumdum bullets were the most famous type. The following appeared, quite surprisingly, in the *Government Bulletin* (cited in *Vestnik Evropy* 1899c: 370): 'The results of the work ... fully justified our expectations.' It was appreciated that, despite the failure to make greater progress in achieving disarmament, the Conference 'unanimously recognized the alleviation of the military burden as highly desirable for the good of all peoples.' The same document once again drew attention to the symbolic significance of this Conference for Russia: 'The careful and comprehensive discussion of certain points of the Russian programme ... indicates the high importance of the questions put on the agenda by the Imperial Government, affecting so closely the interests of all mankind.'

The Hague Conference of 1907 purposely does not form part of this chapter. Even though it was another step in the development of international law, and in particular the laws of war, it carried no significant change from the perspective of disarmament. Most importantly the possibility of disarmament was ruled out by Russia itself because it emerged severely damaged from the Russo-Japanese War (1904–1905) and was in need of restoring its military might and regaining its former prestige (Eyffinger 2007: 203). Keefer (Interview no. 10) particularly noted that Russia nearly lost the entire Baltic fleet at the Battle of Tsushima Strait, meaning the loss of the bulk of its Navy.

3.5 Synthesis of the Approach: A Range of Asymmetric Reactions

This chapter shed light on the process of military-technological innovation in Imperial Russia during the nineteenth century. It opened with a detailed elaboration of the role of the Crimean War in Russia's initial decision to react, in one way or another, to the advantage in military technology enjoyed by Western nations. Not only did this war expose Russia's technological inferiority, it also challenged, even reversed, its favourable great power status. The Russian authorities were sincere in their aspiration of catching up with the West. However, they found themselves needing to pursue two seemingly incompatible paths: increasing their defence efforts while also maintaining a low defence budget. Nevertheless, Russia could not afford – at least it was so claimed – to lag behind its Western competitors and embarked on the ongoing RMA. First, it launched a massive process of re-arming its army initially with rifled and then also with breech-loading weapons. Second, appropriate operational principles were selected to exploit the advantages of new conventional weapons to the fullest. The principles of loose formation and concentration of fire, themselves not entirely new, came to the fore. Finally, organizational structures and processes were adapted accordingly with the objective of quickly catching up with the West. First of all, such a multi-faceted transformation of the Russian military was part of – and, in fact, would not be possible without – large-scale changes in the social, economic, political, and cultural spheres, with far-reaching implications for the economy as a whole, taking place in Imperial Russia. Steps were taken to facilitate domestic defence orders, even though progress on this front was slow at best, and make military training more efficient. With regards to the former, there were pressures – and even efforts – to help domestic arms manufacturers. But top-down processes slowed the development of defence-industrial capabilities at home. Tenants for arms factories were appointed rather than competitively selected, and the tsar was more fascinated with sophisticated weapons of foreign origin. Despite the steps taken towards a better organized society and a more efficient economic model, the evidence presented in this chapter indicate that Imperial Russia was a *proto*-developmental state, at least from the perspective of how the ecosystem of military-technological innovation was organized.

What deserves a separate note is that there was an emulative logic driving Russia's desire for technological parity with the West. It was expressed in at least two ways. First, Russia's re-armament programme depended heavily on foreign technology and the tsar himself did not particularly rush to end dependence on foreign arms suppliers. Second, the idea that reaping the fruits of others' labour was a better strategy for Russia than investing resources into own experiments was articulated. This particular tendency endured for centuries, as the following chapters will show.

Another important caveat is that Russia's exploitation of this RMA was accompanied by firm intent and clear vision. Rather than setting out with their own experiments (though there were rare exceptions to this rule), Russia observed the advantages of Western weapons and aspired to have the same. Four revolutionary qualities of rifled breech-loading weapons were most actively discussed by Russian military experts. As they repeatedly highlighted, the possiblity to quickly reload breech-loading weapons significantly increased not only the *speed* of fire but also, by implication, its *destructiveness*. Rotary cannons and magazine-equipped weapons contributed to the same effect. The impact of rifling technology consisted, in their view, in the *improved range and accuracy* of new-generation weapons.

However, Russia still lacked a broad-based capacity to actively explore the possibilities offered by this RMA. It is for this reason that the rest of the chapter explored the asymmetry of responses available to Russia. First of all, there was a deep distrust of technology in Russian military circles, even though the growing role of technology was still carefully recognized. Instead, emphasis was placed on Russia's supposedly unique advantage: the fighting spirit of the Russian soldier. The use of operational art to Russia's advantage was seen as a way to compensate for the imbalance in military technology. Russian military experts even argued that, contrary to the surge of techno-euphoria, the role of *high-quality* soldiers increased with the introduction of new weapons systems. This was linked to the increase in weapons complexity and, consequently, the growing importance of military training.

Yet there was a more pragmatic reason for Russia to explore outside of direct responses to the Western RMA. Russia's poor financial situation, especially after the Russo-Turkish War of 1877–1878, was among the key factors preventing Russia from keeping pace with the accelerating arms race. Meeting their Western enemies on the battlefield was highly undesirable for the Russians. So Russia came up with another asymmetric response driven by the need to put its Western competitors under pressure to reevaluate their own strategy: disarmament advocacy at the international level. Russian authority figures and military experts associated arms races and war preparations with enormous economic costs, the risk of widespread destruction, and terrible humanitarian costs. With respect to the latter, Russia took an active part in promoting humanitarian causes not only to make the case stronger. Archival documents reveal that Russian political and military officials were truly committed to humanitarian ideals at that time. Russia even called to ban those weapons which it already possessed, supposedly for humanitarian reasons. Russia's cultural predisposition and strong commitment to lead the process were highlighted by key government officials. This finding is particularly significant because it reveals that part of the motivation for the tsar to advocate for humanitarian disarmament was to restore Russia's status as a major European power. By promoting the discourse of civilized humanity, with itself at the lead, Russia sought, inter alia, to increase its international authority at the time when its military might could no longer fulfil this ambition. Russia's leadership on this front culminated in the adoption of the St Petersburg Declaration of 1868 and the Hague Conventions of 1899.

The above makes it possible to conclude that Russia primarily explored asymmetric responses to Western military-technological innovation in the nineteenth century. Be they the only available options or not, two were particularly preferred: offsetting the enemy's technological strength by superior operational performance of the Russian soldiers; and restoring the relative balance that existed before the introduction of new technologies through disarmament. The quest for symmetry between military technologies available to Russia and those at the disposal of its Western competitors persisted, but it did not appear to be the dominant trend (Fig. 3).

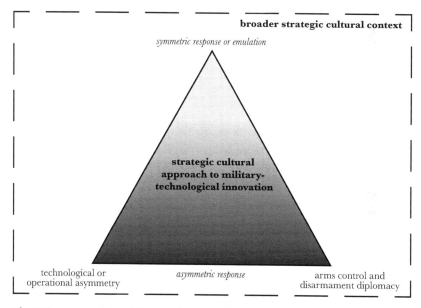

Fig. 3 The approach to military-technological innovation in Imperial Russia. The author's own figure.

4. Nuclear Weapons and Delivery Vehicles

This chapter focuses on the greatest Soviet military-technical revolution of the second half of the twentieth century: the introduction of nuclear weapons and the means of their delivery. Another major transformation which took place earlier in the same century and could have otherwise been a case study in this book was the accelerated build-up of the military-industrial potential of the Soviet Union in the first half of the twentieth century. However, the author's choice fell to the nuclear revolution for four reasons. First, the significance of nuclear weapons for the Soviets' overall military strategy in the twentieth century was comparably greater than that of industrial weapons, even though the latter should not be underestimated, especially in the context of World War II. Second, the ever-growing destructiveness of Soviet weapons within the realm of nuclear weapons (thermonuclear bombs, MIRVs) was comparably higher than the trends in the US's arsenal. Third, it was precisely the category of nuclear weapons that elevated the Soviet Union from a great power to a superpower, on par with the US within a new bipolar macro-structure. Finally, the choice was determined by the availability of primary data, seriously lacking for the first half but plentiful for the second half of the twentieth century.

This chapter opens with a discussion of the immediate Soviet reaction to the atomic bombings of Hiroshima and Nagasaki. It then proceeds to examine, in two consecutive sections, further steps taken by the USSR in response to American nuclear superiority, including those facilitated by the Cuban Missile Crisis. The concluding section summarizes the key findings and offers their graphic representation (Fig. 4).

Before proceeding to the discussion itself, it is important to draw attention to one initial contextual condition: the USSR's great power status that was tested and proved in World War II. In 1945, Soviet Minister of Foreign Affairs V. M. Molotov (1945: 12) highlighted the growing might and prestige of the Soviet Union:

> The Red Army emerged from the war with the glory of a winner. ... Everyone knows how much the international prestige of the USSR has grown. ... The war showed everyone how our country has grown and strengthened in military and economic terms. To no lesser extent, the war also showed how much the Soviet Union had grown in the eyes of other peoples in moral and political terms.

Baz' (1947: 9) agreed that different factors contributed to the Soviets' unparalleled military victory but particularly stressed that the military art of the Soviet Army was 'one of the most important factors in the military might of the *great* [emphasis added] Soviet state.' This once again testifies to the fact that a narrow realist understanding of *greatness* has dominated Russian and Soviet strategic thought.

4.1 Asymmetric Response to the World's First Atomic Bombings

The atomic bombings of the Japanese cities of Nagasaki and Hiroshima constituted a major turning point for the USSR. However, the Soviet response to it was circumspect and cautious. Soviets did not immediately rush into the nuclear arms race to the fullest for two reasons. First, they did not originally believe – at least it was so claimed – in the revolutionary potential of nuclear weapons. For example, Tolchenov (1949: 77) argued that an atomic bomb would be 'inapplicable' against combat groups widely dispersed along the front and in depth. He also stressed that no capitalist state was able to manufacture the quantity of bombs sufficient to defeat the multi-million-strong army of a large state. Khlopov (1950: 75) similarly insisted that the effect of using atomic bombs against troops and military equipment, especially if dispersed and sheltered, would be 'far from the same' as the bombardment of Japanese cities with dense populations and light urban buildings. Even though the US tried to convince the world that these two bombs decided the outcome of the war, according to Poltorak (1950: 47) it was the entry of the Soviet Union into the war, not the American atomic bombs, that decisively contributed to the surrender of Japan. Soviet military experts argued, instead, that the 'American imperialists' carried out the atomic bombings of Hiroshima and Nagasaki primarily with the aim of strengthening their positions in the struggle against the USSR (Ilyin 1967: 42).

This underestimation of the revolutionary nature of nuclear weapons informed the broad political-military strategy of the USSR. Sokov (Interview no. 2) noted that Soviet political leadership stated openly at the very beginning of the nuclear age that the only possible function of nuclear weapons was 'deterrence'. Stalin (1946/1997: 38) himself believed – and shared this idea with A. Werth, Moscow correspondent of the English newspaper *The Sunday Times*, on 17 September 1946 – that atomic bombs were designed primarily for 'deterrence' (устрашение) and could not 'decide the fate of a war'. For the sake of comparison, the US treated atomic and later hydrogen bombs as 'ultimate weapons' throughout the 1940s–1950s, and only at the end of the 1950s did the concept of 'deterrence' come to the foreground of American strategy (Arbatov 2017: 36–37).

Second, and rather unsurprisingly, the USSR took a diplomatic initiative to ban nuclear weapons as its immediate asymmetric response to the American RMA. The Soviet nuclear disarmament plan was presented by A. Gromyko, the Soviet delegate to the UNAEC. According to the Gromyko Plan, the USSR called for a prohibition on the production and use of atomic weapons, as well as the destruction of existing stockpiles of such weapons within three months (*Pravda* 1946: 5). This plan was an alternative to the so-called Baruch Plan for the international control of atomic energy, presented by B. Baruch, the US representative to the UNAEC. The Baruch Plan was criticized for the fact that it would, in essence, create an international cartel dominated by the monopolies that already controlled the American nuclear industry. Stalin himself denounced the content of the American plan for the international control of atomic energy, calling it 'a mockery of control' (cited in Monin 1953: 94). Soviet military experts eventually spoke about the emergence of two different tracks in international politics: the USSR, demanding an immediate ban on atomic weapons and the establishment of international control over the production and use of atomic energy; and the US, thwarting Soviet proposals in every way possible and seeking the legalization of these 'means of mass destruction' (Poltorak 1950: 46). The existing data suggest that the Soviets had both idealogical and strategic reasons to pursue their preferred course. On the one hand, witnessing the experiences of Hiroshima and Nagasaki, Tolchenov (1949: 77) called atomic bombs 'a *barbaric* [emphasis added] instrument ... intended for the mass destruction of the civilian population.' Poltorak (1950: 48) similarly condemned them as being 'a *barbaric* [emphasis added] means of mass destruction of people.' On the other hand, in Stalin's (1946/1997: 39) view, a ban on nuclear weapons would be a remedy to the American 'monopoly on the secret of the atomic bomb.' The necessary steps in the interests of preserving peace, according to him, were 'the elimination of such a monopoly, and then an unconditional prohibition of atomic weapons' (cited in *Voennaya Mysl'* 1951: 3–4).

4.2 Forced into the Revolution in Military Affairs

Having not achieved its stated goal of nuclear disarmament (essentially for the US), and perhaps not believing in the success of this enterprise from the very beginning, the USSR itself embarked on the ongoing RMA. The logic of doing so was communicated by Stalin:

> As you know, the Soviet Union several times demanded a ban on atomic weapons, but each time it received a refusal from the powers of the Atlantic bloc. This means that in the event of a US attack on our country, the US ruling circles will use the atomic bomb. It was precisely this circumstance that *forced* [emphasis added] the Soviet Union to have atomic weapons in order to meet the aggressors fully armed (cited in *Voennaya Mysl'* 1951: 3–4).

Ilyin (1967: 41–42) confirmed the same a few years later, saying 'the creation of new means of combat was a forced matter for the Soviet state.' In retrospect, D. F. Ustinov also agreed that the creation of Soviet nuclear missiles was 'a *forced* [emphasis added] but necessary measure' (cited in Yakovlev 1999: 17). Later Russian military experts also argued, in retrospect, that the USSR was always the 'catch-up side' (догоняющая сторона), systematically 'dragged' into further and further rounds of the arms race by the US and NATO. The latter, according to them, wanted to undermine the Soviet economy by inflicting 'the unsustainable burden of military spending' (Yakovlev 1999: 7–8). Stalin (cited in *Voennaya Mysl'* 1951: 3–4) eventually portrayed the nuclear revolution in Soviet military affairs as an effort, primarily, to bring the US to the negotiating table: 'I think that the supporters of the atomic bomb can go to ban atomic weapons only if they see that they are no longer monopolists.' This finding contradicts the existing literature which points towards the fact that it was the Kremlin that 'preferred' not to negotiate until it had achieved strategic parity with the US (Brands 2008: 3). However, the data show that a reverse logic was adopted in the USSR. In the eyes of Soviet political leadership, as claimed publicly at least, their decision to eliminate the American monopoly – and later to match US capabilities, as discussed below – was seen as a necessary step towards nuclear disarmament pursued for principled and instrumental reasons.

Progress was soon achieved at all possible levels from the introduction of new concepts and technologies to various organizational adaptations, testifying to the initial success of the *Soviet* nuclear RMA. From the organizational perspective, centralized control was the guiding principle. The organizational logic of Soviet party bureaucracy and related bureaucracies was the *nomenklatura*. It was a top-down system in which politically reliable officials were appointed, as opposed to self-recruitment. Not only were key party and government posts part of the Soviet nomenklatura, itself representing 1–3 per cent of the overall population, but important positions in multiple sectors of the economy and society (e.g. heads of research institutes, enterprise directors and shop heads, chief engineers, newspaper editors) were also included (Snegovaya and Petrov 2022: 332). Pipes (1993: 444) drew a parallel between the ways Soviet and tsarist bureaucrats were appointed to their positions. This same continuity is demonstrated here, with further details on the tsarist regime presented in Chapter 3.

The implementation of the Soviet uranium project dates back to 20 September 1942. Having found out that research on utilizing atomic energy for military purposes had begun in capitalist countries, the State Defence Committee issued a decree in which it charged the Academy of Sciences with investigating 'the possibilities of creating a uranium bomb or uranium fuel'. But it was only after the atomic bombings of Hiroshima and Nagasaki that the decision was taken to actually produce a Soviet weapon (Simonov 2000: 150–152). Nikitin and Baranov (1968: 6) clearly articulated that a powerful Soviet atomic industry was created under the 'direct leadership' of the party and its Central Committee. Of particular importance was Decree No. 9887 of the State Defence Committee of 20 August 1945, signed by Stalin, ordering the creation of the First Main Directorate under the Council of People's Commissars of the USSR and subordinating it to the Special Committee at the State Defence Committee. This Directorate would, according to the same document, be responsible for 'the direct management of research, design and construction of organizations and industrial enterprises for ... the production of atomic bombs' (Yakovlev 1999: 17). In view of the previous chapter, this is obviously the recurring tendency of Moscow to keep innovation under absolute control stemming at least from the nineteenth century. At the same time, there was great immediate attention on developing the scientific, technical, and production potential of the Soviet nuclear industry, and new organizational infrastructure was gradually being built to serve as the basis for the Soviet RMA. Numerous production, research, and design organizations were subordinated to the First Main Directorate. Contiguous issues were tackled by enlisting institutes and design bureaux of other agencies but this process was also coordinated from above (Simonov 2000: 156). All of this testifies to the fact that the USSR did not simply wait for the US response to their disarmament initiatives of the 1940s. One may argue that those disarmament initiatives were driven only by the need to 'buy time' before the USSR could bridge the technological gap with the US (cf. Shoumikhin 2011: 101). That being so, this chapter illustrates that Soviet motives were more complex and mixed.

Besides changes in organization, the USSR aimed for a series of technological breakthroughs during the late 1940s to early 1950s. The Soviet Union detonated its first atomic device on 29 August 1949. On 25 September 1949, there was an official announcement by TASS that the USSR had acquired nuclear weapons (Yakovlev 1999: 19). The significance of this achievement was not only practical but also symbolic. The very fact that the USSR succeeded in ending the American monopoly on nuclear weapons in just four years had, according to Povaliy (1967: 72), 'a decisive influence on the further strengthening of the international position of the Soviet Union.' On 12 August 1953, there was the first Soviet test of a hydrogen bomb (Krylov 1967: 16–17). The tests of new, thermonuclear charges, which took place in 1953 and also in 1955, confirmed, in Artemov's (2014: 273) view, the ability of the Soviet Union to 'independently develop new nuclear weapons systems.' In October 1961, the Soviets tested the 'Tsar Bomba' ('Царь-бомба'), a thermonuclear bomb that produced the most powerful human-made explosion ever recorded (*Reuters* 2020).

V. I. Zhuchikhin, a direct participant in the creation of Soviet nuclear weapons, particularly highlighted the existence of independent knowhow possessed by the USSR: 'the development of both the technology for the production of fissile materials and the design of the atomic bomb were carried out by domestic engineers and scientists *without borrowing from anywhere* [emphasis added]' (cited in Yakovlev 1999: 21). However, this was not necessarily true. The Soviet atomic project originally relied – and to a considerable degree – on German expertise and technology. Not only did Soviet atomic scientists conduct trips to Germany but German scientists even worked on related projects in the USSR. In terms of the availability of raw materials, the USSR was 'catastrophically' short of uranium, and the uranium confiscated from Germany, including from the Sudetenland, greatly contributed to the Soviet atomic project. Even the electronic components that the Soviets used in their atomic project were imported from Germany for nearly five years after 1945 (Oleynikov 2000: 5, 8, 10–17, 24). Oleynikov (2000: 26) also argued that, even though the Soviet Union had the capacity to become a nuclear power without German input, German resources saved it 'up to five years of time.' The USSR also concluded a uranium treaty with Czechoslovakia in November 1945. According to this longterm agreement, the Soviet Union was to be the sole buyer of Czechoslovakian uranium for a 'reasonable' price. It is notable that the Russians did not even hide the fact that they needed Czech uranium for military purposes (Zeman 2000: 12). The raw material was transported from Czechoslovakia to the Soviet Union virtually until the depletion of the Jáchymov and Příbram deposits in the 1950s (Knápek, Efmertová, and Mikeš 2011: 61). Another important finding is that the Soviets had US technical drawings at their disposal and likely relied on them while designing their own atomic bomb (Oleynikov 2000: 24). Artemov (2014: 272) also recorded that the first Soviet atomic bomb was a 'copy' of the American one. He clarified, however, that the goal was to move from this 'catching up', 'imitative' model to their own 'innovative' model in the development of nuclear weapons. However, the Soviet atomic scientist P. L. Kapitsa captured the Soviets' general reluctance to proactively experiment with technological innovation in the following words: 'suspicion of scientists and engineers was a major reason for the Soviet Union's poor record in developing technologies that were new in principle ... Soviet ideas did not receive full support until and unless they had been proved by Western experience' (cited in Harrison 2000: 128).

Since the USSR's first atomic test, the nuclear revolution was primarily about the means of delivery. When it came to rocket technology, Soviet experts acknowledged that the USSR originally 'learned a lot' from Germany (Yakovlev 1999: 29). Major success was achieved in the late 1950s. On 21 August 1957, the world's first ICBM R-7 was tested in the USSR. Of particular importance, especially in terms of delivering a clear message to the US, was the launch of the world's first artificial Earth satellite by the USSR on 4 October 1957. Sputnik 1 was launched by an ICBM (Ivanov, Naumenko, and Pavlov 1971: 5). It was precisely that moment when it became clear that the USSR was ahead of the US in the development of modern rocket technology and, perhaps even more importantly, that American territory was no longer invulnerable to Soviet nuclear attacks (Kozlov 1959: 70; Ivanov 1962: 47). On 15 December 1959, the State Commission signed an act on the commissioning of the first combat complex of ICBMs. Soviet nuclear missiles came to be seen as 'a reliable shield of the state' (Yakovlev 1999: 47).

The most important element of Soviet organizational adaptation to all the aforementioned technological changes was the creation of a qualitatively new arm of the Armed Forces: the Strategic Rocket Forces. This decision was taken by the Soviet government on 17 December 1959 (Yakovlev 1999: 53). The Strategic Rocket Forces became 'the main branch of the Armed Forces', according to Kulakov (1964: 14). What is remarkable is that this branch of the Soviet Armed Forces controlled solely land-based capabilities, as noted by Sokov (Interview no. 2). According to him, the USSR's emphasis on land-based capabilities (even though air- and sea-based capabilities existed and fell under the Air Force and Navy) was 'quite logical'. The American model of sea-based deterrence, which was not America's immediate choice but eventually became the strongest leg of the triad, was not readily applicable to the USSR. Not only did the Soviet Union have very few suitable exits to the oceans, especially where the Americans could not regularly detect the activities of Soviet submarines, but it also had vast territories of land that were the property of the state, unlike in the US.

What deserves separate note is that economic conditions for the Soviet RMA were favourable and it is a question if the same results could have been achieved, had it been otherwise. The Soviet atomic project relied upon a highly centralized and relatively strong economic basis. The Stalinist system, and particularly the command economy, were formed in the pre-war years and created almost unprecedented opportunities for military buildup, as successfully exploited before and during World War II. Unsurprisingly, the atomic project was given unconditional priority and the command economy made it possible to find the necessary resources for it, including by infringing on the interests of other sectors of the economy (Artemov 2014: 267–268, 271). However, there is a fact, related primarily to non-nuclear industries, that has often been overlooked which carries great significance for the argument developed in this book. While the centralization of effort was the key defining feature of the Soviet economy in general and the Soviet nuclear industry in particular, as discussed above, these constraints were not fully applicable to military R&D. The Soviet military R&D system in the aircraft, tank, and armament industries, with direct implications for the new postwar missile industry, was already then characterized by pluralism and competition among rival design bureaux. It was 'a quasi-market' bringing together Soviet weapon designers and defence suppliers, as well as their only real client – the Ministry of Defence (Harrison 2000: 127–128). Therefore, the USSR could be best characterized as a *command* developmental state, at least from the perspective of its approach to military-technological innovation. The Soviet state, building on a coterie of politically loyal bureaucrats and having exclusive control over resource allocation, determined the priority industries to be developed, such as the nuclear industry, and exercised full control of the process. At the same time, there were 'developmental' tendencies. The Soviet state's initiatives supporting innovation in nuclear weapons and the means of their delivery were clearly driven by the need to close the industrial gap between the USSR and the US. To achieve greater success in the shortest possible time, selected military industries, including the missile industry, were made more pluralistic, competitive, and hence market-like.

In the Report of the Central Committee of the CPSU to the Party Congress in 1961, Khrushchev confirmed that the USSR had made a great leap forward, saying 'the re-armament of the Soviet Army with nuclear missile technology has been fully completed' (cited in Lomov 1963: 14). It was essentially the official announcement of the ultimate success of the Soviet RMA. What deserves special note is that all these achievements had important symbolic value for the USSR. Poloskov (1958: 39–40) argued that the launch of Sputnik 1 was a 'crushing blow to the scientific, technical and industrial prestige' of the US. Kulakov (1964: 12) called the fact that the USSR created the atomic and hydrogen bombs in a very short time and outperformed the US in the development of rocket technology 'a historically necessary victory.' The Soviets' competitive spirit and tendency to innovate with an eye on the enemy, and particularly with the desire to be no worse, but even better, characterized their approach to military-technological innovation. As the other empirical chapters show, it is a rooted cultural feature of the Russian state. Also remarkable is the fact that the Strategic Rocket Forces themselves were referred to as 'the embodiment of the military might of the Soviet state, a concentrated expression of its unlimited possibilities in the field of science, technology, industrial production and the training of first-class military personnel' (Krylov 1967: 16).

However, two major developments – as seen by the Soviets – fueled the arms race from the late 1950s to early 1960s. First, Soviet military experts were alerted to the development of low-yield nuclear weapons in the US. The USSR perceived it as an effort to 'exchange' a total nuclear war for a series of local wars (Kozlov 1959: 66). It is because, according to Marudin (1962: 66), tactical atomic weapons would make 'close combat' possible in a nuclear war. Reznichenko (1972: 56) additionally warned that equipping NATO with low-yield nuclear weapons moved 'the danger of instantaneous mass losses ... close to the battle line.' However, it is not a complete, accurate representation of the logic behind the flexible response strategy adopted by the US and NATO. From the US standpoint, this strategy was an important step towards a more '*credible* [emphasis] deterrence' of the USSR (Witteried 1972: 14). Witteried (1972: 11) also mentioned that the Soviet Union systematically 'tested' US resolve to defend its interests and commitments on the Indian subcontinent, in Africa, the Middle East, the Western Hemisphere, Southeast Asia, and Western Europe. He (1972: 14) argued it was important to broaden the range of options actually available to the US if deterrence failed and hinted at the idea of strategic ambiguity, saying 'it does not mean that every time deterrence fails the United States *must* [emphasis added] choose to defend.' The Soviets were apparently unwilling to accept or extensively discuss certain facts. Eventually, the USSR itself engaged in the construction of non-strategic nuclear weapons but these programmes were – and, essentially, have been ever since – 'hidden by a veil of secrecy.' According to some reports, the Soviets possessed 22,000 units of such weapons by the end of the 1980s (Arbatov 2010). However, for reasons explained later in this section, the concept of using tactical nuclear weapons was never part of an 'open' military doctrine in the USSR (Fenenko 2012: 38).

Second, the Cuban Missile Crisis of October 1962 was another major turning point in the Cold War. Sedin (1962: 16) called it 'the most difficult test since the Second World War.' In view of this, he (1962: 21) called on the Soviets to be alert, saying 'we have no right to weaken our vigilance and our combat readiness in the slightest degree.' Most importantly, the Cuban Missile Crisis clearly showed that simply breaking America's monopoly was not enough. As specifically highlighted by Sokov (Interview no. 2), it revealed that the US outnumbered the USSR in strategic nuclear weapons nearly 7:1 and spurred the idea on the side of the latter that parity was 'desperately needed'. Other Russian experts also admitted that the USSR experienced 'a catastrophic backlog' at the beginning of the 1960s. This facilitated 'a mass construction' of combat missile systems for the Strategic Rocket Forces, which started in 1963 (Yakovlev 1999: 68).

The 'qualitative and quantitative build-up' of the combat potential of the Strategic Rocket Forces in the late 1960s and early 1970s led to the establishment of 'military-strategic parity' between the USSR and the US (Yakovlev 1999: 7). This achievement had historic significance and symbolic meaning for the USSR. Having reached strategic parity with the US – albeit not in terms of labour productivity or living standards but solely in military power, which once again testifies to the fact that Russia's greatness could be understood primarily from a narrow realist perspective – the Soviet Union gained the status of 'a world power of the highest class' and considered itself 'equal' to the US (Kirilenko and Trenin 1992: 15). Indeed, the following statement appeared in one of the articles published in *Voennaya Mysl'* (1969: 61): 'Only *such mighty industrial powers as the Soviet Union and the US* [emphasis added] could begin the full range of production of nuclear weapons and their delivery vehicles.' Therefore, this sense of equality had an important symbolic value for the Soviet Union and the Soviets would immediately move ahead to codify it on paper, as discussed later in this chapter.

Besides rapid technological advancements and appropriate organizational adaptations, an entirely new conceptual framework was being developed in the USSR. It was yet another dimension of the Soviet RMA, as of any other RMA. In Soviet terms, the focus was on the development of 'rocket-nuclear weapons' (ракетно-ядерное оружие) (Skovorodkin 1963: 14). Ballistic missiles were considered to be the most advanced strategic carriers of nuclear warheads (Anureev 1963: 12). The possibility to equip a missile – especially an ICBM – with a nuclear charge was explicitly called 'a revolution in military affairs' in Soviet military publications (Kulakov 1964: 12; Ivanov, Naumenko, and Pavlov 1971: 8). Going broader, Cherednichenko (1973: 39) even characterized this revolution as 'a revolution in strategy'. Interestingly, almost the same term ('a revolution in strategic affairs') would later be applied by Payne (2018) to characterize the AI-RMA.

Soviet military experts extensively discussed the revolutionary nature of nuclear weapons, giving a clear vision of the purpose of the Soviet RMA. According to Skovorodkin (1963: 16), rocket-nuclear weapons were 'the most powerful and most promising weapons.' Lomov (1963: 24) made particularly clear that such weapons became 'a decisive means of achieving the main strategic goals of armed struggle and, consequently, the political goals of war.' In his speech at the 22nd Party Congress in 1961, the Minister of Defence commented on their revolutionary potential, linking it with the newly acquired ability 'to achieve decisive military results in the shortest possible time at any range and over a vast territory' (cited in Lomov 1963: 22).

Transformative or revolutionary qualities of nuclear weapons were actively explored. First of all, attention was immediately drawn to the destructiveness of nuclear weapons. According to Lomov (1963: 23), these weapons had 'exceptionally high destructive power'. Bronevsky (1963: 31) explicitly associated them with 'mass destruction'. Another game changer was certainly the speed at which such destructive strikes could be delivered. According to Skovorodkin (1963: 16), modern rockets could travel at 'huge speeds', covering 'many thousands of kilometres in just tens of minutes.' Bronevsky (1963: 29) agreed that, for a nuclear warhead delivered by missile, the time necessary to approach the target was significantly reduced.

Soviet military experts also recognized that the role of distance had changed dramatically with the increasing range of immediate destruction. If war was to erupt, it would immediately become 'intercontinental', as noted by Lomov (1963: 22) and Skovorodkin (1963: 17). As seen from one of the statements by N. S. Khrushchev, there was a clear idea in the USSR that nuclear missiles could hit any object deep in enemy territory overseas:

> The war will begin primarily in the depths of the warring countries, and there will be not a single capital, not a single large industrial or administrative centre, not a single strategic region that would not be attacked, not only in the first days but also in the first minutes of the war (cited in Lomov 1963: 23).

The ability to extend nuclear strikes into the deep areas of enemy territory, including on other continents, revived the Soviet theory of 'deep battle' or 'deep operations.' Developed in the 1930s, this theory promoted the idea of simultaneous impact on the entire depth of the enemy's defence. Rockets, in conjunction with aviation, made it possible to fully implement this idea in practice, according to Skovorodkin (1963: 20). Dzhelaukhov (1966: 33) agreed that the possibilities for applying the principles of 'deep battle' and 'deep operation' expanded with the development of strategic nuclear missiles. Krylov (1967: 19) noted the line between front and rear areas was increasingly blurred.

At the same time, improvements in rocket technology made long-range strikes more accurate. Skovorodkin (1963: 16) identified 'accuracy strikes at long range' as one of the the key revolutionary qualities of missiles. For example, he recorded that, during tests conducted in 1960, a Soviet ballistic missile covered a distance of 12,000 km and deviated from the assigned point of landing by only 2 km.

To achieve high accuracy at long ranges, rocket weapons increasingly relied on automation, and in particular the use of electronic computers, as noted by Skovorodkin (1963: 26). This is why he (1963: 14) associated the ongoing transformation in military affairs not only with nuclear munitions and rocket delivery vehicles, but also with radio electronics that made it possible to control this type of weapon in the first place.

These technological advances changed the way human-machine interaction was perceived in Soviet political and military circles. This discussion is important since it captures another dimension of the Soviet RMA, as of any other RMA, in the Russian view: a qualitatively new approach to the problem of man-technology. Kulakov (1964: 15) argued that technology received an 'increasing share' in the qualitative and quantitative 'ratio' between human masses and military equipment. One example, according to him, clearly illustrated this. In the period from 1955 to 1960, the size of the Soviet Armed Forces was reduced by one third, but their firepower simultaneously increased many times due to the introduction of the latest types of modern military equipment. Ilyin (1967: 51) captured basically the same change but from a slightly different perspective. In the past, he noted, the lack of military equipment or the inability to master it could be compensated for by the physical strength, high morale, and psychological preparation of personnel. But nuclear missile weapons, in his view, significantly lowered the probability of successful performance for troops that were not well equipped with the latest technology. Progress in automation encouraged even more ambitious ideas. For example, Zheltikov and Polyakov (1966: 57) speculated that a nuclear war could, in essence, be started by 'the press of a button'.

However, automation came to be viewed with suspicion in the USSR. Kulakov (1964: 18) clarified that new weapons could not 'replace' people but only enhance their combat capabilities. Zheltikov and Polyakov (1966: 57–58), who contemplated the possibility of a push-button war as mentioned above, made particularly clear that such a war was not sustainable in the long run. According to them, it was almost impossible to disable or destroy all of the enemy's missile equipment, aircraft, submarines, and other military objects dispersed over a large area 'with a single blow'. Not only would a retaliatory strike follow, but massive armies would also be called to action. The same authors stressed that only a human could reason logically and improvise in an unfamiliar environment, and be capable of an accurate reconstruction of events, a correct assessment of the combat situation, and even prediction. These arguments also led them to conclude that technology, no matter how perfect it was, could not 'replace' a human. Therefore, it was not technology but the people who controlled it that eventually played a 'decisive role' in the determination of military outcomes, as additionally noted by Tolchenov (1949: 78). Essentially the same ideas were articulated by Soviet political leadership, in particular L. I. Brezhnev himself:

> The experience of history and modern wars allow us to conclude that only those who have the necessary weapons and personnel who are proficient with these weapons can defeat a strong enemy. *Technology without man is dead* [emphasis added]. It is impossible to bring everything in war to full automation, at least at the present stage (cited in Andrushkevich 1973: 79).

Others were even less optimistic. Karpovich (1952: 59) argued that even the most advanced technology was 'powerless' against man.

That said, it is important to understand how the increasing role of technology, which was even reflected in the reduction of military personnel, still co-existed with the decisive role assigned to humans in Soviet military thinking. What may shed light on this is the relationship between quantity and quality. Even though the role of human masses (quantity) was reduced, the demand for professional military expertise (quality) increased. This trend takes root in the nineteenth century, as discussed in Chapter 3, but it was in the twentieth century, and mainly with the introduction of nuclear weapons, when it manifested fully. Kulakov (1964: 19) made clear that the high degree of mechanization and automation of nuclear weapons made it possible to carry out the necessary manoeuvering of forces 'with much less effort, but with more qualified people.'

At the same time, Krylov (1967: 23) insisted that the ongoing military revolution sharply increased the importance of 'the moral-political factor' (морально-политический фактор) in modern warfare. This logic provided a solid basis for promoting the image of Soviet superiority. Pechorkin (1962: 27) wrote: 'The moral superiority of the army of the socialist power over the bourgeois armies is so obvious that it does not need any proof.' Kulakov (1964: 20) expressed a similar idea: 'The moral, political and fighting qualities of the working people of the socialist countries, drafted into the armed forces, are incomparably higher than those of the soldiers and sailors of the imperialist countries.' Basically, the same statement appeared in another article published in *Voennaya Mysl'* (1971: 11): 'The moral, political and combat qualities of Soviet soldiers are incomparably higher than in the armies of the imperialist countries.' Ilyin (1967: 46–47) further developed and captured this idea:

> The decisive nature of war and the use of new weapons in it will require exceptional stamina, courage, and the ability to overcome the greatest trials from personnel. ...this proposition is also well understood by many bourgeois military leaders. They would very much like to have in their armies such conscientious soldiers, convinced in the right spirit, as the soldiers of the Soviet Army and Navy. ... In this light, the imperialists see their main task in cultivating in their soldiers a spiritual strength that would be equal to that of the opponent. To put it bluntly, vain hopes.

Therefore, Soviet military experts took up the challenge of developing a more dialectical approach to the relationship between humans, representing both professionalism and spiritual strength demanded in battle and technology. Bogomolov and Alekseev (1967: 22) clarified that Soviet military science assigned a 'decisive role' to the human factor but did not in any way diminish the role of technology in warfare. Therefore, compared to nineteenth-century dynamics discussed in Chapter 3, the ratio between human and machine input was clearly shifting, albeit only slightly, throughout the twentieth century.

There was also a series of conceptual innovations linked to the Soviet RMA. The concept of *deterrence* constituted a major component of Soviet military thinking from the very beginning, as also discussed above. Even though a broader set of strategic and operational concepts and principles was eventually introduced, this one provided the logic on which most, if not all, of the others were based. For example, one of the guiding principles for the USSR in its nuclear arms race with the US was 'the struggle for military-technical superiority' (Kulakov 1964: 13). In particular, it was the quest for '*qualitative and quantitative* [emphasis added] military-technical superiority' (Sokolovsky 1963: 258). This shows that the Soviets' ultimate objective was to create *reverse asymmetry* by surpassing America's originally superior nuclear capabilities in qualitative and quantitative terms. Kulakov (1964: 14) made clear that superiority in rocket-nuclear weapons was 'a decisive factor' in defining this military-technical superiority. Achieving nuclear superiority was important, according to Tyushkevich (1969: 31), because success in a nuclear war would depend on the 'ratio' of forces that had developed before it began.

However, Soviet military experts admitted that the USSR had to find a balance between its expanding ambitions on the one hand and its limited material resources on the other. It was a rather typical situation for the Russian state, as demonstrated also with respect to Imperial Russia in Chapter 3. According to Kornienko and Korolev (1967: 33), the USSR's desire to achieve military-technical superiority, while limited in resources, led it to 'choose the most cost-effective solutions, [i.e. to] achieve maximum combat effectiveness at minimum cost.' Kulakov (1964: 21–22) also mentioned that it was 'extremely important' for the Soviet Union to maintain military-technical superiority with the 'minimum' expenditure of financial, economic means and human resources. Despite the benefits of the command economy for the atomic project, as discussed above, it did not mean that the government sought to achieve results at any cost. The government had to take into account the needs and possibilities of the entire economy of the country, and a balanced approach, as well as the optimization of costs and results in the atomic project were necessary when making costly decisions (Artemov 2014: 282).

It is interesting that, in line with the discussion presented above, the human-machine nexus, not technologies themselves, was seen as the basis for military-technical superiority. Kulakov (1964: 14) argued that the best military equipment and the highest quality personnel who mastered this equipment formed 'an organically unified basis' of one's military-technical superiority over the enemy. Achieving an 'optimal' ratio between these two constituent elements could be beneficial even from the economic perspective, according to Kornienko and Korolev (1967: 32).

If such superiority was achieved, it would, according to Soviet military experts, fulfil two functions. In the first place, it would be an 'impressive deterrent' to imperialist aggression. But if the war was 'unleashed by the imperialists', which literally meant if deterrence failed, the USSR's military-technical superiority would be 'the most important condition for *achieving victory* [emphasis added]' (Kulakov 1964: 21). Indeed, there was a belief in the US that the Soviets had a war-fighting, war-winning nuclear strategy. In his seminal work titled 'Why the Soviet Union Thinks It Could Fight and Win a Nuclear War', Pipes (1977: 21) contrasted the American and Soviet nuclear doctrines, saying the former maintained that a nuclear war could have 'no winner', while the latter was set on the idea that the side better prepared and having a superior strategy 'could win'. Brodie (1959: 274–281) also differentiated between the logics of 'a deterrence strategy' and 'a win-the-war strategy'. Half a century later there persists the idea that '[d]eterrence was not a central concept in Moscow's strategic thinking' based on the reasoning that 'Soviet military strategists, in contrast to their NATO counterparts, never abandoned the aim of war victory and had a coherent nuclear warfighting strategy' (Adamsky 2014: 111–112).

However, war-fighting and war-winning ambitions were not contrary to deterrence rationales in Soviet military thinking. Veselov (Interview no. 9) explained that the rhetoric of Soviet readiness to 'go all the way' constituted a form of 'deterrence', especially until the USSR achieved strategic parity with the US. Soviet military experts concurred that the only possible way for the USSR to be dragged into the next war would be if the other side launched it (e.g. Bronevsky 1963: 28; Krylov 1967: 18–19). The Soviets, at least from their own perspective, were not going to launch war on the US and NATO. Official statements and speeches by Soviet leaders, the Programme of the CPSU, and the decisions of the 22nd and 23rd Party Congresses of 1961 and 1966 repeated the same message: the USSR did not want war and did not ever intend to attack anyone (Ivanov 1969: 44). In his book *History Teaches Vigilance*, Ogarkov (1985: 77) highlighted the following point, seemingly a mere matter of terminology but, in fact, an important difference in the perception of Soviet nuclear weapons at home and in the US: 'the strategic nuclear forces of the USSR were never called "strategic *offensive* [emphasis added] forces," as they are eloquently referred to in the United States.' Sokov (Interview no. 2) noted however, that, both the USSR and the US assumed that if a war was to erupt that it would be started by the other side. So this feeling of insecurity was mutual.

Snyder (1977: 18) grasped it more accurately arguing that 'Soviet military writings typically *equate* [emphasis added] effective deterrence with superior war-fighting capability'. This statement captures the very fact that war-fighting – and, eventually, war-winning – ambitions constituted the basis of the Soviet logic of deterrence. However, it does not capture the depth and breadth of the Soviet conceptualization of war-fighting and deterrence either. Besides the quest for qualitative and quantitative superiority, the Soviet Armed Forces had to maintain 'constant combat readiness', as underlined by Moskalenko (1969: 19). Skovorodkin (1963: 19) clarified that nuclear missile strikes sharply increased the importance and role of 'constant combat readiness' simply because they were themselves, in essence, surprise actions. The nature of nuclear weapons and the speed with which they could be delivered made Soviet military experts adapt the traditional notion of combat readiness to new circumstances in the nuclear age. First of all, combat readiness came to be seen as 'a deterrent' against a new world war being unleashed by the aggressor (Moskalenko 1969: 19). Korobeinikov, Shabaev, and Sokolov (1967: 44) also made clear that the degree of combat readiness had to be newly measured 'not in days and months, as in the past, but in hours, minutes and even seconds.'

Operational principles of the possible use of nuclear weapons were developed as well, giving a still more solid conceptual shape to the Soviet RMA. The USSR originally believed that, if a war broke out, both sides would use all the force and means at their disposal, primarily strategic nuclear weapons, 'from the very beginning' (Zemskov 1969a: 20). Such a 'massive use' of nuclear weapons could, according to Koyanovich (1959: 35–36), be successfully executed by both the attacker and the defender. Therefore, the main strategic task of the Soviet Armed Forces was 'to disrupt the aggressive plans of the enemy and seize the strategic initiative in their own hands from the very beginning of the war' (Lomov 1963: 25). Rodkin (1963: 48) even noted the following, hinting at the possibility of a pre-emptive strike in a nuclear war: 'The fact that the defender has nuclear weapons, missiles and other modern means of combat allows him to defeat the enemy *even before the latter goes on the offensive* [emphasis added].' However, these conceptual innovations eventually boiled down to the fundamental logic of deterrence, at least from the Soviet perspective. It is because the ability to inflict a destructive strike on the aggressor in the shortest possible time, and subsequently the Strategic Rocket Forces themselves, were seen primarily as 'the main military means of deterring the aggressor' (Krylov 1967: 21). Brezhnev (1970: 541) himself openly declared that the Soviet strategic nuclear forces were 'a reliable means of deterring any aggressor.' In retrospect, Russian military experts even argued that the Strategic Rocket Forces effectively served as 'the main deterrent' during the Cuban Missile Crisis, and have been seen then as 'the primary means of deterring aggression against the Soviet Union and Russia' (Yakovlev 1999: 19).

One caveat is essential in light of this. Some Western experts argued that the Soviets 'never accepted' (Paulsen 1994: 11) and 'never adopted' the mentality or the policy of MAD (Hearing 1980: 44). Snyder (1977: 18) was convinced that even '[t]he SALT experience ... led to no discernible Soviet doctrinal convergence toward American concepts'. Sokov (Interview no. 2) called it 'a big analytical mistake'. The existing data proved the same. Other Western analysts recorded that it was the SALT process that 'represented Soviet acceptance' of the logic of MAD (Flynn 1989/2021: 17). This statement is more accurate but it communicates the way the USSR's thinking was understood in the West. However, Soviet military experts themselves came to realize the logic of MAD, even though they did not use the same phrase. Ivanov (1969: 47–48) clearly realized the danger of mutual destruction in case either side resorted immediately to nuclear weapons: 'The risk of *destroying one's own states* [emphasis added] is too great and the responsibility to mankind for the fatal consequences of a nuclear war is too heavy for an aggressor to easily decide to put nuclear weapons into action immediately from the very beginning of the war'. Looking at it from a more practical perspective, he also added that it was 'practically impossible' for either side to completely destroy the other side's nuclear arsenal with a single blow, and therefore it was 'impossible to prevent a destructive retaliatory strike.' Zemskov (1969b: 60) also came close to realizing the possibility of mutual destruction and the need to prevent a first strike by either side: 'In fact, as already noted, in modern conditions, any [nuclear] attack option does not exclude crushing responses from the other side. Therefore, under any conditions, *measures must be taken to exclude such an attack* [emphasis added].' Even the top political leadership of the Soviet Union accepted the general logic of MAD. In his book of memoirs, *The Memorable*, Gromyko cited a conversation between US President Nixon and Soviet General Secretary Brezhnev upon the former's arrival to Moscow at the end of May 1972. 'According to American data, – said Nixon, – the US and the Soviet Union have accumulated so many weapons that they can repeatedly destroy each other.' Brezhnev replied: 'The same is true according to our calculations' (both cited in Yakovlev 1999: 77). All of the above indicates that the Soviet leadership did not just '[i]ntuitively' (cf. Adamsky 2014: 112) follow the logic of MAD. Soviet military strategists themselves participated in its theorization. Woolf (2022: 6) noted more precisely, therefore, that '[d]uring the 1960s, *both* [emphasis added] countries [the US and the USSR] recognized the reality of the concept of [MAD]'. Evidence from later years shows even more clearly that the logic of MAD deeply penetrated Soviet military circles, though unofficially. For example, Andreev (1989: 45) defined military-strategic parity as each side's capacity to retaliate at an 'unacceptable' level of damage, which he defined with great precision, and considered the inevitability of this as the basis of mutual deterrence:

> The essence of military-strategic parity, hidden behind the existing balance of military forces, in our opinion, consists: firstly, in the fact that each opposing side possesses an equal ability to take effective military actions in the event of a preventative outbreak of war by the side that decided to do so; secondly, in the inability of the attacking side to avoid a retaliatory strike with unacceptable damage (60 per cent destruction of industrial potential, 30 per cent and more losses of the population). The inevitability of such retribution is one of the decisive factors in deterring a potential aggressor from starting a war.

> (Cf. Robert McNamara's original concept defining the level of destruction necessary as 30 per cent of the population and 50 per cent of the industrial capacity, with these numbers evolving thereafter to 20 per cent of the population and 75 per cent of the industrial capacity.)

Even though the Soviets clearly realized the revolutionary potential of nuclear weapons, they never believed in a nuclear 'blitzkrieg' which was, in their view, popular in the US (Tolchenov 1949: 73). Soviet military experts rather believed in a close dialectical connection between conventional and nuclear weapons. Originally, they argued that conventional weapons would be used on a residual basis. While the 'decisive role' was assigned to nuclear weapons, joint efforts of all branches of the Armed Forces were considered necessary to achieve 'the *final* [emphasis added] victory over the aggressor' (Pechorkin 1962: 30; Lomov 1963: 24). Zemskov (1969a: 22) even assumed that the role of conventional weapons would increase because the parties would be able to maintain the initiative and consolidate the results of previous nuclear strikes only by using 'surviving' ground forces, naval forces, and aviation forces.

Later the USSR also accepted the possibility of an initial conventional phase in a nuclear war. In essence, it was a response to the emerging Western idea of a 'phased war', which would begin with the use of non-nuclear forces, then involve tactical nuclear weapons and possibly end up with the use of strategic nuclear missiles (Zemskov 1969a: 23). Ivanov (1962: 52) immediately spotted an 'obvious contradiction': on the one hand, the political and military leadership of the US and NATO believed that a general nuclear war was problematic but, on the other hand, they adopted a new, more flexible, strategy which still implied the ability and readiness to wage an all-out nuclear war. Soviet military experts generally agreed that, if war erupted, hostilities could be carried out for some – most likely a relatively short – time using only conventional means of armed struggle (Krylov 1967: 19–20; Shtrick 1968: 58). They accepted this possibility due to ideological, humane, and political-military (the favourable balance of conventional forces in the European theatre) considerations (Vishnevsky and Golomb 1970: 65). However, the Soviets rejected the idea of a limited nuclear war which would otherwise be the next stage in NATO's phased war. Cherednichenko (1970: 41) stressed that the US was most interested in such a war because it hoped to avoid a crushing retaliatory nuclear strike against itself. In view of this, the intention of the USSR was not to allow for a nuclear war to be limited to Europe, as Sokov (Interview no. 2) clarified. 'No one will be able to localize the nuclear fire that has begun,' warned Zemskov (1969a: 24). Sokov (Interview no. 2) added that it was the continuation of the logic of deterrence.

Some Western analysts called the USSR's more flexible approach to possible hostilities its 'own strategy of flexible response' (Scott 1992: 182–183). But, in light of the aforesaid, it is crucial to make clear that a limited nuclear war was never part of it. Even calling the Soviet approach 'flexible' is problematic in this context. In fact, the Soviets rejected the very term as captured, for example, by Vishnevsky and Golomb (1970: 64): 'We are fundamentally and resolutely opposed to any concept that traces its lineage to the [American] strategy of "flexible response."'

Soviet military experts also explored new approaches to defence planning in the nuclear age. In conceptual terms, three basic principles defined the USSR's general approach: strategic defence, which relied on close collaboration between all branches of the Armed Forces and required 'centralized control'; active defence, which allowed for tactical manoeuvers, as well as targeted offensive operations and counterattacks for defensive purposes (Koyanovich 1959: 37–38); and civil defence, which implied nationwide defence measures aimed at ensuring the protection of the population and increasing the sustainability of the national economy and agricultural production (Tolstyakov 1964: 34). In regards to the latter, the Soviets considered it important 'to equip the country's territory as [if it were] a theatre of military operations' (Ivanov 1969: 49). Other principles were applied at the tactical level as well.

In Bronevsky's (1963: 30) view, the dispersal of forces was necessary to protect them from enemy fire. He expounded that this principle entered the art of war since the use of firearms but received 'a new quality' in the nuclear age. The difference lied, according to him, in the neccessity to disperse not only battle formations, but also military and industrial facilities, as well as the populations of large cities in the rear, far beyond the theatre of operations. With regard to this, the Soviet Union enjoyed advantageous geographic conditions, as Khrushchev hinted in his report at the fourth session of the Supreme Soviet of the USSR: 'a state that has undergone a sudden attack, *if, of course, we are talking about a sufficiently large state* [emphasis added], will always be able to give a proper rebuff to the aggressor' (cited in Bronevsky 1963: 31–32). Korneychuk (1962: 50) added that the reliable protection of one's personnel from nuclear strikes could be achieved not only through their dispersal, but also their camouflage from all types of enemy reconnaissance, the use of natural shelters, as well as the construction of artificial shelters.

Most importantly, Soviet military experts realized the significance of missile defences. It can be argued that missile defences were both an integral part of the Soviet RMA and an important part of the Soviet asymmetric technological response to the American RMA. In strategic terms, missile defences came to be seen as no less important than nuclear strikes themselves, as noted by Skovorodkin (1963: 19). Provorov (1972: 92) also recorded a steady increase in the role and importance of air defence, in particular aerospace defence. There is one caveat. Revolutionary changes in the perception of space and time in the missile age, as discussed above, led to the adoption of different standards for air defence against nuclear missile attacks. First, Bronevsky (1963: 34) admitted that modern air defences (likely meaning missile defences, as he extensively discussed nuclear attack scenarios) had to extend to the entire territories of the belligerent states. Second, he acknowledged the speed at which these air defence systems had to operate increased the demand for their automation. Systematic work on the creation of an experimental missile defence system began in the USSR on 28 October 1953. Given the limited amount of time available for intercepting incoming hostile ballistic missiles and the impossibility of human intervention in this process, almost the entire process was fully automated using the M-40 digital electronic computer. On 4 March 1961, 'for the first time in the world', the experimental missile defence system intercepted and hit the warhead of an R-12 ballistic missile flying at a speed of more than 3 km/s (Antsupov and Zhikharev 2015: 28–30). However, the development of missile defence systems became a destabilizing factor in the Soviet-American arms race, initiating the development of strategic offensive weapons. Soviet military experts gradually started to realize the close relationship between strategic offensive and defensive forces. For example, Provorov (1972: 92) emphasized: 'The share of aerospace defence in the overall balance of military efforts ... is becoming increasingly significant.' That was the logic that underlied the ABM Treaty, one of the key outcomes of the first round of SALT. Representing a widespread opinion, Shoumikhin (2011: 104) stressed that SALT was a turning point which clearly signalled that MAD became the 'dominant' strategic paradigm, yet only on an unofficial level, in US-Soviet relations. However, there likely remained doubts in the US about whether the Soviets fully and sincerely accepted the logic of MAD. Effective missile defences could obviously undermine MAD. In 1985 the Reagan administration expressed concern that the USSR was preparing a nationwide defence against missiles. Moscow made a similar charge against the US (Gwertzman 1985).

4.3 The Circle Closes: The Role of the USSR in Nuclear Arms Control

During the 1950s to early 1980s, the Soviet Union continued to take systematic steps to curb the arms race and facilitate arms control discussions and disarmament understandings. It means that even at the height of the nuclear revolution in Soviet military affairs, as discussed above, the USSR did not abandon the idea of nuclear – as well as general and complete – disarmament. Anureev (1963: 6) clearly articulated the USSR's unchanged position in one of his articles published in *Voennaya Mysl'*: 'The Soviet Union firmly and resolutely advocated and continues to advocate for the complete ban of nuclear weapons, the cessation of production and the destruction of their stockpiles, and complete and general disarmament.' The USSR stayed true to these objectives from the very beginning because, according to Zemskov (1969b: 57), it continued to promote the policy of 'preventing a world war, including a nuclear one'.

However, the Soviets' motivation in pursuing this course was based primarily on self-interest rather than on moral commitment. There were strategic and budgetary issues. First, the Soviets feared losing their competitive position as they recorded the beginning of a whole new round in the never-ending spiral of their arms race with the US. In particular, they were becoming concerned about America's efforts to sharply increase the striking power of their nuclear weapons by equipping a new generation of strategic missiles with multiple warheads, also known as MIRVs. These efforts were perceived in the USSR as the desire 'to achieve strategic superiority over the countries of socialism' (Trofimov 1970: 81, 84). It should be noted, however, that the Soviet Union eventually proceeded with the development of their own MIRVs, making them more destructive than those of the US. There is evidence that the US could equip a missile with three warheads, while the USSR – eventually with ten, as noted by Sokov (Interview no. 2). Second, the arms race was becoming an increasingly heavy burden for the Soviet economy. Ermakov (1970: 87) warned that, by means of the arms race and brinkmanship, the US sought to impose '*exhausting* [emphasis added] military-economic competition' on the USSR.

Nevertheless, the Soviets aspired to make disarmament, in particular nuclear disarmament, a common purpose of all nations. In doing so, they appealed to emotion and reason. Milko (1961: 61) argued that general and complete disarmament would save mankind from the 'horrors' of bloody wars and save millions of lives, relieve the population of the 'heavy burden' of military expenditures and free up enormous resources for constructive purposes, and open up enormous opportunities for the development of international trade and the use of the greatest scientific discoveries, particularly in the fields of atomic energy and outer space, for peaceful purposes. Lagovsky (1970: 59) put forward a purely logical argument in favour of disarmament:

> History shows that the cost of equipping and maintaining the army from century to century, from one war to another, has continuously increased, depriving the national economy of huge amounts of money. But economic resources are far from unlimited. And the less money the state spends on maintaining the army and navy, on maintaining their combat readiness (without prejudice, of course, to defence purposes), the more remains for the needs of the national economy.

The arguments in favour of nuclear disarmament in particular relied heavily on emotional appeals. The 1960 Statement of the Conference of Representatives of the Communist and Workers' Parties was more specific in this regard. It contained that a nuclear war would 'cause unprecedented destruction', 'turn the largest centres of world production and world culture into ruins', as well as 'bring death and suffering to hundreds of millions of people, including in those countries not participating in the war' (cited in Zemskov 1969b: 57). Bronevsky (1963: 28) similarly argued that 'no state' could consider itself 'safe' as long as the world's major powers were equipped with nuclear weapons. Zemskov (1969a: 23) also associated a possible nuclear war with 'unheard-of disasters for all mankind', 'great destruction', and 'millions of deaths'. Therefore, it was 'the business of all the peoples of the world' to prevent a general nuclear war, as stressed by Cherednichenko (1970: 45). Despite the image of Russia as a pioneer of humanitarian disarmament, as discussed in Chapter 3, the Soviet language of human suffering should be taken with a grain of salt in the general context of state-sanctioned mass killings and detentions, which culminated during the Stalin era, as well as the use of psychiatry for the purpose of political repression in the Soviet Union. But this language was a powerful tool of persuasion, contributing to the success of the Soviet policy agenda, especially in the developing world.

Meanwhile, the USSR took a series of important steps towards comprehensive and balanced, primarily nuclear, disarmament. Indeed, the Soviet Union played a lead role in the international arms control efforts of the 1950s–1980s. In 1955, the USSR came up with a revised disarmament programme that included the conclusion of an international convention on the reduction of arms and the prohibition of nuclear weapons. On 18 September 1959 at the 14th Session of the UN General Assembly, Khrushchev put forward a proposal on the general and complete disarmament of all states and on three successive stages of disarmament in four years: a significant reduction in conventional aircraft and weapons under international control; liquidation of the remaining contingents of the Armed Forces and military bases in foreign territories; and destruction of all types of nuclear and missile weapons, completing measures for general and complete disarmament (Naryshkina 2017: 70).

Shavrov (1975: 19) insisted it was also the Soviet government's initiative that culminated in the successful conclusion of the Treaty Banning Nuclear Weapon Tests in the Atmosphere, in Outer Space and Under Water, also known as the Partial Test Ban Treaty (1963). Signed in Moscow, this treaty was of 'universal significance' according to him. But the result was not satisfactory for the USSR. In 1976, Brezhnev put forward a new proposal – on the complete and general cessation of nuclear weapons testing – in his report at the 25th Congress of the CPSU (Anureev 1976: 20).

The next important step towards reducing the threat of nuclear war, according to Shavrov (1975: 19), was the Soviet Union's suggestion to conclude a Treaty on the Non-Proliferation of Nuclear Weapons. Soviet political leadership believed that nonproliferation was a pre-condition for further arms control and disarmament. Brezhnev himself mentioned in his conversation with Romanian leader N. Ceaüescu in 1967 that the Nuclear Non-Proliferation Treaty could 'serve as a solid step towards further struggle for reducing the production of nuclear arms and complete disarmament' (Sokov 2021: 197–198).[4] However, there are doubts as to whether it was a sincere intention of the USSR. The Soviet Union itself contributed to the proliferation of nuclear weapons. Even though Soviet authorities denied this fact, there is sufficient evidence that the USSR transferred technology for nuclear weapons production (although no actual samples of atomic bombs) to China between 1957–1959 (Gobarev 1999: 22).

It was also the Soviet Union that contributed actively towards the containment of the arms race in the late 1960s to early 1970s. After both sides agreed in July 1968 that it was necessary to commence negotiations, the Soviet government was the first to make an official statement about the USSR's readiness to actually enter into negotiations with US. This statement was issued on 20 January 1969. In February 1969, the Soviet government once again confirmed its readiness to exchange views on this issue but, according to the documents currently available in Russia, the US government did not immediately respond (Kashirina 2011: 124).[5] Full-scale negotiations began in November 1969 and culminated in SALT. Sokov (Interview no. 2) drew particular attention to the fact that it was the Soviet Union that originally insisted on the inclusion of offensive weapons in the SALT agenda. Eventually, arms control proved to be a reliable asymmetric tool by which the Soviets could control their military-technological balance with the US.

The above is not an exhaustive list of the agreements that were reached '[w]ith the active participation of the USSR and ... its perseverance, [its] constructive and flexible approach to decision-making.' Among them was also the Agreement on the Prevention of Nuclear War (1973) (Chervov 1983: 5). By signing this document, the Soviet Union and the US agreed that their common objective was 'to eliminate the

---

4   This quote is derived from the Memorandums of Conversations of L. Brezhnev with C. Mănescu, N. Ceaüescu, and I. G. Maurer, L. Brezhnev's Handwritten Notes Made During Conversations, Messages by L. Brezhnev, RGANI, Fund 80, File 1, Case 761.

5   Both initiatives are documented in the Archive of the Foreign Policy of the Russian Federation (Russian abbreviation: АВП РФ).

danger of a nuclear war and the use of nuclear weapons.'[6] In a speech on American television, Brezhnev said: 'I think I will not be reproached with exaggeration if I say that this is a document of historical significance' (cited in Shavrov 1975: 19–20).

Further Soviet initiatives were outlined in a specific Peace Programme presented at the 24th Congress of the CPSU in 1971. There it was stated that the Soviet Union would insistently seek the creation of nuclear-free zones in various regions of the globe, an end to all nuclear weapons tests, including underground ones, and the conclusion of a treaty banning nuclear weapons. In his own report, Brezhnev made clear that the USSR's ultimate goal was the general and complete elimination of nuclear weapons: 'We stand for the nuclear disarmament of all states possessing nuclear weapons, for the convening of a conference of five nuclear powers for this purpose – the USSR, the USA, the PRC, France, England' (cited in Shavrov 1975: 18). It is particularly interesting to find this out because these were official declarations made at the height of the Soviet RMA in the early 1970s. Apparently, the Soviets did not abandon their original goal of complete nuclear disarmament even after having achieved absolute parity with the US. This fact, in combination with the foregoing, makes the author argue that the Soviets' intention of reducing the role of nuclear weapons in global politics was part of the big picture.

It is noteworthy that the Soviet Union had not given up on the key points of this original agenda up until its dissolution in 1991. During the 1980s, however, other-regarding intentions, if there were any, probably faded away, especially as the Soviet Union invaded Afghanistan and started to fall apart. Seeking reciprocity, the USSR took a unilateral obligation to not use nuclear weapons first. The first official declaration to this effect was made by Brezhnev at the Second Special Session of the UN General Assembly on 15 June 1982 (Shoumikhin 2011: 106). This is a good illustration of a politico-diplomatic signal, whose symbolic meaning was much greater than practical in the realm of arms control and disarmament, as also mentioned in Chapter 2. On 15 January 1986, M. S. Gorbachev proposed a programme that provided for the achievement of 'Global Zero'[7] by the year 2000. At the first stage, the Soviet Union proposed to stop nuclear testing, eliminate the means of delivery (starting with the INF Treaty), and reduce the strategic nuclear arsenals

---

6 The text of the document is available (in Russian) online at: https://docs.cntd.ru/document/901865688.

7 The term that refers to the worldwide elimination of nuclear weapons.

of both superpowers by 50 per cent. The second stage involved the elimination of tactical nuclear weapons and the involvement of other nuclear powers (France, Great Britain, and China) in the general process. The goal of the third stage was to achieve actual 'Global Zero'. However, on 12 October 1986, at the Reykjavik summit, US President Reagan did not support the Soviet initiative for complete disarmament (Naryshkina 2017: 71–72). Three caveats are necessary. First, even though Gorbachev is sometimes seen as the only real driving force behind the shifts in Soviet strategic thinking, his proposals were, in fact, a reflection of the deeply-rooted Soviet disarmament philosophy, as shown previously. Second, even though the 'Global Zero' proposals are most often associated with US President Obama, they apparently originated in the Soviet Union. Third, Gorbachev's disarmament initiative came up against the background of Reagan's SDI, aimed at rendering nuclear weapons, especially those of the Soviet Union, impotent and obsolete, so it should be taken with a grain of salt.

The draft project of the Soviet Military Doctrine of 1990 reiterated that the USSR considered the prevention of war to be a priority, opposed the arms race, advocated for the transition to 'real disarmament', and pledged to 'never be the first to use nuclear weapons' (cited in *Voennaya Mysl'* 1990a: 25). It is remarkable that, when it comes to the latter statement, even the draft project of the Fundamentals of Russia's New Military Doctrine of 1992 contained that Russia would 'not use nuclear or any other weapons of mass destruction first' (cited in *Voennaya Mysl'* 1992: 3). This promise would, however, be withdrawn from the actual Military Doctrine issued in 1993 (Schmemann 1993).

4.4 Synthesis of the Approach:
Two Seemingly Incompatible Paths

This chapter focused on the dynamics of military-technological innovation in the Soviet Union in the twentieth century. It opened with a discussion of the role of the world's first atomic bombings. The bombings of Hiroshima and Nagasaki signalled a new era in Western, particularly American, technological and military superiority. Since the Soviets were not convinced of the military necessity of these strikes in the first place, they believed that their main purpose was to strengthen the US's position in their struggle with the USSR. The Soviet immediate response was clearly asymmetric and lied primarily in the diplomatic realm. In particular, Soviet officials put forward an action plan on nuclear disarmament, aimed primarily at eliminating America's monopoly on the atomic bomb. Interestingly though, and this fact has been overlooked in the existing literature, Soviet military experts originally denied the battlefield utility of nuclear weapons and Stalin himself came up with the idea of nuclear deterrence. This finding challenges the deeply held and taken-for-granted assumption that deterrence is a Western concept.

The Soviet initial disarmament initiative failed and archival documents indicate that the Soviet Union was 'forced' (as per their own language) into the nuclear RMA and, in particular, into closing the technological gap between itself and the US. It was very soon later that the Soviets would develop atomic weapons of their own, as well as the means of delivering them to American targets. Besides technological advancements, many organizational adaptations were made in line with the Soviet atomic project. The nuclear industry was built under the direct leadership of the Communist Party. The Soviet nomenklatura and command economy created a solid basis for the state's centralized control over the development of nuclear weapons and related R&D. More importantly, the conditions under which the military dimension of the atomic project could be prioritized vis-à-vis other industries had been created. Competitive market-like mechanisms found their way into the missile industry but they were also managed by the Soviet state. In this context, the USSR was addressed as a command developmental state. A separate branch of the Soviet Armed Forces – the Strategic Rocket Forces – was also established. This move was unprecedented. What is remarkable is that the Soviets did not hesitate in pursuing this course and, even against the background of their own disarmament calls, would soon announce that the American secret of the atomic bomb had been uncovered. Soviet records contain that Stalin embarked on this revolution to bring the US to the negotiation table. Regardless of whether it was a sincere intention or not, it would not turn into practice any time soon. Instead, there came another turning point – the Cuban Missile Crisis. It was precisely this moment that Soviet technological inferiority became apparent and the USSR headed towards the full symmetrization of its nuclear arsenal with that of the US. The qualitative and quantitative buildup of Soviet strategic nuclear capability allowed the USSR to achieve parity with the US by the early 1970s. It was a historic moment for the USSR. The achievement of nuclear parity implied the completion of the Soviet transformation into a superpower on par with the US.

There was a clear understanding among Soviet military experts of the nature of revolutionary weapons, which they called rocket-nuclear weapons. The unprecedented destructiveness of nuclear weapons came to be viewed through the prism of mass destruction. Rocket technology allowed for their delivery to targets over a great range and at a great speed. The accuracy of such strikes was increased, inter alia, through automation. The same four revolutionary qualities were distinguished in rocket-nuclear weapons as in rifled breech-loading weapons in the nineteenth century, as shown in Chapter 3. This finding reveals a tendency for a particular way of defining revolutionary technologies in Russian military thought. Yet there was one major change compared to nineteenth-century thinking. The idea that traditional military qualities demanded of the soldier in battle could compensate for the country's technological inferiority no longer resonated in military-political circles in Moscow. However, emphasis on the moral, political and combat qualities of Soviet soldiers persisted. Technology was not assigned a decisive role, which was still supposedly played by humans. Soviet experts realized that technology could substantially reduce the effort required to achieve certain military outcomes, but placed even greater emphasis on the professional qualities of operators.

Opportunities for conceptual innovation in nuclear thinking were also actively explored. The concept of deterrence became the basis of Soviet military doctrine. The objective of qualitative and quantitative superiority in nuclear capabilities, with an optimal balance between human and machine input, and the principle of constant combat readiness were both perceived as contributing factors. The discussion presented in this chapter inquired into every nuance of the Soviet approach to deterrence, war-fighting, and war-winning, and refined the existing knowledge on this subject. Attention was particularly drawn to the fact that the Soviets did not originally see deterrence and war-winning as mutually exclusive. Another important empirical contribution in this respect was the analysis of the Soviets' own MAD-like thinking. Archival records were used to challenge the existing assumption that Soviet nuclear philosophy was fundamentally different from the US doctrine of MAD in the late 1960s to early 1970s. In particular, it was demonstrated that the SALT agreements were not the only evidence of the Soviets' unofficial acceptance of the logic of MAD.

The principles relevant to the use of nuclear and, by extension, conventional weapons were also developed. The cornerstone of Soviet deterrence was the threat of a massive pre-emptive strike or retaliation by remaining forces. At the same time, and this is often overlooked in the existing literature, the Soviets rejected the possibility of a limited nuclear war in Europe. Their flexibility was to recognize at some point that a limited war in Europe could begin with the use of conventional weapons only before it escalated into a full-scale nuclear exchange between the US and the USSR. This is how their approach differed from the strategy of flexible response adopted officially by the US and NATO in the 1960s. In fact, the Soviets attached great importance to their conventional arsenal from the very beginning. They originally believed there would still be a follow-up conventional phase even after a massive nuclear exchange. The only change in the Soviets' more flexible approach of the 1960s was the recognition of the possibility of an initial conventional phase in a nuclear war as well.

Nonetheless, the accelerating arms race was exhausting for the USSR. Although the command economy provided a solid basis for the great triumphs and achievements of the Soviet atomic project, the government still had to take into consideration the needs and possibilities of the entire economy, and hence could not operate with unlimited resources. At the same time, the Soviets could not afford to concede to America's military-technological superiority. It is for these reasons that the Soviets never gave up on their initial disarmament objective. Throughout the 1940s to 1980s, Soviet political leaders and military experts consistently advocated for war prevention, as well as nuclear non-proliferation, arms control, and disarmament. In doing so, they expressed concern about the relentless search for increasingly barbaric weapons, the danger of mass destruction, mainly of the civilian population, and the increasing cost of preparing for war. The language was very similar to that used by Imperial Russia in the nineteenth century.

So two paths were simultaneously pursued by the USSR in response to America's technological advantage: the path to the full symmetrization of capabilities and the path to nuclear disarmament. Efforts at achieving asymmetric advantages were part of the story too. For example, the world's first operational anti-ballistic missile system was successfully tested in the USSR. What is more interesting, however, is that the Soviets originally sought to surpass America's superior nuclear capabilities in qualitative and quantitative terms, meaning to create reverse asymmetry in the technological realm. Although this objective was not met on a broad scale, this thinking involved, inter alia, the creation of weapons of unparalleled destructive power (e.g. the 'Tsar

Bomba').[8] Nevertheless, it can be argued that the search for advantages through asymmetric technologies or methods of applying them was not a dominant trend (Fig. 4).

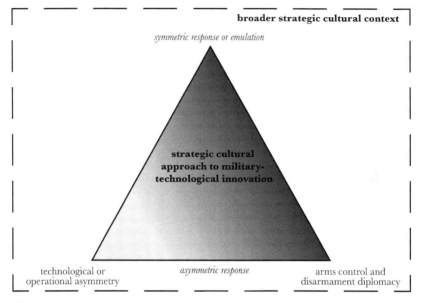

Fig. 4 The approach to military-technological innovation in the Soviet Union. The author's own figure.

---

8   A more recent example of the same aspiration is Russia's aviation thermobaric bomb of increased power colloquially known as the 'Father of All Bombs', arguably the most powerful conventional weapon in the world (cf. the US-built 'Mother of All Bombs').

5. Precision-Guided Conventional Weapons

This chapter concentrates on Russia's greatest military-technological innovation of the twenty-first century: the development of precision-guided long-range conventional weapons. One caveat is important: this revolution started in the twentieth century, and particularly in the US. Although the Soviets recorded America's growing interest in conventional long-range precision strike capabilities in the late 1970s to early 1980s and even pioneered its theorization, Russia did not embark on this RMA until the twenty-first century. There is another caveat. In the twenty-first century, this revolution almost coincided with another major transformation facilitated by the military application of AI. However, the latter is only marginally touched upon in this chapter for two reasons. First, the actual impact of the AI-RMA on Russia's actual way of fighting has been minimal to date. This is yet a nascent RMA. Precision-guided long-range conventional weapons have, on the other hand, already been tested and proven on the battlefield, mainly in Syria. Second, the author has already studied different aspects of the ongoing Russian AI-RMA in another work (Hynek and Solovyeva 2022: 49–83).

This chapter begins by elaborating on the Soviet conceptualization and theorization of the American RMA beginning in the 1970s–1980s. Different aspects of the Soviet, and later Russian, response to it are treated in five consecutive chapters. Particular attention is drawn to the role of the Gulf War (1990–1991), the 1998 bombing of Iraq (code-named Operation Desert Fox), NATO's air strikes in Yugoslavia (1999), the Chechen Wars (mainly the phase starting in 1999), and the Russo-Georgian War (2008). Also, the final empirical section gives special attention to the differences in Western and Russian understandings of the term 'asymmetric response' in the context of the studied RMA. The concluding section provides a nuanced illustration of the main findings (Fig. 5).

5.1 Conceptualization of Revolutionary Potential

Soviet military theorists started to reflect on radical changes in conventional military technology in the late 1970s and the 1980s. In particular, they recorded the beginning of the American RMA. The inevitability of this revolutionary transformation in the American military was 'first predicted' not by the Americans themselves, surprisingly, but by the Soviet General Staff, primarily Ogarkov (Pechurov 1997: 73). An interesting note is that the tendency towards it was captured by Soviet military experts even earlier. For example, Nikolsky (1954: 84) reported that the use of guided missiles and other unmanned means of attack occupied 'a prominent place' in the war preparation plans of the US. Ogarkov 'won the argument' back then, but there was a lack of resources and technological capacities for implementing this change in practice, as noted by Galeotti (Interview no. 7). Blank (Interview no. 4) also added that 'the status quo was too strong for him to break'. Yet, as the following paragraphs will make clear, this did not prevent Soviet experts from exploring the revolutionary potential of new-generation weapons.

Precision-guided weapons, especially high-precision conventional weapons, were newly in the spotlight (Bulatov 1984: 59; Vorobyev 1984a: 35). Precision-guided weapons under development in the US and NATO were represented, according to Soviet military theorists, primarily by cruise missiles, capable of providing high accuracy at long ranges and overcoming air defence systems (Tikhomirov and Bykov 1978: 77). The same authors (1978: 79) drew particular attention to the TERCOM guidance system used by cruise missiles. This navigation system worked on 'the principle of following the terrain, providing high accuracy in determining the location of the missile in flight and periodically correcting errors in the inertial guidance system.' They (1978: 77 and 81) also emphasized the fact that cruise missiles could be equipped with a nuclear or conventional warhead and concluded that they would, therefore, 'significantly increase NATO's combat power, both nuclear *and conventional* [emphasis added].' This is a great example of how two different RMAs – the nuclear and the most recent conventional – met or, to be more precise, merged. Perhaps the best example of this fusion, as given by Zhuravlev (1990: 79–80), was the high-precision long-range – nuclear-equipped or conventional – cruise missile, the 'Tomahawk'.

Cruise missiles were not the only type of precision-guided weapons distinguished by Soviet military experts. Robotic UAVs, guided (homing) missiles, as well as guided and correctable bombs and shells fell, according to them, under the same category (Vetrov 1984: 46; Korotchenko 1986: 19; Gladkov 1989: 41–42). However, reconnaissance-strike complexes (разведывательно-ударные комплексы) were recognized as the most advanced type of precision-guided weapons. A reconnaissance-strike complex was generally defined as an 'integrated, highly automated system ... combining the functions of searching for the targets and aiming weapons at them' (Afinov 1983: 63–64). Two were identified as the most effective ones at the time – the US PLSS and Assault Breaker. The first was designed to destroy radar stations, the second – mainly armoured objects (Gladkov 1989: 42). The first included reconnaissance aircraft, mobile points of the radio navigation network, a ground control centre, and weapons. The second encompassed reconnaissance and guidance aircraft, a ground-based mobile control centre, and guided weapons. Vetrov (1984: 53) spotted that, during exercises of various scales, the use of high-precision weapons as part of reconnaissance-strike complexes was constantly being worked out. He particularly highlighted that one of the options for a massive air strike tested during these exercises was the launch of remotely piloted aircraft.

Exploring the implications on a broader scale, Filippov (1984: 68) found that the American command had to revise the forms and methods of warfare in view of the increased range, accuracy, and destructive power of their weapons, as well as the adoption and integrated use of automated reconnaissance, target acquisition, electronic warfare equipment, control, and communications. According to him, all of this was reflected in the US concept of 'air-land battle' adopted in 1982. The essence of this operational concept, he continued, lied in the highly manoeuvrable combat operations of ground forces and tactical aviation which were synchronized and relied on a simultaneous application of electronic warfare to destroy the first and second echelons (reserves) of the enemy and decisively seize the initiative. The success of an 'air-land battle' was, as Zhuravlev (1990: 78–79) pointed out, directly dependent on the availability and optimal use of three components: highly effective means of ground, air, and space-based reconnaissance; surveillance and target acquisition; long-range high-precision weapons with great destructive power; and automated control and communication systems. Reconnaissance-strike complexes were seen as the basis for developing such capabilities (Afinov 1983: 64). The same author (1983: 63) expressed the concern that the Pentagon developed this operational concept 'to wage war in Europe without the use of nuclear weapons.' Zhuravlev (1990: 79) also assumed that, since none of the neighbours on the North American continent were going to attack the US, the implementation of this concept was entrusted to the groupings of American troops abroad, mainly in the European area. NATO's concept of 'follow-on-forces' raised even greater concerns in the USSR. It further developed the provisions of US 'air-land battle' and was adopted in 1984 (Levadov 1985: 70). Leonidov and Viktorov (1986: 77–78) warned that, in accordance with this concept, NATO would transfer hostilities to the territory of the Warsaw Pact from the very beginning of the war, striking with precision weapons. Citing Western military experts, they stressed that NATO's success would result from 'the destruction of communications and the destruction of second echelons (reserves) [of the enemy] at the maximum achievable depth.' Levadov (1985: 71) and Leonidov and Viktorov (1986: 77–78) particularly highlighted the role of high-precision weapons, especially reconnaissance-strike complexes, in the execution of such operations.

Afinov (1983: 63) comprehensively covered the issues which the USSR was most concerned with in just a couple of sentences:

> The Pentagon has embarked on a radical modernization of conventional weapons. We are talking about the creation of a qualitatively new high-precision guided weapon *with a conventional warhead* [emphasis added] capable of hitting small-sized ground targets *at a great distance from the first launch* [emphasis added].

Vorobyev (1984b: 47–48) was even more precise in capturing the revolutionary potential of such weapons. According to him, they would exceed existing weapons 'in range by several times, in power – by tens of times, and in accuracy – by hundreds of times.'

As for their accuracy, the Vietnam War clearly demonstrated the effectiveness and military utility of this type of weapon. Vetrov (1984: 46) spotted that, at the beginning of the war, the low accuracy of American unguided munitions was 'offset' by simply dropping a higher number of them. One specific example perfectly illustrated the change that was taking place. American pilots could not destroy the Thanh Hóa Bridge for a long time, despite using more than 4,000 bombs and many unguided rockets. Eventually, one bomb with a laser guidance system, first used in

Vietnam, destroyed it from the first launch (Vetrov 1984: 48–49; Gladkov 1989: 41–42). The Maverick missile was invoked as another example. Reminding readers that the rate of precise strikes with air bombs did not exceed 7 per cent during World War II, Bulatov (1984: 62) revealed that the probability of the Maverick missile with a television guidance system directly hitting the target amounted to 80 per cent. A closely related outcome and yet another testimony to the military utility of precision-guided weapons was the ability to reduce the number of weapons needed for the successful execution of the attack. According to Vetrov (1985: 26), a modern fighter-bomber was capable of destroying its target with high probability so there was no more need to create large air formations to destroy individual objects.

As for the increased range of precision-guided weapons, reconnaissance-strike complexes were designed to deliver 'massive strikes', i.e. the simultaneous defeat of a large number of targets, 'in the depths of the enemy troops' without the need to bring one's own troops into enemy territory or to penetrate their airspace with manned aircraft. Having clarified this, Afinov (1983: 64) went on to further argue that these strike systems were 'fundamentally new … not only from a military, but also from a technical point of view.' Vorobyev (1984b: 53) similarly noted that reconnaissance-strike complexes such as the Assault Breaker would operate 'at a considerable distance from the front line'. In view of this, he (1984b: 48–49) concluded that the US concept of 'air-land battle' was about transferring 'the centre of gravity' of the fire effort 'deep' into the location of enemy troops. NATO's concept of 'follow-on-forces' was seen as yet another 'deep strike' capability under development (Leonidov and Viktorov 1986: 77–78). Recalling the theory of 'deep battle' (теория глубокой операции) developed by Soviet military scientists in the 1930s, Pechorov (1992: 12) arrived at the conclusion that, in principle, the US and NATO's new operational concepts replicated it just 'at a higher level of the development of weapons and military art.'

Many authors of *Voennaya Mysl'* linked the increased accuracy of precision-guided weapons at a greater range with the development of complex automated systems for reconnaissance and weapon control (e.g. Bulatov 1984: 59; Vorobyev 1984a: 36–37). Bulatov (1984: 66) explicitly linked the effectiveness of any precision-guided weapon or strike complex with the availability of reliable data on the location of its target. Besides reconnaissance-strike complexes showing considerable progress, this is what motivated NATO, according to him, to develop and use high-precision navigation systems such as Navstar GPS. The US

Department of Defense decided to create Navstar GPS in 1973. Dmitriev and Mashchenko (1983: 79–80) noted that the Pentagon had high hopes for this navigation satellite system and assumed that it would significantly expand the capabilities of reconnaissance-strike complexes being developed in the US.

As for the destructive power of precision-guided weapons, Gladkov (1989: 39) explained that the accuracy of hitting the target could be offset by increasing the area of destruction, as was the case with first-generation nuclear weapons. High-precision weapons could, according to him, compensate for the power of the warhead, at least to an extent, with the accuracy of firing. Shishkin (1990: 18) also argued that conventional weapons could indeed make a difference: 'Pre-emptive strikes by high-precision weapons ... can cause such damage to the other side that it would significantly change the ratio of combat potentials.' As a result, many authors of *Voennaya Mysl'* explicitly stated that by skillfully using high-precision weapons, especially with the help of reconnaissance-strike complexes, NATO could bring the combat capabilities of conventional weapons up to the effectiveness of tactical nuclear weapons (Afinov 1983: 70; Vorobyev 1984a: 38; Vetrov 1985: 25; Leonidov and Viktorov 1986: 74; Gladkov 1989: 41–42; Zhuravlev 1990: 79).

Possibly the last major advantage of new precision-guided weapons, as recognized by Soviet military experts, was their speed. New high-precision combat weapons were, according to Vorobyev (1984a: 36–37), interfaced with automated reconnaissance assets which allowed for a quick (seconds-long) preparation of initial data for targeting and firing. He added that, as a result, it became possible to successfully implement the principle of 'quickly discovered – quickly and reliably hit' within minutes. Dmitriev and Mashchenko (1983: 79–80) also noted that new military navigation satellite systems such as Navstar GPS would provide navigation data not only at any time of the day and under various meteorological conditions, but also at great speed – within 0.2–5 minutes.

5.2 Going (A)symmetric: Failed Ambitions of the USSR

The idea that all these developments were indicators of a new and destabilizing arms race deeply penetrated the minds of Soviet military experts and, subsequently, the pages of *Voennaya Mysl'*. Afinov (1983: 63) expressed these concerns precisely: 'The work unfolding in

NATO countries in the field of high-precision weapons, including their most advanced version to date, reconnaissance-strike complexes, is … aimed at achieving military superiority and is leading to the next round of the arms race.' Bulatov (1984: 59) reiterated the idea that NATO sought to 'achieve *superiority* [emphasis added] over the Warsaw Pact countries in conventional weapons.' From the Soviet perspective there were two major problems with the US and NATO pursuing this course. First, this arms race would 'negatively impact the ratio of the military potentials' of the USSR and the US (Zhuravlev 1990: 78). This is particularly because it would be burdensome for the USSR. According to Podberezkin (1989: 58), the arms race into which the USSR was being drawn was about 'the economic and technological *exhaustion* [emphasis added] of socialism.' What made the USSR feel even more vulnerable was President Reagan's SDI. While the USSR clearly lagged behind in the sophistication of conventional weapons, this initiative, putting the reliability of Soviet nuclear weapons at risk, could further widen the gap between Soviet and US military capabilities. As Yu. V. Andropov said, 'the intention to get the opportunity to destroy the corresponding strategic means of the other side with the help of anti-missile defence, that is, to deprive it of the ability to strike back, is calculated to *disarm* [emphasis added] the Soviet Union' (cited in Chervov 1983: 12–13). Second, the USSR perceived this arms race as a way of preparing for war on the part of the US and NATO. Leonidov and Viktorov (1986: 80) warned that the directions of military modernization and combat training in the US and NATO 'testify to the buildup of their efforts to prepare for a conventional war against the USSR and its allies.' That said, Vorobyev (1984a: 34) captured all the concerns shared in Soviet military circles in just one sentence: 'The US imperialists and their NATO allies, having set themselves *the goal of achieving military superiority* [emphasis added] over the USSR and other states of the Warsaw Pact, are *intensifying the arms race more and more and speeding up military preparations* [emphasis added].'

Soviet response to these developments was shrouded in confusion and uncertainty. On the one hand, the narrative of catching up with the West was particularly prominent. 'Fighting to prevent a new war,' emphasized Ustinov (1982: 73), USSR Defence Minister, 'we are doing everything in order to prevent the aggressive circles of imperialism from achieving superiority over the USSR in conventional weapons as well.' Afinov (1983: 71) also felt it was a path worth pursuing: 'It is quite understandable that the side against which new types of weapons are being prepared will not only *not* remain indifferent [emphasis added to highlight the original formulation], but will also do everything to have no less effective weapons at its disposal.' Bulatov (1984: 59–60) generally agreed: 'It goes without saying that these military preparations cannot go unanswered on our part.' As further clarified by Vorobyev (1984a: 35), the Soviet state was 'doing everything necessary to equip the Armed Forces with first-class weapons that are not inferior in their characteristics and fighting qualities compared to the best foreign models.' The draft concept of a military reform presented in 1990 confirmed that the goal was 'to reduce the military-technical lag behind the armies of NATO countries, primarily in such types of weapons as conventional long-range precision-guided missiles and automated command and control systems for troops and weapons' (featured in *Voennaya Mysl'* 1990b: 7–8). But due to the lack of financial resources, this decision came with a compromise: quality was prioritized over quantity. The same draft concept (1990b: 16) made clear that 'in the new economic conditions', improving the 'quality parameters' of weapons and military equipment was of particular importance for the Soviet Armed Forces 'to maintain strategic parity' with the West. The idea was that an increase in the effectiveness of a single weapon model would allow for the reduction of the number of units necessary for the successful execution of combat missions, thus reducing the overall procurement costs. Pozharov (1990: 41) also drew attention to the political economy of 'quality parameters'. Making them a priority would, in his view, help the Soviet Armed Forces 'achieve the maintenance of military-strategic parity with the least possible expenditure of public funds.' Podberezkin (1989: 58) made a very similar argument a year earlier. According to him, the prioritization of 'quality parameters' of the Soviet defence industry would help Soviet Armed Forces maintain their combat power – importantly, without having to further expand their numbers – 'at a level that excludes the military superiority of the enemy.'

On the other hand, Soviet military experts realized that the USSR was not necessarily keen to engage in direct competition with the West. Arguing for a broader definition of 'military-strategic parity', Korovushin (1990: 30) insisted that 'the superiority of one side in any means ... can be balanced by the advantage of the other side in other means'. Therefore, the USSR would, according to Chirvin (1990: 9), apply 'asymmetric measures' to maintain parity with the US. As a result, asymmetric measures at the technological level were actively explored. First of all, Tretyak (1990: 5) drew attention to the significance of 'air defence capable of solving problems in a conventional war.' At the same time he acknowledged that the tension between quantity and quality remained a hallmark of Soviet military modernization. In particular, he (1990: 8) stressed that, when defence appropriations were reduced, the USSR had to place more emphasis on the quality of air defence. Besides the significance of air defence, the role of radio-electronic countermeasures such as the timely detection, suppression, and destruction of enemy reconnaissance systems and various fire control systems were also brought to the fore (Shishkin 1990: 20).

Aware of the time needed to achieve parity, the USSR developed a different asymmetric response to US technological improvements. It lied mainly in the politico-diplomatic, rather than technological, realm. Colonel V. F. Andreev was cited as saying that 'maintaining a military-strategic balance on the basis of the "action-reaction" principle was a *mistake* [emphasis added] of military policy; the expenditure of huge material resources' (cited in *Voennaya Mysl'* 1990c: 33). So the USSR moved in the direction of disarmament negotiations and identified 'general and complete disarmament' as its ultimate goal (Chervov 1983: 5). The same author (1983: 15) further clarified the position taken by the Soviet Union: 'There is no type of weapon that it would not agree to ban if, of course, this is done on a reciprocal basis.' Before this could be achieved, the USSR unilaterally adhered to the principle of 'defence sufficiency'. In accordance with this principle, the quantitative and qualitative composition of the Soviet Armed Forces was to be 'determined by the minimum necessary to ensure the security of the state' (Korovushin 1990: 29). It is important to note that this principle applied to both nuclear and conventional weapons (Chirvin 1990: 6). A more detailed discussion of Soviet nuclear disarmament ambitions can be found in Chapter 4. To be more precise, 'sufficiency' in conventional weapons would be defined by the minimum necessary to ensure reliable defence, but likely insufficient for conducting large-scale offensive operations (*Voennaya Mysl'* 1990a: 27).

What deserves special attention is the fact that the tension between quantity and quality played out here too. Chirvin (1990: 10) explained that, with respect to conventional weapons, 'sufficiency' particularly implied 'the minimum required quantity and high quality.' To demonstrate goodwill and serious intent, the USSR proceeded with a considerable unilateral reduction of its military spending and Armed Forces. The latter was reduced by 500,000 people, 10,000 tanks, 8,500 artillery systems, and 820 combat aircraft (*Voennaya Mysl'* 1990b: 3). In the hope that the opponent would reciprocate, the USSR clearly communicated its longterm strategic objectives. These were: the prevention of an arms race, the transition to real disarmament beginning with the reduction of nuclear arsenals and conventional armaments, the dissolution of military blocs, and the reduction of military spending (*Voennaya Mysl'* 1990a: 25; 1990b: 3).

Going further, the USSR declared its concurrent objective to be the prevention of both nuclear and conventional war (Podberezkin 1989: 58; Tretyak 1990: 2). In other words, it no longer perceived war – at least it was so claimed – as a foreign policy instrument and as a means of achieving political goals or resolving interstate disputes and contradictions (Podberezkin 1989: 53; *Voennaya Mysl'* 1990a: 24; 1990b: 3). For example, the following was noted in the Political Report to the 27th Congress of the CPSU: 'the nature of existing weapons leaves no hope for any state to protect itself only by military-technical means ... Ensuring security is increasingly presented as a political task, and it can be solved only by political means' (CPSU Materials 1986: 64). In Soviet eyes even a non-nuclear war was 'meaningless' because, given the destructive power of modern conventional weapons, it would have as 'disastrous consequences' as a nuclear war (Chirvin 1990: 5).

According to Chervov (1983: 15), the USSR's position in these matters 'should not be mistaken for its weakness.' On the contrary, Chirvin (1990: 6) insisted that such statements and moves required 'considerable courage' from Soviet political and military leadership as it was 'difficult to break the stereotypes.'

5.3 The Gulf War as a Major Turning Point

The Gulf War was a catalyst of further and much greater change in Soviet – and eventually Russian – strategic thinking. It was called 'a turning point', triggering the era of high-tech wars (Vorobyev 1992: 68), and the 'prototype' of future wars by military experts in post-Soviet Russia (Erokhin 1991: 41; Sizov and Skokov 1992: 37). What this war showed them, most importantly, was that one's technological (qualitative) superiority could 'negate' another's quantitative superiority in manpower and conventional weapons (Vorobyev 1992: 69). The latest weapons and professional training of military personnel appeared to be decisive in achieving victory as even an army of many millions and a large arsenal of tanks, aircraft, and guns did not bring success to the Iraqis (Korotchenko 1991: 23;

Vorobyev and Kiselev 2006a: 5–6). The coalition many times surpassed the Iraqis in ultra-modern types of weapons, including precision-guided weapons (Vorobyev 1992: 69). It was during this operation that the US tested new systems and types of weapons, including a number of high-precision weapons and especially cruise missiles, and 'worked out the tactics of their use' (Manachinsky, Chumak, and Pronkin: 1992: 92).

The revolutionary potential of new-generation weapons, precisely as Soviet military experts previously imagined it, was tested and proven during the Gulf War. The increasing accuracy of weapons became a persistent trend ever since: 70 per cent of all bombs were guided in Operation Desert Fox in Iraq (Zakharov 1999: 69); 90 per cent of all aviation weapons used in Yugoslavia in 1999 were precision-guided (Krasnov 1999: 72); and the share of high-precision weapons used in Operation Shock and Awe in Iraq reached 85 per cent (Vorobyev and Kiselev 2011: 22). These examples once again illustrate that Russian military experts were grasping the revolutionary potential of new-generation weapons by observing the effects of their application by others.

At the same time, the Gulf War demonstrated the prominence of space assets in establishing a high degree of awareness of the environment and the enemy's actions and raising the effectiveness of reconnaissance, communications, and command and control (Romanov and Chigak 1991: 76; Ionov 1992: 80). Iraq's most important military and economic assets, as well as the operational formation of its armed forces were determined with high accuracy. The navigation field created by Navstar GPS was widely used during this operation. With the help of this space system, the accuracy of aviation and cruise missiles significantly increased (Romanov and Chigak 1991: 78–79). The Gulf War, according to Politsyn (1992: 69), opened 'a new period of wars of the space age.' Russian military experts expected this trend to continue in the coming decades. A few years later, for example, Zakharov (1999: 69) discovered that the use of space-based reconnaissance contributed to the destruction of 85 per cent of all targets in Operation Desert Fox.

The possibility for the destruction of individual and even group objects 'with one blow' implied an increase in the destructive power of conventional weapons (Zakharov 1991: 13). Manachinsky, Chumak, and Pronkin (1992: 89) openly stated that, during the Gulf War, the coalition brought down on Iraq such a number of bombs and missiles that their total destructive power was 'comparable to the explosion of several nuclear weapons.' Sizov and Skokov (1992: 37) went even further to argue the following: 'The role of nuclear weapons ... fades into the background.'

Besides the increased accuracy and destructive power of the new generation of Western conventional weapons, the Gulf War was also an excellent example of 'remote combat', as spotted by Vorobyev (1992: 70). The substantial and clearly growing role of aerial force in modern operations allowed for this (Rudyuk 1991: 61; Ionov 1992: 80). In particular, it was during the Gulf War that reconnaissance-strike complexes developed in the US underwent combat testing (Vorobyev 1992: 74). Most importantly, the US concept of 'air-land battle', in particular its integral component – an air offensive operation, was tested and proved promising (Manachinsky, Chumak, and Pronkin 1992: 90). Further progress was made over the next few years. While the US primarily tested the conduct of an air campaign during the Gulf War, the ground phase of the operation began simultaneously with air strikes during Operation Shock and Awe (Vorobyev and Kiselev 2006a: 8). Inter alia, UAVs have proven themselves in combat, particularly in the Gulf War and later also in Yugoslavia, Afghanistan, etc. (Romanchuk, Dulnev, and Orlyansky 2020: 73). Observing NATO's operations in Yugoslavia, Krasnov (1999: 73) even insisted that aerial force assumed a 'priority role' in modern warfare. The key revolutionary feature of air-launched precision weapons was the increasing range of fire (e.g. the distance from one's own front line to enemy targets increased to 600–1,200 km) (Ionov 1992: 80), i.e. the additional 'depth' these weapons provided to the battlefield (Zakharov 1991: 9–15). Korotchenko (1991: 21) arrived at the conclusion that aerial force could eventually decide the war's outcome. The intrusion of the attacker's ground forces into enemy territory was no longer a necessity. Instead, long-range fire which the coalition's air force achieved during the Gulf War went 'far beyond the limits' of ground operations (Vakhrushev 1999: 23).

In the Soviet view, such an increase in the quality of weapons levelled out, at least to some extent, the need for their large quantities. In Vakhrushev's (1999: 27) view, the experience of the Gulf War and NATO's air operations in Yugoslavia clearly showed that an increase in the combat power and range of certain types of aircraft made the application of much smaller aviation groups increasingly effective. While 2,300 aircraft were initially involved in Operation Desert Storm, the aviation grouping at the beginning of NATO's operation in Yugoslavia consisted of only 460 aircraft, even though their number gradually increased during the operation itself (Krasnov 1999: 71).

5.4 Asymmetric Assurance:
The Nuclear Escalation Ladder

Besides most clearly realizing the revolutionary potential of the new generation of Western conventional weapons early on, the USSR – and eventually Russia – learned more from the involvement of the US and NATO in local wars. Citing an article titled 'Battle in the Steppe' by one American military observer, Erokhin (1991: 38) contemplated the possibility and feasibility for the US to repeat Operation Desert Storm in the steppe, i.e. against the USSR (later, in particular, Russia). Vorobyev (1992: 67) drew attention to another important detail: 'Iraqi troops were mostly equipped with Soviet weapons. It is no coincidence that the Western press believes that the war in the Persian Gulf zone is a "mirror image" of future operations with the CIS Armed Forces.' Krasnov (1999: 71) voiced similar concerns about NATO's military operation in Yugoslavia: 'The scenario that played out in Yugoslavia, under certain conditions, can be realized in our country as well.' What increasingly concerned Russia was that the US and NATO could intrude into the territories of sovereign states even without UN Security Council approval, 'ignoring the generally recognized norms of international law' (Pavlov, Belsky, and Klimenko 2015: 4). Sokov (Interview no. 2) drew attention to the role of NATO's aerial bombing campaign during the Kosovo War. He made clear that it was the war that made Russia understand that international law was not necessarily decisive; instead, military force was. He especially highlighted that this understanding came to Russia nearly against the background of the resumption of military action in Chechnya. Russia was, according to him, concerned about the possible repetition of the Kosovo scenario in Chechnya.

At the same time, there was a huge and growing gap between the capabilities of post-Soviet Russia and that of NATO. The latter had a great and increasing advantage in conventional forces 'for the first time in many decades', as particularly stressed by Korotchenko (1991: 20). In 1999, Levshin, Nedelin, and Sosnovsky (1999: 34) reported that Russia would not be sufficiently equipped with high-precision conventional weapons at least until 2010. Barvinenko (1999: 26) clarified that even Russia's best – and increasingly high-precision – weapons could not be fully exploited 'due to the imperfection of reconnaissance and command and control systems.' Kokoshin (2009: 49) also explained: 'Today, even for purely economic reasons, we cannot afford straightforwardness and symmetry.' Even though this argument was made in 2009, it has remained generally relevant since then. Elsewhere, he (2002) mentioned that looking for 'more reliable and much cheaper' countermeasures was even more relevant for post-Soviet Russia than it was for the USSR. Gorbunov and Bogdanov (2009: 6) agreed that Russia had to explore 'asymmetric', not direct, response options as its economic and military power were 'incomparable with the capabilities of the USSR and the US.'

Russia's immediate and relatively inexpensive asymmetric response, mainly at the doctrinal or conceptual (and not as much at the technological) level, was a re-evaluation of the role of tactical nuclear weapons. Its non-strategic nuclear arsenal was seen as the best available tool to 'compensate for the imbalance' in conventional forces. Non-strategic nuclear weapons would, therefore, serve not only as a 'political means' of preventing war, but also as a 'military means' of counteracting the possible use of nuclear weapons, other types of weapons of mass destruction, as well as conventional weapons (Ivasik, Pis'yaukov, and Khryapin 1999: 72). The latter option was particularly defined as a means of 'de-escalating' hostilities (Levshin, Nedelin, and Sosnovsky 1999: 35). The same authors (1999: 35–36) proposed the following nuclear escalation ladder:[9]

- *demonstration* (delivering single demonstrative nuclear strikes on unpopulated territories or secondary military installations of the enemy with either limited military personnel or not serviced at all);
- *intimidation-demonstration* (delivering single blows on transport hubs, engineering structures, and individual elements of enemy forces leading to the disruption of control but not causing large losses);
- *intimidation* (inflicting group strikes on the main groupings of enemy troops in one operational direction to change the balance of forces in this direction);
- *deterrence-retaliation* (inflicting concentrated strikes on groupings of enemy troops in one or several operational directions for a decisive change in the balance of forces in the event of an unfavourable development of a defensive operation);
- *retaliation-deterrence* (inflicting a massive blow to defeat the aggressor's military forces in the theatre of operations and radically change the military situation);

---

9   Russian experts have themselves used the term 'nuclear escalation ladder' (*лестница ядерной эскалации*) (Kokoshin 2002).

- *retaliation* (inflicting a massive strike or a series of strikes against the enemy with the maximum use of available forces and means, including strategic nuclear forces).

The concept of de-escalation was primarily seen as 'an additional ... element of the deterrence mechanism' (Kreidin 1999: 75). Non-strategic nuclear weapons became an important deterrent in regional and local wars (Levshin, Nedelin, and Sosnovsky 1999: 37). The idea of 'global nuclear deterrence', relying primarily on strategic nuclear weapons, was, as a result, complemented by that of 'regional nuclear deterrence' (Kreidin 1999: 73). Russia's Military Doctrine of 2000 clarified the relationship between regional and local wars: 'A regional war may be the result of an escalation of a local war.'[10] Kreidin (1999: 77) particularly highlighted that an important conceptual principle for regional deterrence to work was 'the uncertainty of the nuclear threshold', according to which the attacker would not have prior information about the possible moment of nuclear escalation by the defending side when repelling non-nuclear aggression.

Russia also began to put greater emphasis on the sophistication of air defence as yet another means of technological asymmetry, having learned from Iraq's failure in 1991. The catastrophic results of the war for Iraq were, according to Rudyuk (1991: 65), 'the result of its insufficient work on its own air defence, and underestimation of the role of its means under modern conditions.' Similarly assessing the results of the Gulf War, Manachinsky, Chumak, and Pronkin (1992: 89) concluded that air defence had 'outgrown tactical limits and ... had become an important operational-strategic factor.' The overthrowing of legitimate state regimes in Yugoslavia, Iraq, and Libya were, in Zaretsky's (2015: 27) view, also the result of the 'suppression (inaction)' of their air defences. A very important step in creating the basis of Russia's modern system of air (aerospace) defence was taken in 2011 with the establishment of an entirely new branch of the Armed Forces: the Aerospace Defence Troops (Aksenov, Tretyakov, and Filin 2015: 19). It was seen as yet another layer in Russia's deterrence mechanism. Building a promising aerospace defence system, as the same authors explained (2015: 21), would 'create a fundamentally new deterrence system', cotributing to the

---

10 The text of the document is available (in Russian) online at: https://docs.cntd.ru /document/901759209.

'strategic deterrence of possible aggression with the use of both nuclear and non-nuclear high-precision weapons.' New technologies were being developed for this purpose too. At a more general level, Russia's Unified Space System (Единая Космическая Система), designed to detect and track ballistic missile launches towards Russia, took up experimental combat duty in December 2017 (Podymov 2018: 33). Also, Russian forces have reportedly acquired an automated control system that uses AI elements to coordinate the work of air defence complexes (S-300s, S-400s, Pantsirs) (*Izvestia* 2018).

However, information about the incapacity of Russian air defences to detect and intercept precision missiles launched from the the US-supplied HIMARS had been disseminated broadly during the war in Ukraine in 2022 (e.g. Ayad 2022; Drake 2022). Ukrainian military expert Sergey Kuzan explicitly stated that the American weapons 'defeated all those laudatory reports that the Russians used to address their S-300s, S-400s about the fact that they are invincible' (cited in *NV* 2022). Another expert, Yuri Fedorov, explained that S-400s have anti-missile capabilities with respect to medium-range missiles but they are 'not designed' to destroy missiles with a range of around 80 kilometres launched by HIMARS (cited in Chernovol 2022). This is despite the fact that the Russian media has been strongly advocating the narrative of their effectiveness, even against HIMARS. Military expert Vladislav Shurygin was cited (Sokirko 2022a) as claiming the following: 'Even complexes such as the S-300, not to mention the S-400 and S-500, will cope with HIMARS'. Boris Dzherelievsky, another Russian expert, similarly characterized HIMARS as 'quite vulnerable' to missile defence systems. Gennady Alekhin, also a military expert cited by the Russian media, offered the following explanation concerning the alleged ineffectiveness of Russia's defence against HIMARS: 'the Ukrainian army often fires at unprotected objects where there are no missile defence and air defence systems of the Russian army' (both cited in Sokirko 2022b). Ukrainian forces were reported to have destroyed Russian ammunition stockpiles (Drake 2022).

5.5 Seeking Symmetry: Embarking on the Revolution in Military Affairs

At the same time, Russia came to the realization that it was losing what the USSR had uneasily gained. In the early 1990s the USSR, and eventually Russia, lost the position of 'superpower' (Kirilenko and Trenin 1992: 15). The common aspiration was restoring Russia's status – at least – as being a great power so lagging behind in modern weaponry was unaffordable in the long run. Gareev (1992: 39) set the goal clearly early on: 'The main idea that unites all personnel is that Russia can and must be revived and develop only as a great power.' Local conflicts in which Russia was involved additionally demonstrated that it was not prepared for modern warfare. For example, the war in Afghanistan showed that Russia's approach and military tools were 'completely unsuitable for combat operations in Afghan conditions.' Gareev (1993: 39) went even further to argue the following: 'We have had and still have a dismissive view of local wars and conflicts, and this is a big mistake.' The Russo-Georgian War revealed further deficiencies in the equipment and operation of Russian Armed Forces such as the lack of high-precision weapons and UAVs, including modern reconnaissance UAVs, as well as problems with target reconnaissance, communication, and data transmission systems (Bogdanov, Popov, and Ivanov 2014: 9; Sinyatkin, Bozhkov, and Gorchakov 2018: 87). Not only did Russia's strike complexes appear '[t]echnically and morally obsolete', but its theory of operational art also proved outdated as it prioritized 'traditional large-scale terrestrial operations' (Bogdanov, Popov, and Ivanov 2014: 9). The priority was to revive Russia as both 'a great power' and 'a high-tech state' (Gorbunov and Bogdanov 2009: 4).

Galeotti (Interview no. 7) noted that it was mainly since 2009, and particularly the Serdyukov-Makarov reforms, that original Soviet ideas about the ongoing revolution in warfare were 'beginning to be fed into practical military change' in Russia.[11] But he noted that, even then, Russia 'was still dealing with the legacies of technological backwardness, but also two decades of under-spending and neglect.' Sitnov and Rakhmanov (1999: 2) also admitted, even earlier, that Russia was originally working with 'extremely limited resources'. So, at this very basic level, the starting point was almost no different from that at which Imperial Russia found itself in the nineteenth century.

Kirillov and Kryuchkov (2008: 11) associated the beginning of the twenty-first century with 'a *gradual* [emphasis added] rise in the economy and in the social sphere' in Russia. Yet favourable economic conditions

---

11 Blank (Interview no. 4) clarified that Russia has not been implementing Ogarkov's original vision 'literally' but has been 'influenced by it'.

for future military modernization were being created slowly and unsurely. A massive drop in the GDP between 1990–1997 was remedied during the next ten years. However, if the entire post-Soviet period is assessed, the country's GDP grew by only 19 per cent (0.7 per cent per year) in the period from 1990 to 2014. Also, the raw material orientation of the Russian economy even increased with the start of these reforms, which did not meet the original expectations and held back economic growth (Baranov and Bessonov 2018: 144, 148–149). It is no surprise then that Russia had a considerable delay in embarking on this revolutionary venture and has experienced difficulties in subsequently exploiting its benefits to the fullest, as additionally revealed by Russia's military invasion of Ukraine in 2022. However, at the time of writing this text, changes have taken place at all possible levels from the introduction of new concepts and technologies to various organizational adaptations. Commenting generally on the reported results, Miles (Interview no. 3) concluded that there has been 'a lot of success' by Russian standards.[12]

One of the most important novel related concepts introduced in the pages of *Voennaya Mysl'* was 'high-precision combat' (высокоточное сражение), defined as 'the next, higher step in improving the methods of warfare' (Vorobyev and Kiselev 2006b: 15). Another innovative concept that increasingly penetrated Russian military thinking was 'non-nuclear deterrence'. It appeared for the first time in Russia's Military Doctrine of 2014. There it was defined as 'a complex of foreign policy, military and military-technical measures aimed at preventing aggression against the Russian Federation *by non-nuclear means* [emphasis added].'[13] Polegaev and Alferov (2015: 5–6) defined non-nuclear deterrence with greater precision, elaborating more on the expected threshold of damage and defining it precisely as 'the threat of causing *unacceptable damage* [emphasis added] using non-nuclear means.' Unacceptable damage is, according to them, the damage that 'would call into question the achievement of the goals of armed conflict, but would not deprive the enemy of an alternative to de-escalate it.' The term itself was seemingly borrowed from Soviet terminology on nuclear deterrence, as shown in Chapter 4, even though the precise definition of this term differs. Ponomarev, Poddubny, and Polegaev (2019: 99) even suggested calling it '*predetermined* [emphasis added] unacceptable damage', especially for local and regional wars.

---

12 The interview was conducted prior to February 2022.

13 The text of the document is available (in Russian) online at: https://docs.cntd.ru /document/420246589.

As a matter of fact, the idea of non-nuclear deterrence was articulated much earlier in Russian military circles than it appeared in official military doctrine. For example, Danilevich and Shunin (1992: 49 and 53) introduced the term 'non-nuclear deterrence forces' – or alternatively 'strategic non-nuclear forces' – and clarified that they could 'complement the deterrent effect of strategic nuclear forces.' Burenok and Achasov (2007: 12) put forward more subtle arguments in favour of such deterrence: first, it would raise the threshold for the use of nuclear weapons in the event of a conflict between countries possessing such weapons; second, it would help verify the seriousness of hypothetical aggression (if non-nuclear means failed to deter the start or continuation of aggression, the transition to the use of nuclear weapons would be 'natural and inevitable'). To a certain extent, non-nuclear deterrence was, therefore, considered as 'pre-nuclear' (Khryapin, Kalinkin, and Matvichuk 2015: 19).

Particularly important is the fact that the philosophy of active defence, taking root at least in the Soviet Union, as shown in Chapter 4, has continued to dominate Russian strategic thinking in the twenty-first century. Chief of the General Staff V. Gerasimov himself stressed that the basis of Russia's current responses to external security challenges is based upon the 'active defence strategy' (стратегия активной обороны), which provides for a set of measures to pre-emptively neutralize threats to the security of the Russian state (cited in Sviridova 2019). What deserves attention is that arguments of the same kind have been invoked in relation to Ukraine in 2022. President Putin (2022) justified Russia's supposedly 'pre-emptive' armed intervention there as follows:

> Everything indicated that a clash with neo-Nazis, Banderites, whom the United States and their younger partners staked, would be inevitable. ... The danger grew every day. Russia gave a *pre-emptive rebuff* [emphasis added] to aggression.[14]

Opinions from independent Western sources are generally in agreement. *The New York Times* reported in one of its recent articles, for example, that Russia's initial objective was to capture Kyiv, topple the Ukrainian government, and subsume Ukraine into Russia's orbit (Bilefsky, Pérez-Peña, and Nagourney 2022). Another article published by BBC News also

---

14 The full transcript of his speech from 9 May 2022 is available (in Russian) online at: http://kremlin.ru/events/president/news/68366.

contained that Russia's original goal was to overrun Ukraine and depose its government, or at least conquer Donbas (Kirby 2022a). An article accidentally or prematurely published by the official Russian news agency RIA Novosti (and subsequently deleted from their website) also contained a different interpretation of the country's objectives in Ukraine: 'Russia is restoring its historical fullness, gathering the Russian world, the Russian people together – in its entirety of Great Russians, Belarusians and Little Russians [supposedly Ukrainians]' (Akopov 2022). The publication of this article pointed out a discrepancy between the public discourse of the government and the information that leaked through a state-run news agency. Comparing himself with Peter the Great, President Putin ironically remarked that the return and consolidation of territories fell to the share of modern Russia (BBC News 2022). In this context, he particularly referred to the transfer of Donbass to Ukraine under the leadership of Lenin (Khaneneva 2022). The illegal annexation by Russia of Ukraine's Donetsk, Luhansk, Zaporizhzhia and Kherson regions in September 2022 clearly demonstrated that there is ample room for manipulation within the so-called 'active defence strategy'.

Besides conceptual innovations and adaptations, the technological quest for precision-guided weapons and related technologies also was gaining pace and momentum, constituting yet another core element of the Russian RMA. Russia developed its own global positioning system, GLONASS, 'analogous' to the Navstar GPS system operated by the US (Borisov and Evdokimov 2013: 134). A 'real breakthrough' in equipping the Russian Armed Forces with high-precision long-range weapons was made between 2012–2017. The troops began to be serially supplied with operational-tactical missile systems (Iskander-M), long-range cruise missiles for surface ships (Kalibr-NK) and submarines (Kalibr-PL), as well as new long-range air-launched cruise missiles (Kh-101) which facilitated the modernization of long-range aircraft too (Podymov 2018: 33). In 2021, Russia's Minister of Defence S. K. Shoigu declared that the number of high-precision cruise missiles in the Russian army has increased more than 30 times since 2012, and the number of their carriers more than 12 times (cited in TASS 2021a). Russia also made progress in the development of UAVs. It had more than 900 complexes with UAVs, including more than 2,400 units of UAVs for various purposes by 2021 (Goncharov and Ryabov 2021: 67). The creation of such a large fleet of UAVs in a relatively short time span, 'starting from far behind in the 1990s', can be considered a 'success' according to Bendett (Interview no. 5). However, he clarified that Russia is gaining 'near-peer' capability when it comes to ISR UAVs but lags far behind the US, Israel, and China in combat UAVs. He also added that Russia is still competing mainly with Turkey and Iran 'for the same spot in the global UAV market.'[15] Russian military experts also admitted that Russia's newest combat UAVs emulate American UAVs. For example, the Inokhodets medium-altitude long-flight drone is, according to Sinyatkin, Bozhkov, and Gorchakov (2018: 88), 'close in its characteristics to the American MQ-1 Predator.' The Altius medium-altitude long-endurance drone is 'an analogue of the American MQ-9 Reaper.' The latest State Armament Programme adopted for the period 2018–2027 also gave priority attention to, among others, high-precision weapons and UAVs (Gaydunko and Makarova 2019: 12).

Organizational adaptations were made as well. However, it is appropriate to begin their analysis with the discussion of continuities. Although post-Soviet Russia seemed to make a clean break with the past, centralizing tendencies in the state bureaucracy did not disappear. Quite the opposite, they have endured in principle but assumed a different form. Exploring the Soviet nomenklatura ties of Putin elites, Snegovaya and Petrov (2022: 329) argued that the proportion of those with professional and family nomenklatura backgrounds constitute approximately 60 per cent. In fact, their share is 'significantly higher' than the *siloviki*, on which recent studies have primarily focused. Industrial bases were largely integrated through the nationalization of the country's most valuable assets and the creation of large state corporations. Much of the banking system ended up 'in state hands' too (Szakonyi 2020: 2–4). Russian military experts immediately recognized the need for the 'centralizing role' of the Ministry of Defence in planning and financing high-tech R&D (Nikolaev 1992: 30). All of this made it easier for the Russian government to determine the priority directions for industrial R&D. Particular emphasis was placed on the development of Russia's military-industrial complex. Nepobedimy and Prokofiev (2006: 71) captured the general spirit:

> The majority of the population has no doubt that our country should be a self-sufficient, independent and strong state. Therefore, it must be ready to defend its interests by armed means, that is, by having a strong army, *modern weapons and their foundation – a military-industrial complex* [emphasis added].

---

15 The interview was conducted prior to February 2022.

In 2015, President Putin even stressed that the defence industry should 'set the bar for technological and industrial development and continue to remain one of the main locomotives for innovation' (cited in Bowen 2021: 6, with reference to TASS). In 2016, Deputy Prime Minister Dmitriy Rogozin also expressed the hope that the military-industrial complex would come to play a principal role in the country's national economy: 'Military-industrial enterprises must be subordinated to the logic of the parallel development of high-tech civilian products so that they become *a driver for the most important sectors of the economy* [emphasis added]' (cited in *Primgazeta* 2016). For example, it was reported that defence industry enterprises would be engaged in the production of medical equipment (Zgirovskaya 2016).

What deserves special attention in this regard is the entrepreneurial model of Russia's military industry. Despite raw materials' dominance of Russian exports, arms exports is one of the few areas of manufacturing in which Russia has truly achieved the position of 'a world leader'. The volume of arms exported by Russia has surpassed the value of respective exports by China, Germany, France, and the UK, all recognized as significant arms exporters, and, in some years, even the US (Connolly and Sendstad 2017: 6–7). Russia has fewer arms export destinations than the US but it has indeed developed a culture of entrepreneurship in the military industry: it delivered major weapons to 47 states and to rebel forces in Ukraine between 2013–2017 (SIPRI 2018: 4). These findings are particularly interesting in that they testify to the general primacy of the military-industrial sector over other sectors of the economy in Russian strategic thinking, as also discussed with respect to the Soviet Union in Chapter 4.

However, as Zysk (2021b: 12) rightfully remarked, 'advanced military-industrial sectors are no longer the main sources of technological innovation', which is increasingly '*driven* [emphasis added] by the commercial sector, with dual-use potential'. Therefore, efforts have been made to create synergies between the military and the civilian sector but a culture that would prioritize the development of civilian technologies has never developed in Russia. For example, the Advanced Research Foundation, a state fund created in 2012, has facilitated the development of high-tech innovative technologies and products for 'military [listed first], special and dual-use' applications (*FPI*, n.d.). It is also reported that the Ministry of Defence, with the participation of the Russian Academy of Sciences, financial development institutions, as well as leading research centres and universities, has formed and operates an 'innovation system' that interacts with more than 1,200 subjects from the country's innovation sectors from 25 regions, with which 151 cooperation agreements have been concluded (MoD, n.d.). Attractive working conditions are reportedly created 'for [both] civil and military specialists' at the Era Technopolis, the first military innovation city established in 2018, and the Ministry of Defence discloses that the results of research at the Technopolis 'will be used not only to strengthen the country's defence capability, but also for peaceful purposes'. More than 500 organizations currently interact with the Era Technopolis but 80 per cent of them are enterprises of the military-industrial complex (MoD 2020).

The above clearly illustrates that military-technological innovation is given priority and has been pursued under the direct guidance and supervision of the Russian state. At the same time, the Russian state increasingly draws on technological expertise from the civilian sector and appreciates the dual-use potential of research. It is fair to note that the civilian-to-military transfer of technology is not automatic and often rather difficult. Verbruggen (2019: 340) rightly warned, for example, that civilian companies may not want to cooperate with the defence sector for ideological reasons. For example, the services conglomerate Sistema, one of the key private investors in Russia, publicly announced on 4 May 2022 that it had divested its holdings in the Russian defence companies RTI and Kronstadt and owned no stake in the defence industry (*Sistema.com* 2022). However, Russian (and Chinese) companies are arguably more immune to normative pressures of the wider society than those in the West.

Nevertheless, Russia has failed to strike a competitive balance between business and the state in terms of facilitating dual-use R&D. Kryshtanovskaya and White (1996: 719–721) convincingly illustrated that the privatization process of the 1990s was basically the '[p]rivatisation of the state by the state', and that the nomenklatura sold itself its own property at 'nominal' prices. The problem has been further exacerbated by Putin's 'crony' (Sharafutdinova 2011; Åslund 2019) or even 'comrade' capitalism, as detailed, for example, in a continuing investigation by Reuters.

To create a sustainable ecosystem of entrepreneurship and innovation, engender a startup culture, and encourage venture capitalism, the Russian government created the Skolkovo Innovation Center, a high-tech business area on the outskirts of Moscow, and its managing entity, the Skolkovo Foundation, in 2010. But the civilian innovation ecosystem remains underdeveloped despite considerable achievements on this front by Russian standards. The establishment of Skolkovo did not turn Russia into a viable innovation economy (Arcuri 2022). Heavy bureaucratic control and corruption, poor enforcement of intellectual property rights, as well as shortages of professional expertise ('brain drain') are among the factors that constitute an unfavourable business climate in Russia (Zysk 2021b: 20). As a result, the core of dual-use R&D ended up in the hands of state-owned, state-financed, or state-controlled corporations. For example, Sberbank, Yandex, Gazprom Neft, Mail.ru Group, MTS, and the Russian Direct Investment Fund jointly constitute the so-called *AI Alliance* and play the leading role in the country's innovation ecosystem in the field of AI. Rather unsurprisingly, the Ministry of Defence has performed the centralizing role in AI R&D (Hynek and Solovyeva 2022: 66–67). The significance of AI within the context of the current RMA for Russia is discussed later in this chapter. Last but not least, the Russian invasion of Ukraine in 2022 has 'seriously handicapped' the country's emerging market-based innovation economy (Arcuri 2022).

Therefore, Russia displays the characteristics of a developmental state in politico-economic terms in its effort to catch up technologically with the West, but it is a stretch to call it a capitalist developmental state. In addition to the market distortions discussed above, it has always been a state with 'a *top-priority* [emphasis added] commitment to [the] economic development' that lied at the heart of South Korea, Taiwan, Hong Kong, Singapore, and Japan's success (Kim 1993: 228). Despite similar aspirations, Russia's proportionally greater emphasis on military innovation programmes and military-oriented entrepreneurship moves it farther away from other capitalist developmental states. As part of Russia's response to international sanctions over its invasion of Ukraine, the government even adopted a law according to which it can introduce 'special measures' in the economic sphere during Russia's counter-terrorist and other operations outside its territory. If such measures are adoped, legal entities, regardless of their organizational form and form of ownership, will not be entitled to refuse agreements and state contracts for the supply of goods, the performance of work, and the provision of services necessary to ensure the conduct of such operations. Special measures can also interfere with the legal regulation of labour relations, including procedures related to work outside regular working hours, at night or on weekends, as well as to paid annual leave (*Interfax* 2022a). Therefore, the Russian ecosystem of military-technological innovation is embedded in what can be characterized as a *quasi-capitalist* developmental state, with elements of a market economy, a predatory crony-capitalist economy, and a command economy.

Regardless of the limitations of Russia's innovation ecosystem, the idea of '[t]echnological independence' became increasingly popular (Gaydunko and Makarova 2019: 10). To facilitate progress on this front, some experts of *Voennaya Mysl'* highlighted certain dangers posed by Russia's technological dependence from a more general perspective. For example, as revealed by Selivanov and Ilyin (2020a: 53), 72 per cent of the components and parts of Sukhoi Superjet 100 were imported, 22 per cent of which were American-made, and it happened that the US refused to issue an export certificate to Russia for the sale of a batch of Sukhoi Superjet 100 aircraft to Iran. Bendett (Interview no. 5) warned, however, that the imported high-tech technologies on which Russia currently relies to a considerable degree are 'difficult to replace'. He assumed it could be possible for such companies as the Russian defence company Kronstadt, which supposedly produces hardware and software on its own. He also added that, even under sanctions, Russia could possibly obtain technologies on the secondary market or import them from other partners such as China.[16] Chinese exports of microchips and other electronic components have increased since Russia's invasion of Ukraine (Spegele 2022).

Further and more specific organizational changes were intended to make more effective use of precision-guided weapons. The unification of Russia's Air Force and Aerospace Defence Forces into a new unified branch named the Aerospace Forces took place in 2015. This step allowed Russian political and military leadership to ensure 'unified responsibility' for the organization of aerospace defence, as well as the construction and development of forces conducting combat operations in the aerospace sphere, their combat training, and use. Their unification clearly reflected the idea that offensive and defensive military capabilities were increasingly inseparable even in the domain of conventional arms and forces. Indeed, the country's system of aerospace defence was seen as a 'passive component' of the strategic forces of non-nuclear deterrence, while long-range high-precision weapons were identified as their 'active component' (Podymov 2018: 33). Bodner (2015) assumed that the focus of this newly created branch was on countering advanced conventional capabilities developed in the US under the banner of the Prompt Global Strike programme. Gerasimov also noted that there were newly 'formed administrative bodies and special units planning the use of

---

16 The interview was conducted prior to February 2022.

[high-precision long-range weapons] and preparing flight missions for cruise missiles of all basing types' (cited in Podymov 2018: 33).

The feasibility and effectiveness of non-nuclear deterrence of local threats to Russia's military security was, in Sterlin, Protasov, and Kreidin's (2019: 14) view, 'convincingly confirmed' during the Syrian campaign. Miles (Interview no. 3) also remarked that the Syrian campaign demonstrated, inter alia, 'successes' of the ongoing military modernization, especially as Russia's intervention there became 'decisive'. Russia's new high-precision long-range weapons were tested on the battlefield in Syria. 'The widespread use of reconnaissance-strike assets based on reconnaissance, control and communications complexes made it possible to implement the principle of "one target – one bomb"', as pointed out by Gerasimov (cited in *RIA FAN* 2017). For example, it was during this campaign that Russia for the first time fired cruise ship-based missiles at a real enemy located at a distance of almost 1,500 km from the launch site. The missiles that traveled 1,500 km and destroyed 11 terrorist targets in Syria were launched by the Kalibr-NK missile system (*Vesti.ru* 2015). Gorenburg (Interview no. 8) characterized the introduction of Kalibr missiles as 'one of the biggest changes' because these weapons have 'a significant strategic value' for Russia. According to him, systems of this kind allowed Russia to conduct a military operation at a considerable distance from its immediate borders, as demonstrated in Syria. Noteworthy is the fact that Kalibr missiles are being embedded into the military-oriented entrepreneurial model of the Russian state, as introduced above. Russia has already exported submarines and ships armed with Kalibr missiles, promoting the narrative of their 'high efficiency during the anti-terrorist operation in Syria' (*Interfax* 2021a). More recently, the Russian Defence Ministry was cited as reporting on the destruction – by Kalibr cruise missiles – of a large depot with US and European weapons in Ukraine's Ternopil region (*Reuters* 2022).

From a more general perspective, even Western experts recognized that, by the time of its invasion of Ukraine, Russia had 'developed' C4ISR capabilities and 'integrated' them into Russia's own systems of 'reconnaissance strike complexes', allowing for accurate targeting in high-precision long-range strikes (Jones 2022: 4). Russia's UAVs also proved effective in combat. In January 2018, Shoigu underlined that, '*thanks to unmanned aircraft* [emphasis added], Russian troops gained full control over the situation in the entire territory of Syria' (Milenin and Sinikov 2019: 57). President Putin also announced in 2018 that

Russia's Armed Forces were being armed with new models of strategic weapons, including conventional, high-precision, high-speed, and long-range weapons, such as the missile system with a heavy intercontinental ballistic missile named Sarmat, the Avangard hypersonic missile system, the Peresvet combat laser complex, the Kinzhal aviation missile system, the Burevestnik cruise missile complex, and the Poseidon unmanned underwater vehicle (Evsyukov and Khryapin 2020: 27).

Discourse on the emergence of Russia as a leading power and even a superpower (сверхдержава) became increasingly popular. 'Russia should be among the leading states, and in some areas the absolute leader in the construction of a new generation army' said President Putin in his speech at the meeting of the board of the Ministry of Defence in December 2017 (cited in Maslennikov et al. 2019: 58). Gaydunko and Makarova (2019: 11) were among the experts who explicitly stated that Russia's current objective was 'to *remain* [emphasis added] and gain a foothold as a superpower'.

The increasing sophistication and automation of new-generation weapons facilitated ever more ambitious hopes, pointing to a considerable shift from Soviet strategic thinking. When battlefield conditions become too dangerous for people and public opinion is more sensitive to military casualties, military robots may, according to Novozhilova (2011: 8), 'successfully ... replace' humans in the future. Bendett (Interview no. 5) agreed that Russian political-military figures have increasingly put emphasis on 'new military technology that would be able to save their soldiers, make missions more effective, minimize civilian casualties and potentially win a conflict.' Gerasimov (2013a) himself admitted that: 'In the near future, it is possible to create fully robotized formations capable of conducting independent combat operations.'

However, traditional ways of thinking have not been shelved. Kokoshin, Baluevsky, and Potapov (2015: 14) generally highlighted the significance of 'human capital', without 'a sufficient critical mass' of which neither the development of the most modern technology, nor the construction of effective control systems, nor the conduct of successful military operations were possible. Emphasis on the supposed high morale qualities of the troops has persisted as well. President Medvedev gave 'the highest assessment of the morale of the Russian troops' following the Russo-Georgian War (Gorbunov and Bogdanov: 2009: 9). The Russian operation in the Crimea in 2014 'demonstrated both the qualitatively new capabilities of [Russia's] Armed Forces and the high morale of the personnel', according to President Putin (*RG* 2014).

Tonkikh (1985: 59–60) argued that, in modern warfare, not only would humans play a 'decisive role', but their role would even be enhanced. It is because the ever-increasing complexity of military equipment and the development of automation requires 'a significant intellectualization of military activity'. The expert suggested putting emphasis on abstract thinking, concentration, efficiency, and other higher-level cognitive skills in the training and education of military personnel. Novozhilova (2011: 7) agreed that the improvement of technology 'increases the role of the human factor, making it decisive.' She explained it as follows: 'The modern army ceases to be *massive* [emphasis added] and becomes *highly professional* [emphasis added]'. In 2021, Head of the State Duma Defence Committee V. Shamanov confirmed that only 30 per cent of Russia's military personnel were left on conscription; the rest were all contract soldiers (TASS 2021b). Miles (Interview no. 3) agreed that Russia's 'high degree of effectiveness' in Syria would not have been possible without 'technologically sophisticated command and control networks and also technologically sophisticated operators.' However, he stressed that the baseline level of technical training or 'technical sophistication' of operators was still a challenge for Russia. For instance, he noted that an average Russian private is 'less technologically skilled and worse trained' than an average American private.

Indeed, the Russian way of fighting in Ukraine in 2022 challenges its claims of military professionalism and testifies to the Russian state's continuing inclination to manpower-intensive approaches. The study of Mediazona and volunteers on the deaths of Russian soldiers in Ukraine disclosed that most of the dead in the first months of the invasion were servicemen from poor regions, mainly Dagestan and Buryatia. Moreover, most of them were younger than 27 and many younger than 24. Last but not least, there were conscripts among them, including conscripts that were persuaded into signing on as contract soldiers (Mediazona 2022). The Russian state recognized, however, that the use of high-precision weapons required highly professional specialists, including those from closely related civilian professions, and who become specialists by the age of 40–45 (*Interfax* 2022b). The Russian state eventually announced the recruitment of volunteers up to the age of 60 and, according to more recent data published by BBC News, more than 40 per cent of dead volunteers were over 45 years old (Ivshina 2022). However, this change did not solve the basic problem. As one of the state-controlled television channels reports, 'there are more and more people [fighting on the Russian side of the conflict] who quite recently were far from military affairs'

(1tv.ru 2022). Partial mobilization which would allegedly concern only those who had already served in the army, primarily those with combat experience and a military specialty, was announced in September 2022 (TASS 2022). However, in practice, the Russian army has ended up with a lot of untrained and underequipped recruits on the front line (Axe 2022; MacFarquhar 2022).

Thousands of volunteers and law enforcement officers from the Chechen Republic have also fighted on the side of Russia (RIA Novosti 2022). Syrian army veterans and former opposition fighters signed up as volunteers to fight alongside the Russian army too (*Izvestia* 2022). Shoigu reported that more than 16 thousand volunteers from different Middle Eastern countries expressed their readiness to participate in the armed hostilities on the side of Russia (*Interfax* 2022c). Even lower standards of recruitment were observed in the so-called Donetsk People's Republic (DNR) and the Luhansk People's Republic (LNR) (Glikman 2022; Lotareva and Ivshina 2022). Perhaps as a way to compensate for the lack of highly skilled professional military forces, paid fighters from the Wagner Group and the Redut have stepped in to reinforce the Russian army and pro-Russian armed groups in Ukraine (Meduza 2022). However, the Wagner Group and later the Russian Ministry of Defence itself have also recruited prisoners to join the fight in Ukraine (Shevchenko 2023).

Even from a purely technological perspective, Russia's forces of non-nuclear deterrence are yet of limited use. As admitted by Selivanov and Ilyin (2020a: 49), the development of high-tech production 'continues to be at a critically low level' in post-Soviet Russia. Brychkov, Dorokhov, and Nikonorov (2019: 21) specifically underlined that the 'disparity' of NATO's and Russia's conventional forces would not disappear in the near future 'for economic reasons'. Bendett (Interview no. 5) was rightfully more sceptical, saying that 'Russia cannot match the US or NATO when it comes to military capacity.' However, he admitted there are technologies, including strategic and tactical nuclear missiles, as well as a robust undersea nuclear capability, hypersonic missiles, and strategic aviation, which would allow Russia to compete, symmetrically or asymmetrically, with the West.[17] Gorenburg (Interview no. 8) also made clear that there is a 'strong belief' in Moscow that they cannot win a conventional war against NATO.

---

17   The interview was conducted prior to February 2022.

Interestingly though, some Russian military experts sought to justify the Russian army's poor performance in the war with Georgia by its staunch reluctance to bomb civilian areas:

> But a number of articles have now appeared in the press, stating that our troops fought in the old way and did not use modern methods of combat operations characteristic of 'democratic countries' and their armies. The aggression of the US and other NATO countries against Yugoslavia in 1999 is still considered a sample model, when power plants, hospitals, bridges, and other infrastructure of the country were destroyed by rocket and bomb attacks on cities, which forced the country's leadership to capitulate, and ground forces were practically not involved. If we follow this example and fight purely 'democratically', then the Russian army should have bombed Tbilisi, Batumi, Kutaisi, Poti, the entire infrastructure of the country and forced Georgia to capitulate. But this is not a 'democratic', but a barbaric way of waging war ... (Gareev 2008).

Russia's current way of fighting in Ukraine is not so different, in principle, from what Russian experts criticized in relation to what they defined as a Western way of war with references to Yugoslavia. Miles (Interview no. 3) observed 'a much higher casualty tolerance amongst the civilian population on the part of Russian military leadership' already during the Syrian campaign. Nevertheless, two different warfighting paradigms meet in its current military operation in Ukraine: precision strikes at a distance, though to a much lesser extent, and a major old-fashioned ground offensive relying heavily on artillery. Likely due to an insufficient supply of precision-guided munitions (Jones 2022: 4), Russia has extensively relied on unguided ones (Ivory et al. 2022). The Russian invasion of Ukraine can, therefore, be largely characterized as a 'traditional large-scale terrestrial operation', Russia's operational dogma which Bogdanov, Popov, and Ivanov (2014: 9) criticized as being outdated after the Russo-Georgian War. Generally commenting on new-generation, primarily non-contact warfare, Galeotti (Interview no. 7) mentioned the following though: 'If you have to manoeuver forces clashing on the battlefield on a tactical level, you've actually missed your chance.'[18] Be it for the insufficiency or unavailability of technologies, the urban environment which supposedly hinders their application, or the rather unusual military

---

18 The interview was conducted prior to February 2022.

objectives originally sought from these attacks (the 'demilitarization' and 'de-nazification' of Ukraine), Russia has generally failed to demonstrate the 'high-precision combat' that their military experts envisioned, drawing inspiration, inter alia, from NATO's operations in Yugoslavia. Bendett also stressed, along with other military analysts, that Russia's edge in drone warfare has diminished (cited in Schmitt, Gibbons-Neff, and Ismay 2022).

This testifies to Russia's persistent inability to exercise non-nuclear deterrence against the US and NATO. Polegaev and Alferov (2015: 6) made clear in 2015 that Russia did 'not yet have the means and capabilities to *inflict unacceptable damage* [emphasis added] on an enemy capable of waging a "remote" war,' meaning it could not effectively *deter* such a war. Ponomarev, Poddubny, and Polegaev (2019: 100) acknowledged basically the same even four years later: 'It should be noted that Russia still does not have enough non-nuclear weapons and the ability to *inflict unacceptable damage* [emphasis added] on an enemy capable of waging a remote war.' Russia's nuclear capabilities were seen as a more reliable strategic deterrent. For example, according to Sterlin, Protasov, and Kreidin (2019: 15) whose article appeared in *Voennaya Mysl'*, 'strategic non-nuclear weapons cannot create a total military-economic alternative to nuclear weapons.' Testifying to the centrality of nuclear weapons in Russia's strategic position vis-à-vis the US and NATO against the background of the ongoing war in Ukraine, President Putin immediately elevated this conflict to the level of one in which nuclear use was an option: 'This is a real threat not just to our interests, but to *the very existence of our state* [emphasis added], its sovereignty' (cited in *Interfax* 2022d). He further lowered the threshold for nuclear use after the illegal annexation by Russia of four Ukrainian regions in September 2022: 'When *the territorial integrity of our country* [emphasis added] is threatened, we will certainly use *all the means at our disposal* [emphasis added] to protect Russia and our people. This is not a bluff' (cited in Movsesyan 2022).

5.6 Twisted (A)symmetries

What is generally missed in the existing literature, however, is that Russian military thinking suggested a dual understanding of asymmetry in relation to modern warfare. On the one hand, military experts discussed the significance of Russia's 'asymmetric responses' to its potential adversaries (Selivanov and Ilyin 2020a: 50), in particular 'asymmetric weapons systems' (Selivanov and Ilyin 2020b: 56). This thinking was reflected, inter alia, in the decision to broaden the functions of non-strategic nuclear weapons and turn them into a means of de-escalating a regional or local conflict. But it is certainly not the only example as shown later in this section. 'A symmetrical response ... only draws the economically weaker side into an arms race, i.e. an economic "war" for the depletion of resources,' as explained elsewhere by Selivanov and Ilyin (2019: 7).

On the other hand, Russian military experts defined asymmetric actions as new (non-traditional) means of armed struggle utilized by weak and strong warring sides alike (Chekinov and Bogdanov 2010: 19). Indirect actions, which would usually play a secondary role, complemented, if not displaced, the 'strategy of force', which consisted in defeating an enemy with numerical superiority. Such an 'asymmetric strategy' was being implemented, according to Vorobyev and Kiselev (2006a: 5–6), in the US. It means that, at least in the eyes of Russian military experts, Russia's – seemingly – asymmetric responses were eventually symmetric to those of the US.

One of the key examples of Russia's dual conceptualization of asymmetry is electronic warfare. Bogdanov, Popov, and Ivanov (2014: 12) clearly conveyed the idea that this type of warfare could negate the technological advantage enjoyed by the US: '[I]t is no secret that well-organized electronic warfare facilities will make the American command and control system useless and inoperative.' Demin et al. (2012: 36) explicitly called it an 'asymmetric measure'. Lastochkin (2015: 16) also characterized electronic warfare as an 'asymmetric response' which could 'nullify the long-term efforts of Western countries in the development of high-tech weapons.' However, the Russo-Georgian War revealed the short-comings of Russia's electronic warfare capabilities (Lyubin 2009: 74). The development of highly effective electronic warfare equipment became 'one of the most important priorities' (Koziratsky, Budnikov, and Skopin 2010: 52–53). Success was not long in coming. Russian forces were 'particularly successful' at using electronic warfare technologies against the US and its allies in Syria (Varfolomeeva 2018). Russian electronic warfare capabilities were also reported as being 'effective' in Ukraine (Lalu 2021: 328). Miles (Interview no. 3) agreed that Russia's electronic warfare operations in Ukraine were representative of a 'modern warfare phenomenon'.[19] There were problems on this front in the first months

---

19   The interview was conducted prior to February 2022.

of the Russian invasion of Ukraine in 2022, but, as noted by Bendett (cited in Shoaib 2022), Russia eventually managed to better organize its electronic warfare capabilities. However, it is often overlooked that Russia learned this type of warfare from the US. Russian military experts immediately identified the Persian Gulf War as 'the first war at the electronic level' (Paliy 1991: 76). It was after this war that they started to perceive electronic warfare as 'an independent type of combat operations' (Manachinsky, Chumak, and Pronkin 1992: 90), and even as 'a special weapon, equivalent in its effectiveness to fire' (Vorobyev 1992: 70). According to Zakharov (1999: 69), an important tendency to consider was that the US placed greater emphasis on the suppression and destruction of the enemy's control systems, communication lines, and nodes, as also demonstrated during Operation Desert Fox.

Another prominent example of Russia's contemporary (a)symmetric efforts is information warfare. Russia's two military campaigns in Chechnya showed that its military command paid 'insufficient attention' to information warfare and efforts were made to overcome these weaknesses. Moreover, Russian military experts came to realize that constant 'information confrontation' – in peacetime, in a threatened period, and in wartime – was the assurance of 'information superiority' (Saifetdinov 2014: 39). Giles (2015: 1) eventually found Moscow's media campaign on the war in Ukraine to be 'surprisingly effective' not only in Russia but also in the West. He even insisted that Russia had built up 'a highly developed information warfare arsenal', with which NATO was 'unable to compete'. Fadeev and Nichipor (2019: 37) eventually concluded that modern wars were '80–90% propaganda and 10–20% violence'. Russia has been accused of systematic disinformation against the background of the ongoing armed conflict in Ukraine. It is fair to say that disinformation has sometimes been spread by the Ukrainian side as well (*DW*, n.d.). Disinformation, especially in the digital space, has generally been perceived in the West as a weapon 'of the weak' (Polyakova 2018). This vision fundamentally contradicts the one held by military experts in Russia. They considered US's Operation Desert Storm to be 'the first information war' (Pechurov 1997: 75). Among the tools used were disinformation in the press and mass radio propaganda, which 'demoralized' Iraqi soldiers and undermined their combat capability (Vorobyev 1992: 72; Vorobyev and Kiselev 2006a: 6–7). Puzenkin and Mikhailov (2015: 13) also underlined that the US-based CNN news service, which disseminated information from the conflict zone and was broadcast in more than ninety countries, tended to paint the operation in a more favourable light. The US-led

2003 invasion of Iraq was presented in a similar manner in *Voennaya Mysl'*. According to Russian experts, the US manipulated 'false intelligence' about the presence of Iraq's weapons of mass destruction to 'mislead' public opinion and 'legitimize' its military intervention in the Gulf (Dylevsky et al. 2008: 8).

However, information warfare has often been considered as a narrow representation of a much broader strategy – hybrid warfare. The term was first introduced in relation to the actions of non-state actors fighting against governments by William J. Nemeth in 2002. It was most widely used to characterize Russia's actions during the Ukrainian crisis of 2014 (Fabian 2019: 309). Even though the term itself originated elsewhere, the very idea of hybrid warfare was grasped earlier by Russian military experts. For example, the 'systemic damaging effect' (системный поражающий эффект) is an alternative term introduced by Konopatov and Yudin (2001: 53). In their view, such an effect could be achieved by directing all the components of state power (informational, ideological, political, economic political, military, scientific, legal, diplomatic, cultural, etc.) against the enemy. What is particularly interesting is that, according to Chekinov and Bogdanov (2010: 22), the primary goal of asymmetric measures of this kind would be 'to cause *unacceptable damage* [emphasis added] in other (non-military) security areas.' So basically the same terminology was applied to non-military measures the Soviets used in relation to nuclear deterrence and post-Soviet Russia used to define non-nuclear deterrence, as discussed above. In 2015, Kiselev and Vorobyev (2015: 41–48) introduced another highly relevant term that has not received sufficient attention in the existing literature: 'hybrid operation'. They defined it as 'an operation to *seize part of the territory of another state* [emphasis added] ... based on the coordinated application of a set of measures of politico-diplomatic, informational-propagandist, financial and economic, as well as military nature.' It was likely the logic that underlied the annexation of Crimea by Russia. Two other terms are also closely related but they mean more than a combination of military and non-military means of warfare; they particularly stand for high-tech wars: 'new generation warfare' (война нового поколения) (Chekinov and Bogdanov 2013) and 'sixth-generation wars' (войны шестого поколения) (Slipchenko 1999).

The original Western term 'hybrid warfare' has also penetrated Russian military thought. Bartosh (2018a: 10) defined the ultimate goal of 'hybrid warfare' (гибридная война) as 'crushing the enemy by defeating him on all fronts: informational, economic, military, diplomatic.'

Brychkov, Dorokhov, and Nikonorov (2019: 25) identified the content and stages of 'hybrid wars' as follows: indirect and asymmetric actions (economic, political, informational, and psychological pressure on the enemy), the use of irregulars (covert deployment of special operations forces and engagement with armed opposition), and only then the 'open' use of military force. One caveat is important here: Fadeev and Nichipor (2019: 41) explicitly called the actions of special operations forces, various forms of informational impact, as well as political, economic, and other non-military types of influence 'asymmetric measures'. It is also noteworthy that Brychkov, Dorokhov, and Nikonorov's conceptualization of hybrid warfare reiterates the key ideas put forward by Gerasimov in 2013. He discussed the changing rules of war in one of his articles which appeared in the *Military-Industrial Courier* and became accidentally known as the Gerasimov Doctrine. There he described the process of modern warfare as the use of political, economic, informational, humanitarian and other non-military measures, covert military measures (including the use of special operations forces and internal opposition forces), and – only at some later stage – the 'open' use of force to achieve final success in the conflict (Gerasimov 2013b). The escalation of the Ukrainian conflict in 2022 testifies to the relevance of this phased conceptualization for Russia.

Hybrid warfare has eventually become a synonym for Russia's actions in Ukraine. Russia has, however, developed its own and essentially different perception of the matter. It has rather perceived itself as the target country. Even if eventually pursuing the same course and taking it to the next level, Russia indicates that it has drawn inspiration from the practices of the West. For example, according to Kalinovsky (2001: 59), the Milošević regime in Yugoslavia fell as a result of a powerful information campaign, an economic blockade, and an aerial bombing campaign by the US and NATO. Bartosh (2018a: 11) used the term 'hybrid wars' to characterize the US involvement in the Balkans, Iraq, and Libya. Elsewhere (2018b: 13) he explained the Ukrainian crisis as 'the skillful use of Ukraine in a hybrid war of the collective West against Russia.'

Even the so-called 'Gerasimov Doctrine' has never been a Russian doctrine because Gerasimov's famous 2013 article addressed what he felt was a Western way of war. The term was created by M. Galeotti, who subsequently recognized it was a misconception (Galeotti 2020). What is especially interesting is that some Russian experts even believe that the USSR was destroyed in a hybrid(-like) campaign by the West, particularly through economic, financial, trade, and technological sanctions, as well as informational-psychological impact (Chekinov and Bogdanov 2011: 8, 10).

The above examples demonstrate that Russia's asymmetric measures have also been seen by Russian military experts as efforts to master the forms of warfare that are symmetrical in relation to the West, and particularly the US. Another example of the same kind are ASATs. In November 2021, the Russian Armed Forces conducted a successful test of an anti-satellite missile which hit the inactive Tselina-D spacecraft launched by the USSR in 1982 (National Defence 2021). Russia's ASATs represent an 'asymmetric response' to the US's 'aerospace superiority', as suggested by one of the articles published by the US-based Arms Control Association (Sankaran 2022). However, Soviet military experts recorded American anti-satellite weapons programmes as early as the 1980s (Korotchenko 1986: 19). Glebovich (1991: 69) even assumed that anti-satellite systems could be created as a 'by-product' of the US SDI programme.

Hypersonic missiles represent another interesting example that is worth examining. On the one hand, they allow one to gain a great asymmetric advantage over the enemy's air defences. It is because, according to Kuptsov (2011: 13), hypersonic aircraft pose a challenge to air defence systems in terms of their detection, tracking, identification, and defeat. Such an asymmetric capability is especially useful for Russia. Gorbunov and Bogdanov (2009: 7) argued that the Americans sought to 'devalue' Russia's nuclear potential by building more sophisticated missile defence systems while simultaneously creating long-range precision conventional weapons. This is why Russia has moved in the direction of developing its hypersonic strike capability 'at a faster pace' than the US and China. Among the key achievements so far are the Kinzhal aviation missile system with hypersonic missiles, the Zirkon shipborne hypersonic missile, and the Avangard hypersonic glide vehicle which can be launched by ICBMs such as the Sarmat (Stepshin and Anikonov 2021: 37). In March 2022, the Russian Ministry of Defence reported the first successful strike with the Kinzhal which destroyed a large underground arms depot in western Ukraine (Kirby 2022b). On the other hand, Selivanov and Ilyin (2019: 7) insisted that Russia's hypersonic weapons should not be seen as 'ideal' tools for an asymmetric response in view of the respective developments and successes in both in the US and China. They (2019: 8) even assumed that such systems as the Avangard paved the way for Russia's own 'global strike' strategy (cf. the US Conventional Prompt Global Strike). It is because systems of this kind made it possible for Russia to destroy the enemy's strategic targets without the use of a nuclear explosion, at higher hypersonic speeds, and from a long distance with the help of ICBMs.

In contrast to the above, asymmetry can be seen more clearly in the development of A2/AD capabilities in Russia. Russian (and Chinese) A2/AD capabilities, i.e. the ability of their Armed Forces to create zones of 'restricted access', are supposed to 'negatively affect' the capabilities of the US Air Force and Navy, according to Khomutov (2021: 28). He defined such zones, with reference to Pentagon military analysts, as areas of land, sea, or airspace in which access is restricted due to the activities of adversarial early warning systems, air defence systems, electronic warfare systems, and long-range precision weapons including hypersonic missiles. For example, Russia has supposedly employed A2/AD capabilities in Crimea (Williams 2017/2018; Giles and Boulegue 2019: 22).

Where Russia believes it could gain a truly asymmetric advantage is the development of qualitatively new and 'unparalleled' technologies such as AI (Selivanov and Ilyin 2019: 9–10; 2020a: 53). The use of AI for military purposes is one of the key priorities for Russia, according to the latest State Armament Programme adopted for the period 2018–2027 (Gaydunko and Makarova 2019: 12). AI will supposedly help Russia create entirely new asymmetric capabilities. Perhaps the best example is Russia's new specialized computing subsystem for an aircraft called SVP-24. Enhanced with AI technologies, mainly for the analysis of data from GLONASS, SVP-24 brings the accuracy of unguided bombs much closer to that of precision-guided munitions. Therefore, it allows for further cost reduction without compromising effectiveness (Maslennikov et al. 2020: 74–75). Also, AI may further advance Russia's existing asymmetric capabilities. For example, as already mentioned above, the Russian Aerospace Forces have reportedly acquired an automated control system that uses AI elements to coordinate the work of air defence complexes (S-300s, S-400s, Pantsirs). Russia's new electronic warfare systems – Palantin and Bylina – are also outfitted with elements of AI (Galkin, Kolyandra, and Stepanov 2021: 115, 118).

5.7 Synthesis of the Approach: Ambitions for Symmetry and Asymmetric Engagement

This chapter examined the process of military-technological innovation in post-Soviet Russia. In particular, the focus was high-precision long-range conventional weapons. Soviet military experts recorded the US having tremendous interest in conventional long-range precision strike capabilities in the late 1970s to early 1980s. Observing the development and incorporation of these weapons into the US doctrine of 'airland battle' and NATO's strategy of 'follow-on-forces', Soviet analysts immediately realized their revolutionary potential. Four revolutionary qualities characterizing new-generation conventional weapons were distinguished: their ability to strike with high accuracy at great range, as enabled by the development of advanced automation; the speed at which they could deliver conventional strikes, newly a matter of minutes; and their destructive power, comparable to tactical nuclear weapons.

Soviet immediate response to these developments consisted to a large extent of failed ambitions and propaganda. The Soviets' initial commitment to catch up with the West at least in quality, if not in quantity, was articulated at the level of discourse but was impossible to implement in practice. Budget constraints and the lack of political will to push forward all of the available resources in this direction led the Soviet Union to explore more asymmetric options. Two paths were eventually pursued. In the hope that the US would reciprocate, Soviet military doctrine contented itself with the principle of defence sufficiency, i.e. the minimum required quantity of high-quality defence capabilities. The Soviets also engaged in disarmament advocacy, calling, eventually, for general and complete disarmament. This objective would not be achieved either.

What deserves greater attention are the dynamics unfolding after the abrupt breakup of the USSR. The Gulf War and NATO's Kosovo campaign of 1999 forced post-Soviet Russia to develop a more workable strategy when the US and NATO were clearly transcending to the next generation of conventional warfare. During the Gulf War, the revolutionary potential of new-generation weapons was tested and proven precisely in ways that Soviet military experts had envisioned years back. Moreover, it was also during the Gulf War that Soviet conventional inferiority became apparent. NATO's aerial bombing in the Yugoslav province of Kosovo additionally signalled that the transatlantic allies were ready to resolve contradictions by force, even bypassing international law. Fully aware of the seriousness of the problem, Russia came up with a reasonable long-lasting asymmetric response from the technological-operational perspective: the right to use nuclear weapons in a conventional war. In particular, limited 'de-escalatory' nuclear strikes were newly allowed in a deteriorating conventional war to compensate for Russia's technological inferiority vis-à-vis its potential adversaries in a major regional war. The Russo-Georgian War, despite the victorious outcome, ever more clearly exposed Russia's relative backwardness in conventional capabilities and operational art vis-à-vis the US and NATO. At the same time, however, it challenged Russia's regional leadership and great power status, pushing it to develop comparable capabilities. Especially as the country's economic conditions began to improve after the economic collapse of the 1990s, Russia gradually embarked on the ongoing RMA.

Russia has devoted considerable attention to developing new technologies, concepts, and organizations in its quest for symmetry. Major technological breakthroughs, including the development of high-precision, long-range, and unmanned conventional weapons with strategic implications, fell roughly to the period between 2012–2017. The concept of 'non-nuclear deterrence' has entered the realm of military doctrine and that of 'high-precision combat' has penetrated specialized military terminology. Indicative of the increased emphasis on the role of air power, particularly air defences, as well as the recognition of a close inter-relationship between space and air operations, an entirely new branch of the Armed Forces – the Aerospace Defence Troops – was created and soon merged with the Air Force. Emphasis was placed on the development of the domestic military-industrial complex, seen as the fastest and most efficient way of achieving greater technological self-reliance and closing the technological gap with the West. Efforts have also been taken to facilitate civilian – and, in particular, business-driven – R&D in consideration of the dual use potential of such work but an innovative ecosystem of startups and venture capitalists has never fully materialized in Russia, even after the establishment of Skolkovo. Having considered some of the shortcomings of Russian capitalism, including the role of the state and its nomenklatura-like political-economic networks, this chapter concluded that Russia is a quasi-capitalist developmental state.

Despite the coming wave of military-technological advances, even Russian military experts admit that Russia still does not have sufficient capabilities to buttress its non-nuclear deterrence against those capable of waging a conventional war in a remote theatre, meaning the US and NATO. Russia's current way of fighting in Ukraine also clearly revealed that, despite considerable advances in high-tech conventional warfare demonstrated in Syria, it is still dealing with the lack of a clear technological edge, given the overwhelming proportion of old-fashioned technologies and outdated tactics, as well as the lack of highly trained and technically skilled professional manpower.

The nuclear escalation ladder remains Russia's most reliable deterrent against a large-scale conventional war in Europe even in 2022. In this context, the elite discourse on the supposed high morale qualities of the Russian troops during the Russo-Georgian War and the conflict in eastern Ukraine may well serve not only as a morale booster, but also as a propagandist compensation for the lack of a strong innovation edge and technical skill. In addition, Russia has explored other possible options of technological and operational asymmetry, including the use of electronic warfare, information warfare, hybrid warfare, as well as the development of anti-satellite and anti-access/area-denial capabilities. Interestingly though, Russian military experts argue that America was first to discover most of these non-traditional and indirect means of armed struggle. Calling them *twisted (a)symmetries*, the author assembled the pieces of their discourse and demonstrated that, even though these measures are asymmetric by nature, Russia has perceived its respective activities as symmetric, rather than asymmetric.

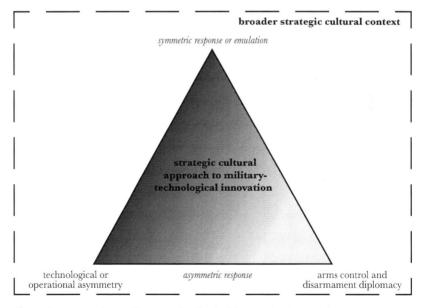

Fig. 5 The approach to military-technological innovation in post-Soviet Russia. The author's own figure.

Therefore, Russia's response to this particular round of the arms race has been largely characterized by an oscillation between the quest for symmetry on the one hand, though limited success has yet been achieved, as further testified to by Russia's poor military performance during its invasion of Ukraine in 2022, and the search for technological and operational asymmetric advantages on the other hand. Soviet immediate proposals for general and complete disarmament were part of the dynamics but were not representative of the general tendency (Fig. 5).

6. Conclusion

This book inquired into the discourses and practices of military-technological innovation in Russia. Though there is a rich body of literature on Russian strategic culture, just as on the history of military technology and military reforms in Russia, the available knowledge on the Russian strategic cultural approach to military-technological innovation is fragmented and incomplete. By asking the question of what the relationship between Russia's strategic culture and its pattern of innovation in the military-technological domain has been, this book filled this gap to the extent possible. In doing so, it took a *longue durée* perspective and examined the traces of a long history of military-technological innovation in Russia. This book covers more than a hundred and fifty years and much of what constitutes the present day, examining three case studies in particular: the introduction of rifled and breech-loading weapons in the nineteenth century, the invention of nuclear weapons in the twentieth century, and the development of precision-guided weapons in the twenty-first century (particularly in Russia as they were developed much earlier in the US). For understanding the process of how revolutionary military technology has been perceived and discursively constructed in Russian political, and especially military, circles over the last hundred and fifty years, extensive archival research was conducted. The value added of this research was the author's ability to read these materials in the original language and grasp the nuances, especially of nineteenth-century spelling and vocabulary.

The relationship between strategic culture and the dynamics of military-technological innovation in Russia was considered from two different, yet complementary, perspectives. From an empirical standpoint, the above analysis was guided by six substantial arguments derived from the existing knowledge and informed by results from the author's previous analysis. In-depth reading of the available scholarship, complemented by a series of expert interviews, was taken as a starting point and made it possible to build some initial knowledge about the Russian cultural approach to military-technological innovation. The goal was to project these assumptions onto the past hundred and fifty years of Russian military history.

Going beyond this, the author switched the reader's attention to show the same picture, but in reverse perspective. The anatomy of Russia's strategic cultural approach to military-technological innovation was disaggregated from the theoretical perspective, which resulted in the introduction of a novel conceptual model (Fig. 1). Its significance was twofold: first, in theorizing the options available for a technological laggard in responding to military-technological innovation elsewhere; and second, in theorizing the relationship between military-technological innovation and strategic culture. Russia's strategic cultural approach to military-technological innovation was represented in the form of a triangle. This triangle captured three possible responses by a technological laggard to an adversary's military-technological innovation (itself conceptualized as a technology-led RMA): a symmetric, possibly even emulative, response; an asymmetric response in the realm of technology or operational art; and an asymmetric response at the diplomatic level. Conflict dynamics were theorized as the trigger for putting the process in motion and making Russia pursue any of these three courses of action. This theoretical discussion stimulated the introduction of yet another argument which would subsequently guide the empirical focus of this book. At the same time, this model integrated strategic culture as an ever-present context for all these processes. Defined in terms of recurring discourses and practices in line with the first generation of scholarship, the concept of strategic culture helped the author to trace continuities in the course of a hundred and fifty years and delineate the Russian style of military-technological innovation.

The introduction of this cultural model of military-technological innovation had both empirical and theoretical importance. Empirically, it showed ever more clearly that Russia's typical response to Western RMAs has been characterized by an oscillation between the development of symmetric vs asymmetric capabilities, catch-up tendencies vs efforts to slow down or reverse the accelerating arms race through arms control and disarmament, and emulation vs creative innovation. To the extent possible, oscillatory tendencies were graphically depicted. The nineteenth century in Russia was largely a history of oscillation between two kinds of asymmetric responses to the introduction of rifled breech-loading weapons in the West: in the operational realm and at the diplomatic level (Fig. 3). In the twentieth century, the Soviet Union experienced an oscillation between a fully symmetric and largely successful response to the American(-led) nuclear weapons programme, and completely reversing the nuclear arms race through disarmament (Fig. 4). Twenty-first-century Russia has oscillated between the development of symmetric capabilities to those possessed by the US and NATO and the exploitation of asymmetric advantages achieved through innovative operational concepts and technologies intended to offset the strength and capabilities of America and its European allies (Fig. 5). The theoretical significance of this model may lie well beyond the studied case. Although partially inspired by the literature on Russian strategic culture, it is well suited to study the dynamics of military-technological innovation in other countries that typically do not initiate arms races but tend to respond to the development of revolutionary technologies elsewhere, especially in an accelerating arms race scenario.

Yet one more theoretical insight was incorporated to better grasp the specifics of the Russian cultural approach. The concept of the 'developmental state' was employed to capture one of the key linkages between Russia's strategic culture and its pattern of RMAs. With this concept taken as the basis, three novel purpose-tailored concepts were introduced to characterize the Russian ecosystem of military-technological innovation from an organizational perspective during each of the studied periods: a *proto*-developmental state (Imperial Russia); a *command* developmental state (the USSR), and a *quasi-capitalist* developmental state (post-Soviet Russia). Besides complementing the literature on – and theorization of – developmental states, this theoretical discussion was taken as the basis for the last substantial argument of this book.

6.1 Synthesis and Outline of the Russian Strategic Cultural Approach to Military-Technological Innovation

Resting on a solid theoretical and initial empirical basis, the analysis presented in the following three empirical chapters made it possible to identify the *seven facets*, i.e. recurring discursive claims and practices, of

Russia's cultural approach to military-technological innovation. The discussion presented below testifies to the fact that there has indeed been a distinct strategic culture of military-technological innovation in Russia. What needs to be kept in mind, however, is that many of these points are not unique to Russia. Galeotti (Interview no. 7) rightfully remarked, commenting on Russian strategic culture, that its 'distinctiveness is less than [it] is often assumed.' He added an important note: 'If Britain or the United States had to, for a century, face more technologically advanced antagonists, [I am] not convinced that they would not actually be thinking about technology and military art the same way as the Soviets/Russians.' Miles (Interview no. 3) concurred that if the discussion focused on the US, there would be many similar trends, even though the problems that they dealt with may be different.[20]

6.1.1 Reactive Innovation

History shows that Russia has typically not been the initiator in new rounds of arms races. Instead, its military-technological innovation has typically been a reaction to Western innovation. In other words, there has always been a time lag between particular categories of weapons being introduced in the West and the same being developed or aquired by other means in Russia. There has been a clear realization of this fact in Russian military circles. For example, military experts, under the leadership of the Commander-in-Chief of the Strategic Rocket Forces (1997–2001) V. N. Yakovlev (1999), put together a comparative table of initiatives for the development of new types of weapons from the 1940s to 1980s. They vividly illustrated and concluded that arms races, at least in the defined time period, were regularly 'provoked' by the West, in particular the US and NATO. According to their estimates, nuclear weapons were developed in the US in the mid 1940s, while in the USSR – in the late 1940s; thermonuclear weapons originated in the US in 1952, while in the USSR – in 1953; intercontinental strategic bombers were produced in the US in the mid 1950s, while in the USSR – in the late 1950s; nuclear submarines appeared in the US in the mid 1950s, while in the USSR – in the late 1950s; anti-satellite weapons were invented in the US in the early 1960s, while in the USSR – in the late 1960s; MIRVs were introduced

---

20 Both interviews were conducted prior to February 2022.

in the US in the late 1960s, while in the USSR – in the mid 1970s; long-range cruise missiles were first designed in the US in the mid 1970s, while in the USSR – in the early 1980s, etc.

Another insight their comparative table conveyed was that the Soviet Union did not even respond to every single weapons programme initiated in the US. Whatever the reasons, the Soviets did not rush, for example, into the development of nuclear aircraft carriers, neutron munitions, stealth technologies, or technologies comparable to the SDI. What becomes clear from this comparative table is that the Soviet Union tended to be the catching-up side in its permanent arms race with the US. There were only rare exceptions to this general logic. For example, missile defence systems were properly developed in the USSR by the mid 1960s, while in the US – by the early 1970s, as the same comparative table reported. The significance of all these examples is in showing the way arms races have been and continue to be approached in Russia. Although these particular illustrations are time- and context-specific, the authors captured quite accurately the general trend and this is what the previous chapters show. Overall, to date, there have been only a few types of weapons in which Russia (and the Soviet Union) originally outstripped the US: the world's first launch of an ICBM, the world's first launch of an SLBM, and modern hypersonic weapons, with the latter two additionally noted by Sokov (Interview no. 2).

The first studied revolution, that is the introduction of rifled breech-loading weapons in the nineteenth century, did not originate in Russia. Russia came to realize its technological inferiority during the Crimean War (1853–1856). Russian experts admitted back then that the insufficiency of the smooth-bore muzzle-loading weapons at Russia's disposal was one of the key reasons for its defeat by the alliance of France, the Ottoman Empire, the United Kingdom, and Piedmont-Sardinia. Clearly driven by the need to catch up with other major European powers, as archival records confirm, Russia embarked on a major military modernization programme. The same tendency was observed in the second case study. The atomic bombings of the Japanese cities of Nagasaki and Hiroshima demonstrated American technological dominance and made Stalin believe that the US could possibly use atomic weapons against the USSR. These circumstances, combined with America's refusal to negotiate a ban on nuclear weapons, 'forced' the USSR, as Russian archives show, to develop their own nuclear arsenal.

The situation was no different in the third case dedicated to the study of precision-guided weapons and related technologies. Soviet military experts observed with curiosity, as archival data suggest, how such capabilities were being developed in the US in the 1970s–1980s, and with especially great caution in how they were put to use in the Gulf War (1990–91). However, Russia has not taken serious steps to implement this revolution up until the Russo-Georgian War (2008). Russia's performance on the battlefield very clearly exposed its inferiority vis-à-vis the US and NATO. Even though victory was achieved, its military equipment appeared to be technically obsolete, and its operational art outdated. In this respect, the lessons learned from this war by post-Soviet Russia were similar to those learned from the Russo-Turkish War (1877–1878) by Imperial Russia. Even the slightest prospect of losing control over events on its periphery compelled Russia to proceed with a massive re-armament and modernization of its Armed Forces, or, in Russian terms, transitioning them to a 'new look' (новый облик) after 2008.

All of the above testifies to the fact that military-technological innovation in Russia has, as a rule, been a reaction to Western innovation. There are two more findings that contribute to the same conclusion. First, the archive of *Voennaya Mysl'* delivers a clear message: historically, Russian military experts have very closely followed military-technological developments abroad, especially in the West. Even though it would usually take Russia both time and effort to catch up, foreign innovations and their implications were always receiving a great deal of attention. Second, history shows that Russia has repeatedly emulated Western innovations while trying to catch up, literally speaking. The habit – and even narrative – of reaping the fruits of Western experience has become deeply entrenched. In the nineteenth century, for example, the tsarist government strongly preferred to order weapons from abroad. The idea was not necessarily to develop domestic production capabilities for manufacturing modern weapons at home, though steps in this direction were also taken, but mainly to have the same weapons at their disposal. Emulative tendencies were also observed in the second case study. For instance, the Soviet atomic project, and especially Soviet rocketry, originally relied on German expertise. It is also a well-known fact that the first Soviet atomic bomb was almost a copy of the American one. Similar examples were found in the third case study. For example, some of the newer Russian UAVs are close in their characteristics to America's successfully employed MQ-1 Predator and MQ-9 Reaper.

6.1.2 Punctuated Innovation

The three case studies presented above also clearly demonstrate that Russia's reaction to Western innovation has never been an automatic reaction. Rather, it has typically been punctuated by different conflict episodes, either with or without violence, either with Russia directly involved or with it observing the development of events elsewhere and assessing the potential consequences for itself. What is particularly important is that there has been a tendency towards *repeated punctuation*, closely linked to Russia's general historical reluctance to innovate. The introduction of rifled breech-loading weapons in Russia in the late nineteenth century was apparently punctuated by Russia's humiliating defeat in the Crimean War. The Franco-Prussian War (1870–1871) was also closely monitored by Russian experts and, referred to repeatedly in *Voennyi Sbornik*, it obviously appeared as another watershed. The brilliant victories of the Prussians contributed to a better understanding of the revolutionary potential of modern weapons in Russia.

Similar tendencies were recorded in the twentieth century. The atomic bombings of Nagasaki and Hiroshima signalled a crucial turning point for the Soviet Union. However, it was not the only trigger. While the Soviets did embark on the nuclear RMA in the 1940s–1950s, they did not unleash a full-scale symmetric response to the US nuclear weapons programme until the Cuban Missile Crisis (1962). Not only did this crisis bring both sides to the brink of a real nuclear war, it also revealed that Soviet nuclear capabilities considerably lagged behind that of the US. The Soviet drive towards nuclear parity and their massive nuclear build-up, both in quantitative or qualitative respects, were facilitated by this crisis. In other words, the Soviet nuclear programme got a second wind as the Cuban Missile Crisis created another punctuation moment.

The results of the third case study were also illustrative of this tendency. Russia's corresponding reaction to the development and use of precision-guided conventional weapons by the US and NATO was similarly punctuated by a series of military escalations. Even though the US had been actively engaged in the research and development of precision-guided weapons for almost two decades by then, it was only the Gulf War that pushed the Soviet Union (and eventually Russia) to realize the need to develop comparable capabilities. The defeat of Iraq, mostly equipped with Soviet weapons, was indicative of Soviet and Russian relative technological backwardness vis-à-vis the West. However, the collapse of Soviet communism and the subsequent transformation of political, economic, and social systems suppressed the stimulus to re-armament in the newly formed, post-Soviet Russia. There was another critical turning point. The message contained in NATO's aerial bombing in the Yugoslav province of Kosovo, from the Russian perspective, was that international law was not necessarily a constraining factor in the deployment of military force. However, the truly decisive moment came with the Russo-Georgian War. Not only did it move the possibility of collision between the Transatlantic bloc and Russia closer to the latter's immediate borders but, as explained previously, it also exposed Russia's relative backwardness in conventional weapons and capabilities vis-à-vis the US and NATO. Only then did Russia initiate an ambitious conventional modernization programme aimed, inter alia, at achieving the capability to strike with high accuracy at a greater range with the help of conventional weapons only. Besides a record of considerable success in Syria, precision strikes at a distance (including attempts at delivering them) constitute only a small component of an otherwise traditional military offensive in Ukraine. Therefore, this armed conflict may well become another turning point in the same direction for Russia.

Fig. 6 Conflict spectra spurring military-technological innovation in Russia.[21] The author's own figure, partially based on the typology by Pfetsch and Rohloff (2000: XIII).

21 Conflicts are listed in chronological order.

Therefore, conflict dynamics have historically had a strong impact on Russia's decision to innovate in the military-technological realm. To be more precise, military-technological innovation in Russia has typically been spurred by violent, rather than non-violent, conflicts (Fig. 6). The only exception perhaps within the context of this study was the Cuban Missile Crisis. This crisis did not spill into a violent armed conflict but came very close to it. This is why it is positioned closer to the upper left quadrant and, therefore, confirms rather than disproves this general finding. At the same time, the question of whether Russia was directly involved in such a conflict did not make much difference in the long run. It appeared that simply observing the revolutionary impact of new-generation weapons elsewhere was often enough for Russia to initiate innovation processes at home (Fig. 6). It is fair to say, however, that the technologically superior side in such armed conflicts would typically be represented by Russia's own adversaries, so it was natural for Russia to evaluate the possible consequences for itself. The list of conflicts in the figure is not exhaustive but representative of the indicated trends.

6.1.3 Compensatory Innovation

In view of the aforesaid, another historical tendency on Russia's part has been to compensate for the difference of the adversary's competitive advantage. Russia has always been, and still is, eager to compensate for the gap in two ways. First, as discussed in more detail above, Russia has historically attempted to develop symmetric advantages by matching its adversaries in terms of military-technological capabilities.

Second, either to buy time or sometimes simply avoid direct competition, Russia has often resorted to asymmetric measures in order to compensate for the adversary's superior capabilities. In the nineteenth century, the fighting spirit of Russian soldiers, which Russian military experts considered to be unparalleled, came to be viewed as an operational advantage, in particular the one that could compensate for Russia's technological inferiority. Russia has never been unique in its emphasis on the role of spiritual power, but, for Russia, it was clearly a *discourse of compensation*.

Soviet response to the American(-led) nuclear weapons programme was primarily symmetric, but the pursuit of asymmetric advantages was in place too, though to a limited extent. For example, as also mentioned above, it was the Soviet Union that developed and successfully tested the world's first working anti-ballistic missile system in order to shield itself against incoming US missiles. What is particularly interesting at the same time is that the Soviet Union tried to create *reverse asymmetry*, that is to eventually surpass America's originally superior technological capabilities in both qualitative and quantitative terms. This included, among others, the creation of weapons of unparalleled destructive power such as the 'Tsar Bomba'.

The Russian inclination to resort to asymmetric action was also recorded in the third case study. Fully aware of America's technological superiority, as belligerently displayed in the Gulf War, and its readiness to bypass international law, as demonstrated by NATO's military intervention in Yugoslavia, Russia had to react quickly. But being unable to match US capabilities any time soon and itself on the brink of the resumption of military action in Chechnya, Russia opted for an asymmetric response and reconsidered the role of tactical nuclear weapons in conventional war scenarios. The idea of a limited nuclear war put forward by the US and NATO in the 1960s was completely rejected by the Soviets on the grounds that it would not be possible to localize nuclear fire, but the thinking has obviously changed in post-Soviet Russia. 'Of course there is a risk of limited nuclear strikes developing into an unlimited nuclear war, but it does not have the character of fatal inevitability,' as explained by Kreidin (1999: 76). In addition, Russia has explored other complementary options of creating asymmetric advantages such as electronic warfare, information warfare, hybrid warfare, as well as anti-satellite and anti-access/area-denial capabilities. However, there was a curious finding in regards to this. Russian military experts systematically argued that Russia's respective activities have been symmetric, not asymmetric, because, in their view, America was first to discover and take advantage of these non-traditional and indirect means of armed struggle.

6.1.4 Reluctant Innovation

The case studies presented reveal one more historical trend. Over the last hundred and fifty years, at least, Russia has been particularly sensitive to the classic 'guns vs butter' dilemma. Going broader, Baev (2020: 6) characterized Russia's persistent problem as 'the evolving contradiction between high ambitions and limited capabilities' (Baev 2020: 6). Every round of military-technological innovation studied here involved difficult choices at home and trade-offs between military and civilian objectives.

More importantly, the costs of armaments have usually been more painful for Russia than for its principal adversaries. It is mostly for these reasons that Russia has often been reluctant to innovate. Its immediate and persistent response to Western military-technological superiority has often consisted of arms control and disarmament initiatives intended to restrain and preferably reverse competition.

Unsurprisingly, then, Russia was at the forefront of international disarmament law in the late nineteenth century, as discussed in Chapter 3. It was a rare moment when Russia aspired to project the image of itself as a modern and progressive country abroad. The key driving force was the humanitarian initiative by Tsar Nicholas II leading to the St Petersburg Declaration of 1868 and the First Hague Conference of 1899.

Leveraging Russia's pioneer role in humanitarian disarmament, its representatives would primarily use the language of human suffering, and then only economic arguments in their calls for arms control and disarmament ever since. However, the sincerity of humanitarian calls is questionable. Both Imperial Russia and the USSR resorted to humanitarian arguments in their disarmament calls at the times when they seriously lagged behind their adversaries in the technological sophistication of their weaponry. There were also moments when their calls for disarmament coincided with their own weapons programmes such as in the Soviet Union of the 1940s. There are even more doubts about the language of human suffering in the general context of state-sanctioned mass killings and detentions, which culminated during the Stalin era, as well as psychiatric abuse in the USSR.

However, evidence suggests that the intention to reduce the role of certain kinds of particularly dangerous weapons in global politics – rarely for strictly humanitarian purposes – was sometimes part of the motivation, besides much more obvious strategic and economic considerations. For example, in the nineteenth century, Russia called for a complete ban on explosive bullets, which it already possessed, purely for humanitarian reasons. What testifies to the sincerity of this intention is that Russia was ready to sacrifice the military utility of explosive bullets equipped with capsules to make sure that explosive bullets without capsules were not used either. Another interesting finding is that, in the twentieth century, the Soviet Union consistently advocated for nuclear disarmament, including during its nuclear parity with the US in the late 1960s to early 1970s.

Russia's historical tendency to promote arms control and disarmament has, therefore, been sustained by varied and often mixed motives.

Archival records contain that it has facilitated and actively engaged in such processes for strategic reasons (i.e. to equalize its position vis-à-vis the most technologically advanced states), economic reasons (i.e. to relieve immediate pressure on its military budget), and, to a much lesser extent, for what appear to be principled reasons (i.e. to reduce the role of certain kinds of weapons in global politics, be it for strictly humanitarian purposes or not).

At the same time, Russia has often been reluctant and, in fact, unable (perhaps except for the rare moment of nuclear parity between the Soviet Union and the US achieved in the late 1960s to early 1970s) to go all the way. Whenever innovation appeared to be unavoidable, as in all the three studied cases, Russia's decision to harness it would often come with a compromise: aiming for the same level of quality that Western technologies had achieved, but not necessarily competing in quantity. It is interesting to note at this point that Russia has been particularly obsessed, at least at the discursive level, not only with the quality of weapons, but also with the quality of their operators. One might say that there is nothing unusual about it, but in the Russian context, this aspiration for the best possible quality was often yet another way to compensate for the lack of financial resources to compete quantitatively and keep full pace with the magnitude of Western RMAs. However, in practice, Russia has usually struggled to compete in terms of the overall quality of its weapons and even more so in terms of quality of training.

Galeotti (Interview no. 7) also noted that there were numerous moments in history when Russia heavily relied on 'mass' (meaning quantity), not only on the battlefield but also as an industrial factor. Recalling World War II, he clarified, for example, that the T-34 was a decent, but not the most advanced tank, whose power consisted, to a considerable extent, in being turned out in very large numbers. Miles (Interview no. 3) made clear that there has not been a reversal since then. He admitted that Russia is indeed 'making investments in tools that require sophisticated operators.' But, recalling the Soviet 'deep battle' doctrine from the Cold War, he highlighted at the same time that it was not just about 'brute force' either. The idea itself, according to him, required 'highly disciplined troops', besides the enabling technologies. So he characterized Russia's historical approach as a 'pendulum swinging' between quality- and quantity-driven ambitions.

6.1.5 Steered Innovation

Since the resources required for innovation have always been very limited, there has typically been little room for experiment and manoeuver in the process of military-technological innovation in Russia. The steering of innovation activities has been expressed in two ways. First, there has been a clear tendency towards the deliberate application of innovative technologies. As recorded in all the three studied cases, their revolutionary potential was grasped first typically through observation of their application by others, and only then were they developed and put to a particular use in Russia. Therefore, as previously recorded by other authors and testified to by the foregoing diachronic analysis in the *longue durée*, the primacy of military science is one of the defining features of the Russian cultural approach to military-technological innovation.

Second, there has been a strong natural inclination to favour the top-down approach to innovation policy in Russia, the reason being that it could provide more efficient mobilization of limited resources. To be more precise, Russia's top-down approach has been deeply rooted in its developmental state mindset. The latter was systematically traced from the organizational perspective of RMA theory. The state has always devised the country's broad industrial policy and guided resource allocation to designated priority sectors, typically the military one, to catch up industrially – the main military concern – with the West. The nomenklatura style of its bureaucracy, i.e. the Soviet nomenklatura system and other nomenklatura-like arrangements in Imperial and post-Soviet Russia, secured the bureaucratic hierarchy and its relatively strong hierarchical control over the industry. This organizational arrangement has, in turn, been firmly buttressed by the country's – more or less – authoritarian political system over the last hundred and fifty years, with the exception of rare periods when there was a decrease in top-down control (mainly the Yeltsin era). At the same time, market-like competition for the development and production of weapons or supporting technologies for the government was a relatively constant feature more or less pronounced in Russia since the nineteenth century.

In the nineteenth century, for example, there was growing demand for the independence of the domestic arms industry. The evidence presented captured ambitious bottom-up initiatives and the rudiments of a business model. However, the tsarist government preferred to acquire modern weapons through foreign orders, seen as more attractive in terms of the balance between speed, quality, and price. Such decisions had a detrimental effect on domestic arms production capability but were motivated by the need to bridge the technological gap between Russia and its potential adversaries in the shortest possible time. Imperial Russia was thus a *proto*-developmental state.

In the twentieth century, it was the command economy, and particularly the choice of priority investment projects which it made possible, that contributed to the success of the Soviet atomic project. However, the Soviet defence industry, including the postwar missile industry, represented at least a degree of market-like relations, characterized by pluralism and competition among rival design bureaux. For these reasons the Soviet Union was considered a *command* developmental state, at least from the perspective of military-technological innovation.

In the twenty-first century, the government, especially the Ministry of Defence, also played a major role in planning and financing high-tech R&D, including in priority areas such as AI. However, as dictated by the character of new and emerging technologies, more emphasis was placed on the construction of civil-military, in particular business-state, relations under the direct leadership of the Russian state. Russia was characterized as a *quasi-capitalist* developmental state. Although market mechanisms did find their way into the Russian economy and innovation ecosystem following the end of the Cold War, several shortcomings were brought to attention: the reluctance of the government to ease its tight control over the economy, as expressed in direct control over business activities or government ownership; a proportionally greater emphasis on the military industry; as well as the backwardness of the civilian sector and its further weakening in light of the new round of sweeping Western sanctions imposed on Russia in response to its invasion of Ukraine in 2022. All of the above clearly demonstrates that exploratory experimentation has traditionally been constrained in Russia by the primacy of military science over technological sophistication and tight government control over innovation.

6.1.6 Symbolic Innovation

There is still one more extremely important aspect of the Russian cultural approach to innovation in the military-technological domain. Bringing the sophistication of Russia's military technology and equipment to the level of Western analogues has often had not only practical but also symbolic value for Russia. One of the key motives behind this endeavour has typically been Russia's obsession with its status as a great power, though in purely military terms. In particular, Russia's catch-up tendencies in its permanent arms race with the West have been driven, historically, by the objective of restoring that great power status, either challenged or lost as a result of impressive leaps forward in military technology made by its Western counterparts. For example, Russia was certainly a great power, at least from a narrow realist perspective, up until the mid-nineteenth century. Not only did the Crimean War expose Russia as a technologically inferior military, but it also seriously undermined Russia's international prestige and greatness. The narrative that Russia would not be satisfied by anything less than returning to the ranks of other major European powers accompanied the re-armament process in the late nineteenth century.

Similarly, the Soviet atomic project carried a great deal of symbolic significance in the twentieth century. The Soviet Union came out most clearly as the country that possessed great power in the aftermath of World War II. To be more precise, two major powers, the US and the USSR, and a rigid bipolar system emerged from World War II. Yet the atomic bombings of Hiroshima and Nagasaki were perceived by Soviet military experts as America's effort to strengthen its position vis-à-vis the USSR. One of the key motives behind the Soviets' own nuclear weapons programme, as archival records show, was to regain its status of a world power and an equal of the US. Only with its own nuclear weapons capability did the Soviet Union reemerge as a superpower on par with the US.

The process of military-technological innovation moved basically along the same track in the third case study. America appeared as the world's only superpower after the dissolution of the Soviet Union and the end of the Cold War, and the revival of Russia as a great power, even a superpower, has been one of the key narratives underlying the ongoing modernization of military equipment. One finding concerning the relationship between Russia's great power status and its arms industry deserves particular mention. The tsar, being unable to bring the domestic arms industry on equal footing with the industrialized countries in a relatively short period after the Crimean War, sought to reassert the country's great power status by ordering cutting edge weapons from abroad. This approach has fundamentally changed. For modern Russia, its position as a first-tier arms producer and supplier is one of the key attributes of its great power status.

To sum up, Russia has often been driven by symbolic motivations in its military-technological innovation. Before its status could be reasserted at the level of military technology, it was to be maintained through diplomacy, and in particular through slowing down, if not reversing, the technological advancements of Russia's potential adversaries. This is where the symbolic function of arms control and disarmament for Russia becomes apparent, in addition to other possible motivations discussed above. What is particularly interesting is that Russia's motivation for its pursuit of the leadership role in nineteenth-century disarmament negotiations was, inter alia, a way to compensate for its declining military power in the aftermath of the Crimean War and recover its status as a great power with influence over European affairs by means other than direct military competition.

What relates closely to the above discussion and deserves separate note is the symbolic construction of military parades in Russia. The significance of these symbolic displays of military might has been in boosting the image of Russia as a major military power both at home and abroad. To be even more precise, military parades have proved particularly useful in creating an idealized image of the Russian army, not always mirroring objective reality. For example, Russia's War Minister (1861–1881) Miliutin, as cited in Chapter 3, voiced the following critique against the general condition of the country's military: 'Everything is just great for parades, and just terrible for war' (cited in Panaeva 1986: 232). This became immediately obvious during the Crimean War. Miliutin's judgement is not necessarily representative in a historical perspective, but it draws attention to the gap that may exist between reality and its representation in countries obsessed with military parades such as Russia. Russia's military invasion of Ukraine in 2022 testifies to the lasting relevance of Miliutin's prophecy. Russia has indeed put to use some of its most advanced and sophisticated weapons in Ukraine (*Lenta* 2022a). So the situation is different from the one Russia found itself in in the mid-nineteenth century. However, the proportion of high-tech weapons and equipment is much higher when displayed during military parades than when actually deployed on the battlefield. The fact that Russia still has not used, at least at the time of writing, some of its latest weapon systems previously showcased in military parades (e.g. the T-14 Armata battle tank) in its major military operation in Ukraine also points to the existence of parade-only weapons in Russia.[22] It would be fair to note

---

22 A few caveats are important to explain why the Armata is listed as an example. The Armata became one of the participants in the Victory Parade in 2015. During its military tests in the territory of Syria, 'a number of problematic solutions were identified regarding the level

that it is not only in Russia that some of the cutting-edge weapons end up being a demonstration of capabilities and do not get produced in the quantities generally required to make a difference. Gorenburg (Interview no. 8) mentioned America's B-1 bombers and Seawolf-class submarines as examples. The key difference is that the US does not proudly parade these weapons. Having also indicated that the Armata has been paraded years before becoming a fully operational combat vehicle, Galeotti (Interview no. 7) believed, however, that Russian military parades have become 'more honest' than they were in the past.[23]

6.1.7 Manpower-Balanced Innovation

Another key finding to emerge from this study is that, from the Russian perspective, the human-technology relationship has changed significantly, but not fundamentally, over the last hundred and fifty years. On the one hand, there has been a growing appreciation for the role of technology. As it comes across clearly in the arguments of Russian military experts, manpower-intensive approaches to warfare are being gradually replaced with technology-intensive ones. In the nineteenth century, there was a deep distrust of technology in Russian military circles, even though the growing role of technology was carefully recognized. The popular idea at that time was that the lack of military equipment or the inability to master it could be compensated for by the personnel's physical strength, high morale, and psychological preparation. However,

---

of sensitivity of the incoming projectile detection system, the optical-location complex, and the power plant,' according to Russian sources (Orlov 2021). One of the Russian language sources refers to a Chinese source, itself citing information from the Americans, to report that five Armata tanks were deployed in the Syrian province of Latakia, with three being allegedly hit by TOW-2B ATGMs and one completely destroyed (*Reporter* 2020). Nevertheless, Armata tanks were paraded through the Red Square in 2022. Besides their seeming immaturity, limited availability, and high production costs, Russia's reluctance to deploy T-14s in Ukraine may also be explained by the desire to avoid bad publicity in case something goes wrong again. The reputation of weapons for export purposes matters within Russia's military-oriented entrepreneurial model, as demonstrated in the example of Kalibr missiles in Chapter 5. At the same time, Russia's willingness to parade them even now may be explained by the intention to stir up foreign interest in these weapons systems, especially as T-14s are still under development and intended for export after the Russian army acquires them (*Interfax* 2021b). It clearly appears that maintaining the image of a first-tier producer and supplier of high-tech weaponry has high symbolic value for Russia. In general though, a military parade of this kind is not only a demonstration of technological advancement, but also a historical legacy for Russia, according to Galeotti (Interview no. 7).

23 The interview was conducted prior to February 2022.

the idea of overcoming technological disadvantages solely through the quality of manpower was slowly losing its appeal with the introduction of more advanced technologies and a gradual reduction in manpower. In the mid- to late- twentieth century, Soviet military experts admitted that technology was receiving an increasing share in the human-machine nexus. Progress in advanced automation and robotics gave rise to more ambitious hopes for the full robotization of military operations in twenty-first-century Russia.

On the other hand, many Russian experts believe that the role of humans in war does not decrease with time, but actually increases in direct relation with the increasing importance given to technology. One clue that may help explain the paradox of the still growing role of humans when martial skills are being gradually replaced by technology is the dichotomy between quantity and quality. The shift has, according to Russian military analysts, consisted of the declining role of massive armies and the increasing importance of highly trained troops equipped with the latest technology. In fact, this idea has its roots in the nineteenth century. It was already then that special emphasis was placed upon training designed to improve technical and combat skills of military personnel. The ever-increasing complexity of military equipment, especially in this day and age, may be one of the reasons for Russia's gradual transition from a conscript army to a professional army. However, as discussed in detail in Chapter 5, there is a gap between the discourse on mastering the latest technology and the practice of the Russian way of war in Ukraine. Low recruitment standards, demonstrated by the Russian(-led) forces in 2022, seriously challenge Russia's claims to military professionalism.

At the same time, emphasis on the supposed high morale qualities of the Russian troops has never been abandoned, as demonstrated by the elite discourse on the Russo-Georgian War and the conflict in eastern Ukraine. The use of this discourse as a morale booster may well serve as a negative function of technological sophistication and a propagandist compensation for the lack of obvious technological edge and technical skill. While technology has been an emerging factor in Russian military thinking, the idea of *expendable* manpower remains fairly constant. In addition to this, there is another relatively constant feature. While Russia's armed forces have traditionally been dominated by Slavs, in particular Russians, there have been marked increases in the percentage of recruits being drawn from ethnic minorities in war time (Curran and Ponomareff 1982; Daugherty 1993). This tendency was clearly seen again from the start of Russia's military invasion of Ukraine in 2022.

6.2 Asymmetric Balancing and Further Contributions

The above-mentioned characteristics constitute the Russian style of military-technological innovation, previously underexplored and sometimes even misunderstood. The key finding is that this style has displayed striking continuity over the centuries. In addition to filling this gap, the analysis presented in this book has a number of issue-specific contributions, and each of these deserves separate note.

First of all, this book contributed to a better understanding of the Russian theorization of strategic culture. The key finding was that it builds primarily upon the first generation of strategic culture scholarship in the West. Most importantly, this book showed, referring to trusted archival records, that these were Soviet military experts that introduced the concept of RMA. The existing literature often discusses their contribution in the context of the Soviet concept of MTR. However, it is a mistake to claim that these were Pentagon officials that broadened the Soviet-sourced concept of MTR to RMA. Drawing distinctions between these two terms based on the country of their origin is inherently flawed. This book distinguishes between them on the basis of Soviet original definitions of both, accompanied by corresponding Western definitions of the same.

Another contribution lies in capturing the way Soviet and Russian military experts have traditionally conceptualized revolutionary technology. One caveat applies. This is something that could not be foreseen immediately, at the level of theory, but came out very clearly of the subsequent empirical analysis. Four revolutionary qualities have been recorded and discussed extensively in Russian military circles in relation to each category of revolutionary weapons: their increased *destructiveness*, increased *speed* of their fire, increased *accuracy*, and increased *range*. Russian military experts often discussed new-generation weapons of increasing range, both nuclear missiles and high-precision long-range conventional weapons, in terms of their depth of strikes. This is where they recall the Soviet theory of 'deep battle' or 'deep operations'. This finding contributes to a better understanding of the technological parameter of RMA, especially as the existing body of knowledge about revolutionary technologies is still scarce (Hynek and Solovyeva 2022: 31). At the same time, it gives hints as to how technology-led RMAs, for example the current AI-RMA, should be studied as seen through Russian eyes.

Besides novel theoretical insights, this book offered two important side contributions with respect to the Soviet period in particular. First, archival data revealed that it would be a mistake to claim, as some Western analysts do, that the Soviets did not think in terms of Mutual Assured Destruction during the Cold War. Even though they did not use the phrase, Soviet political leaders and military experts recognized very clearly that the US and the USSR could destroy each other in a nuclear exchange regardless of who committed to strike first. Second, it was found, contrary to some existing literature, that the Soviet Union never had its own strategy of flexible response analogous to that of the US and NATO. The Soviets did indeed reach a point during the Cold War, at approximately the same time as the US, when they admitted that an initial conventional phase in a superpower war was possible. But they never accepted the possibility of a limited nuclear exchange in Europe. They criticized the American view of flexible response and even rejected the term itself.

From a more general perspective, the contribution of this book to International Relations and Strategic Studies literature lies in demonstrating the insufficiency of the neorealist school of thought to grasp the catch-up character of military-technological innovation in Russia. Realist explanations of Russian behaviour have arguably been most common in Western literature (e.g Lynch 2001; D'Anieri 2019; Feinstein and Pirro 2021; Tsygankov 2022). However, this approach has its shortcomings and this book demonstrated them in the example of the Russian approach to military-technological innovation. The original Waltzian account of neorealism and his 'balance of power' thesis (Waltz 1979) capture Russia's infinite quest for (re)arming, aimed at maintaining parity with – and rarely superiority over – its competitors. It also explains the fact that Russia's waves of military-technological innovation would, as a rule, coincide with the periods of shifting power balances and not in its favour. However, this approach fails to capture the nuances. First of all, it misses the key point: Russia's response to the competitive edge gained by its adversaries was not about restoring the balance per se. Having taken a cultural-historical approach (rather than a deductive-structural one) this book systematically demonstrated that Russia's catch-up tendencies were strongly linked to its claims to great power status. This research showed that possessing cutting edge technology had important symbolic value for Russia, including for the purpose of constructing the country's image as a first-tier producer and supplier of high-tech weaponry. Even if Russia struggled to compete in terms of quantity, it was unimaginable for the leadership in Moscow to give up on the very fact of possessing top-of-the-line military equipment, on par with the most advanced technological powers in the West.

Neoclassical realists, arguing that systemic pressures are always 'filtered' through decision-makers' perceptions, would explain this side of the problem better (Rose 1998: 157). However, there is still more to Russian symbolism than the realist school can accommodate. One of these aspects is the Russian culture of military parades, which do not always accurately reflect reality. In principle, it represents an act of balancing *through signals* and downgrades the notion of balancing, inter alia, to the level of a political message. On a more trivial note, Russia's reaction to shifting balances of power has almost never been immediate or automatic. There would usually be a time lag between a forward leap by Russia's competitors, typically in the West, and the Russian state's respective response. Moreover, this delay was not only a temporal gap between action and reaction. There would always be a trigger for Russia to initiate its own innovation cycle, typically a violent conflict – and often more than one – most clearly revealing its technological backwardness. Walt's (1987) 'balance of threat' theory, another variant of structural realism maintaining that one's balancing behaviour is determined by the threats one perceives, may well explain this. Besides building on its own military-technological failures, Russia often initiated innovation processes after the revolutionary impact of new-generation weapons was tested and proven in a violent conflict between other states. But even in these cases the technologically superior side would typically be represented by its own competitors and Russia would immediately be pushed to evaluate the consequences of a possible armed collision with them. However, Walt's original thesis maintains that states facing an external threat 'will align with others' against it (Walt 1987: 32). This argument is barely applicable to Russia. 'Russia has only two allies – its Army and its Navy', Alexander III used to say, and President Putin referred to this statement in his own speeches (*Lenta* 2022b). Later, Walt (2018) was more explicit about the fact that states may react to threats 'either by seeking allies or by building up their own capabilities'.

Nevertheless, the realist school of thought cannot fully capture Russia's *asymmetric balancing*. For example, one of the historical incidents going beyond the realist logic is Imperial Russia's effort to compensate for the loss of military power through the pursuit of global political leadership within the realm of humanitarian disarmament. This case represents an act of balancing *through diplomacy*, particularly through the construction of Russia's image as a culturally, if not militarily, superior nation. Besides diplomatic balancing, Russia has often engaged in other asymmetric balancing strategies, and not necessarily at the level of technology and military capabilities. For example, the supposed spiritual superiority of the Russian soldier was an illustration of Russia's balancing against the technological superiority of adversaries *through the art of fighting* in the nineteenth century. All of this goes beyond the traditional limits of the realist school of thought. Offering an open-ended and reflexive conceptual framework, this book captured exogenous influences as well as a complex mix of indigenous motivations and internal processes. As it showed, the realist logics may help explain a lot of the nuances but they fail to grasp Russia's approach to military-technological innovation in its cultural-historical complexity. This is largely due to the fact that nineteenth-century dynamics are often ignored by International Relations and Strategic Studies scholars, who focus primarily on the Cold War and the post-Cold War periods.

On a final note, this book was written with the hope of contributing to reducing the current gap between the Western representation of Russian military thought and what it has really been about. In doing so, it tried to avoid the orientalist image of Russian military strategy. While accepting the possible limitations of relying primarily on Soviet and Russian archives, the author considered it to be the most productive way to represent the inter-subjective Russian (and Soviet) understanding of military technology. At the same time, however, the critical perspective was maintained throughout the text and to the author's best knowledge. One caveat for prospective critiques of the approach is important. Since the discourse in the country's main military-theoretical journal is not originally intended for a foreign audience and not readily available in open access, it has often maintained a critical tone. Whenever deemed appropriate and possible, this book juxtaposed and balanced Russian sources with Western expert opinions.

Summary

This book traces the dynamics of military-technological innovation in Russia over the last hundred and fifty years. The analysis relies extensively on primary data obtained from Russian archives, complemented by a series of expert interviews. The goal is to understand whether and to what extent Russia's respective discourses and practices constitute a distinct strategic cultural approach to military-technological innovation. From an empirical standpoint, the analysis is guided by six substantial arguments derived from the existing literature on Russian strategic culture, technology and military doctrine, interviews conducted by the author, and partially from the author's own knowledge of the problematic. In theoretical terms, this book offers and graphically nuances a novel conceptual model, theorizing processes related to military-technological innovation and the role of strategic culture. The last two arguments guiding the empirical focus of this research are derived from the theoretical discussion. This model is applied to three case studies, with the key findings represented graphically at the end of each chapter: the introduction of rifled breech-loading weapons in Imperial Russia in the nineteenth century, the invention of nuclear weapons in the Soviet Union in the twentieth century, and the development of precision-guided weapons in post-Soviet Russia in the twenty-first century. The findings, which identify the existence of a distinctive Russian strategic culture of military-technological innovation in a long-term historical perspective, allow this book to propose a new, seven-dimensional view of this phenomenon.

List of References

Adamsky, D. (2010). *The Culture of Military Innovation: The Impact of Cultural Factors on the Revolution in Military Affairs in Russia, the US, and Israel*. Stanford: Stanford University Press.

Adamsky, D. (2014). 'Nuclear Incoherence: Deterrence Theory and Non-Strategic Nuclear Weapons in Russia'. *Journal of Strategic Studies* 37(1): 91–134.

Adamsky, D. (2018). 'From Moscow with Coercion: Russian Deterrence Theory and Strategic Culture'. *Journal of Strategic Studies* 41(1–2): 33–60.

Afinov, V. V. (1983). 'Развитие в США Высокоточного Оружия и Перспективы Создания Разведывательно-Ударных Комплексов' ['The Development of High-Precision Weapons in the USA and the Prospects for the Creation of Reconnaissance-Strike Systems']. *Voennaya Mysl'* 4 (April): 63–71.

Akopov, P. (2022). 'Наступление России и Нового Мира' ['The Advance of Russia and the New World']. Ria Novosti (February 26). Available at: https://web.archive.org/web/20220226051154 and https://ria.ru/20220226/rossiya-1775162336.html.

Aksenov, O. Yu., Tretyakov, Yu. N., Filin, E. N. (2015). 'Стратегические Оборонительные Системы как Фактор Сдерживания Вооруженной Агрессии' ['Strategic Defence Systems as a Factor in Deterring Armed Aggression']. *Voennaya Mysl'* 6 (June): 15–21.

Alexandrov, Yu. G. (2007). *Может ли Россия Стать 'Евроазиатским Тигром'* [*Can Russia Become a 'Eurasian Tiger'*]. Moscow: Institute of Oriental Studies, Russian Academy of Sciences.

Andreev, V. F. (1989). 'Военно-Стратегический Паритет – Объективный Фактор Сдерживания Агрессивных Сил' ['Military-Strategic Parity – An Objective Factor in Deterring Aggressive Forces']. *Voennaya Mysl'* 2 (February): 45–53.

Andrushkevich, I. (1973). 'Советская Армия и Флот – Любимое Детище Народа' ['The Soviet Army and Navy are the Favourite Brainchild of the People']. *Voennaya Mysl'* (February): 78–85.

D'Anieri, P. (2019). 'Magical Realism: Assumptions, Evidence and Prescriptions in the Ukraine Conflict'. *Eurasian Geography and Economics* 60(1): 97–117.

Annenkov, M. (1866). 'О Применении Железных Дорог к Военному Делу' ['On the Application of Railways to Military Affairs']. *Voennyi Sbornik* 12 (December): 329–352.

Antsupov, O. I., Zhikharev, A. S. (2015). 'Анализ Основных Концептуальных Подходов к Созданию Систем Стратегической ПРО США и Российской Федерации' ['Analysis of the Main Conceptual Approaches to the Creation of Strategic Missile Defence Systems of the United States and the Russian Federation']. *Voennaya Mysl'* 6 (June): 28–36.

Anureev, I. (1963). 'О Влиянии Научного Прогресса на Развитие Военной Техники' ['On the Influence of Scientific Progress on the Development of Military Equipment']. *Voennaya Mysl'* 3 (March): 3–14.

Anureev, I. (1976). 'Научно-Технический Прогресс и Обороноспособность Страны' ['Scientific-Technical Progress and the Country's Defence Capability']. *Voennaya Mysl'* 12 (December): 17–28.

Arbatov, A. (2010). 'Тактическое Ядерное Оружие – Проблемы и Решения' ['Tactical Nuclear Weapons – Problems and Solutions']. *Voyenno-Promyshlennyy Kur'yer* [*Military-Industrial Courier*] 17(333) (May 5). Available at: https://vpk-news.ru/articles/6626.

Arbatov, A. (2017). 'Understanding the US–Russia Nuclear Schism'. *Survival* 59(2): 33–66.

Arcuri, G. (2022) *Lessons from Russia's Dysfunctional Pre-War Innovation Economy*. Center for Strategic and International Studies. April 11. Available at: https://www.csis.org/blogs /perspectives-innovation/lessons-russias-dysfunctional-pre-war-innovation-economy.

Artemov, E. T. (2014). 'Советский Атомный Проект в Системе "Командной Экономики"' ['The Soviet Atomic Project in the System of a "Command Economy"']. *Cahiers Du Monde Russe* [Online] 55(3–4): 267–294.

Åslund, A. (2019). *Russia's Crony Capitalism: The Path from Market Economy to Kleptocracy*. New Haven: Yale University Press.

Axe, D. (2022). 'By Deploying Untrained Draftees, The Russian Army Is Committing "Premeditated Murder"'. *Forbes*. September 28. Available at: https://www.forbes.com/sites /davidaxe/2022/09/28/by-deploying-untrained-draftees-the-russian-army-is-committing-premeditated-murder/?sh=505a06945efb.

Ayad, P. (2022). 'Can US-Supplied HIMARS Be a Game Changer for Ukraine?' *France24*. July 14. Available at: https://www.france24.com/en/europe/20220714-can-us -supplied-himars-be-a-game-changer-for-ukraine.

Baev, P. (2020). 'Transformation of Russian Strategic Culture: Impacts from Local Wars and Global Confrontation'. *Russie.Nei.Visions* 118 (June). Ifri: Russia/NIS Center.

Baranov, E. F., Bessonov, V. A. (2018). 'Взгляд на Российскую Экономическую Трансформацию' ['A Look at the Russian Economic Transformation']. *Voprosy Ekonomiki* [*Issues of Economics*], 11: 142–158.

Bartosh, A. A. (2018a). 'Стратегия и Контрстратегия Гибридной Войны' ['Strategy and Counter-Strategy of Hybrid Warfare']. *Voennaya Mysl'* 10 (October): 5–20.

Bartosh, A. A. (2018b). '"Трение" и "Износ" Гибридной Войны' ['"Friction" and "Wearout" of Hybrid Warfare']. *Voennaya Mysl'* 1 (January): 5–13.

Bartosh, A. A. (2020). 'Стратегическая Культура как Инструмент Военно-Политического Анализа' ['Strategic Culture as a Tool for Military-Political Analysis']. *Voennaya Mysl'* 7 (July): 6–21.

Barvinenko, V. V. (1999). 'Об Автоматизации Управления Группировками Вооруженных Сил' ['On the Automation of Control Over Groupings of the Armed Forces']. *Voennaya Mysl'* 2 (April): 26–29.

Baumgarten, A. (1887a). 'Современное Положение Вопроса об Артилерийских Массах' ['Modern State of the Issue of Artillery Masses']. *Voennyi Sbornik* 11 (November): 51–74.

Baumgarten, A. (1887b). 'Современное Положение Вопроса об Артилерийских Массах' ['Modern State of the Issue of Artillery Masses']. *Voennyi Sbornik* 10 (October): 161–186.

Baumgarten, A. (1888). 'К Вопросу об Артилерийских Массах' ['On the Question of Artillery Masses']. *Voennyi Sbornik* 2 (February): 295–310.

Baumgarten, A. (1890). 'Артилерия в Полевом Бою' ['Artillery in Field Combat']. *Voennyi Sbornik* 3 (March): 99–123.

Baz', I. S. (1947). 'Об Источниках Военного Могущества Советской Державы' ['On the Sources of the Military Power of the Soviet State']. *Voennaya Mysl'* 2 (February): 6–24.

BBC News (2022). 'Путин Сравнил Себя с Петром I и Назвал Своей Задачей Возвращение Территорий' ['Putin Compared Himself With Peter I and Called the Return of Territories His Task']. June 9. Available at: https://www.bbc.com/russian/news-61749842.

Becker, M. D. (1993). *Strategic Culture and Ballistic Missile Defense: Russia and the United States*. Monterey, California: Naval Postgraduate School (NPS). The NPS Institutional Archive DSpace Repository. Theses and Dissertations. June 1993. Available at: https://calhoun.nps.edu/bitstream/handle/10945/39769/93Jun_Becker_M_D.pdf?sequence=1&isAllowed=y.

Belykh, A. A., Mau, V. A. (2020). 'Экономические Реформы в России: Вопросы Теории и Практика XIX – начала XX в.' ['Economic Reforms in Russia: Questions of Theory and Practice in the 19th – early 20th Centuries']. *Voprosy Ekonomiki* 1: 18–46.

Best, G. (1999). 'Peace Conferences and the Century of Total War: The 1899 Hague Conference and What Came After.' *International Affairs* 75(3): 619–634.

Bilefsky, D., Pérez-Peña, R., Nagourney E. (2022). 'The Roots of the Ukraine War: How the Crisis Developed'. *The New York Times* (April 21). Available at: https://www.nytimes.com/article/russia-ukraine-nato-europe.html.

Bloch, I. (1898). *Будущая Война в Техническом, Экономическом и Политическом Отношениях* [*The War of the Future in Its Technical, Economic and Political Relations* (abridgement: *Is War Now Impossible?*)], Vol. 6: 'Общие Выводы' ['General Conclusions']. St Petersburg: Printing house of I. A. Efron.

Bluhm, K., Varga, M. (2020). 'Conservative Developmental Statism in East Central Europe and Russia'. *New Political Economy* 25(4): 642–659.

Bodner, M. (2015). 'Russian Military Merges Air Force and Space Command'. *The Moscow Times* (August 3). Available at: https://www.themoscowtimes.com/2015/08/03/russian-military-merges-air-force-and-space-command-a48710.

Bogdanov, A. E., Popov, S. A., Ivanov, M. S. (2014). 'Перспективы Ведения Боевых Действий с Использованием Сетецентрических Технологий' ['Prospects for Conducting Combat Operations Using Network-Centric Technologies']. *Voennaya Mysl'* 3 (March): 3–12.

Bogomolov, V., Alekseev, V. (1967). 'Современная Война и Некоторые Вопросы Морального Фактора' ['Modern Warfare and Some Questions of the Moral Factor']. *Voennaya Mysl'* 8 (August): 21–29.

Borisov, E. G., Evdokimov, V. I. (2013). *Высокоточное Оружие и Борьба с Ним* [*Precision Weapons and Combat Against Them*]. St Petersburg: Publishing house Лань [Doe].

Borrie, J. (2006). 'Disarmament as Humanitarian Action: From Perspective to Practice'. Chapter 1, 7–22. In *Disarmament as Humanitarian Action From Perspective to Practice*, edited by J. Borrie, V. M. Randin. Geneva: United Nations Institute for Disarmament Research (UNIDIR).

Bowen, A. S. (2021). *Russian Arms Sales and Defense Industry*. Congressional Research Service (October). No. R46937. Available at: https://crsreports.congress.gov/product/pdf/R/R46937.

Brands, H. (2008) 'ABM Treaty', 2–4. In *Encyclopedia of the Cold War*, edited by R. van Dijk. New York: Routledge.

Brezhnev, L. I. (1970). *By Lenin's Course: Speeches and Articles* [*Ленинским Курсом. Речи и Статьи*], Vol. 2. Moscow: Politizdat.

Brodie, B. (1959). *Strategy in the Missile Age*. RAND Corporation, No. R-335. Princeton: Princeton University Press.

Bronevsky, S. (1963). 'Факторы Пространства и Времени в Военных Действиях' ['Factors of Space and Time in Military Operations']. *Voennaya Mysl'* 7 (July): 28–37.

Brooks, L. F. (2020). 'The End of Arms Control?' *Daedalus* 149(2): 84–100.

Brychkov, A. S., Dorokhov, V. L., Nikonorov, G. A. (2019). 'О Гибридном Характере Войн и Вооруженных Конфликтов Будущего' ['On the Hybrid Nature of Future Wars and Armed Conflicts']. *Voennaya Mysl'* 2 (February): 15–28.

Bulatov, A. F. (1984). 'Актуальные Вопросы Современного Наступательного Боя' ['Topical Issues of Modern Offensive Combat']. *Voennaya Mysl'* 11 (November): 59–69.

Bull, H. (1961). *The Control of the Arms Race: Disarmament and Arms Control in the Missile Age.* New York: Frederick A. Praeger Publishers.

Burenok, V. M., Achasov, O. B. (2007). 'Неядерное Сдерживание' ['Non-Nuclear Deterrence']. *Voennaya Mysl'* 12 (December): 12–15.

Chekinov, S. G., Bogdanov, S. A. (2010). 'Асимметричные Действия по Обеспечению Военной Безопасности России' ['Asymmetric Actions to Ensure the Military Security of Russia']. *Voennaya Mysl'* 3 (March 31): 13–22.

Chekinov, S. G., Bogdanov, S. A. (2011). 'Влияние Непрямых Действий на Характер Современной Войны' ['The Influence of Indirect Actions on the Nature of Modern Warfare']. *Voennaya Mysl'* 6 (June): 3–13.

Chekinov, S. G., Bogdanov, S. A. (2013). 'О Характере и Содержании Войны Нового Поколения' ['On the Nature and Content of the War of a New Generation']. *Voennaya Mysl'* 10: 13–24.

Cherednichenko, M. (1970). 'Некоторые Черты Современного Военного Искусства' ['Some Features of Modern Military Art']. *Voennaya Mysl'* 2 (February): 40–50.

Cherednichenko, M. (1973). 'Military Strategy and Military Equipment' ['Военная Стратегия и Военная Техника']. *Voennaya Mysl'* 4 (April): 37–47.

Chernovol, E. (2022). 'С-400 Бесполезна: Как HIMARS Развенчал Миф об Одной из Главных Гордостей Российской Армии' ['S-400 Is Useless: How HIMARS Debunked the Myth of One of the Main Prides of the Russian Army']. *Apostrophe.* July 13. Available at: https://apostrophe.ua/news/society/2022-07-13/s-400-bespolezna-kak-himars-razvenchal-mif-ob-odnoy-iz-glavnyih-gordostey-rossiyskoy-armii/274238.

Chernyavsky, S. I. (2017). 'К 110-летию Второй Гаагской Конференции Мира' ['To the 110th Anniversary of the Second Hague Peace Conference']. *Yuridicheskiye Nauki i Politologiya [Law and Political Sciences]* 7: 30–33.

Chervov, N. F. (1983). 'Разоружение: Кто Против?' ['Disarmament: Who Is Against It?"]. *Voennaya Mysl'* 12 (December): 3–15.

Chirvin, V. A. (1990). 'Оборонная Достаточность и Проблемы Предотвращения Войны' ['Defence Sufficiency and Problems of Preventing War']. *Voennaya Mysl'* 7 (July): 5–12.

Cohen, E. A. (2004). 'Change and Transformation in Military Affairs.' *Journal of Strategic Studies* 27(3): 395–407.

Collection (1903) *Сборник Материалов по Русско-Турецкой Войне 1877–1878 Годов на Балканском Полуострове [Collection of Materials on the Russian-Turkish War of 1877–1878 on the Balkan Peninsula]*, Vol. 41. St Petersburg.

Connolly, R., Sendstad, C. (2017). *Russia's Role as an Arms Exporter: The Strategic and Economic Importance of Arms Exports for Russia.* Chatham House (March). Available at: https://www.chathamhouse.org/sites/default/files/publications/research/2017-03-20-russia-arms-exporter-connolly-sendstad.pdf.

Covington, S. R. (2016). *The Culture of Strategic Thought Behind Russia's Modern Approaches to Warfare.* Belfer Center for Science and International Affairs Harvard Kennedy School. Defense and Intelligence Projects (October).

CPSU Materials (1986) *Материалы XXVII Съезда Коммунистической Партии Советского Союза [Materials of the XXVII Congress of the Communist Party of the Soviet Union]*. Moscow: Politizdat.

Curran, S. L., Ponomareff, D. (1982). *Managing the Ethnic Factor in the Russian and Soviet Armed Forces: An Historical Overview*. No. R-2640/1. Santa Monica: RAND. Available at: https://www.rand.org/content/dam/rand/pubs/reports/2008/R2640.1.pdf.

D-N, A. R. [anonymized] (1859). 'Несколько Мыслей об Организации Пехоты' ['A Few Thoughts on the Organization of the Infantry']. *Voennyi Sbornik* 5 (May): 79–88.

Daugherty, L. J. III, (1993) 'The Reluctant Warriors: The Non-Russian Nationalities in the Service of the Red Army During the Great Patriotic War 1941–1945'. *Journal of Slavic Military Studies* 6(3): 426–445.

D. U. S. [anonymized] (1861). 'О Духе Обучения Войска' ['On the Spirit of Troop Training']. *Voennyi Sbornik* 19: 61–70.

Danilevich, A. A., Shunin, O. P. (1992). 'О Стратегических Неядерных Силах Сдерживания' ['On Strategic Non-Nuclear Deterrence Forces']. *Voennaya Mysl'* 1 (January): 46–54.

della Porta, D. (2008). 'Comparative Analysis: Case-Oriented Versus Variable-Oriented Research.' Chapter 11, 198–222. In *Approaches and Methodologies in the Social Sciences: A Pluralist Perspective*, edited by D. della Porta, M. Keating. New York: Cambridge University Press.

Demin, V. E., Korolev, I. I., Lazukin, V. F., Matveev, D. S. (2012). 'Боевое Применение Разнородных Сил и Средств РЭБ в Общевойсковом Бою' ['Combat Use of Heterogeneous EW Forces and Means in Combined Arms Combat']. *Voennaya Mysl'* 2 (February): 34–40.

Dmitriev, Yu. I., Mashchenko, V. A. (1983). 'Применение Навигационных Спутниковых Систем США в Военных Целях' ['The Use of US Navigation Satellite Systems for Military Purposes']. *Voennaya Mysl'* 10 (October): 79–80.

Drake, D. (2022). 'Rusko Má Problém, Jeho Obrana Je proti HIMARS Krátká' ['Russia Has a Problem, Its Defence is Short Against HIMARS']. *Novinky.cz*. July 14. Available at: https://www.novinky.cz/valka-na-ukrajine/clanek/rusko-ma-problem-jeho-obrana-je-proti-himars-kratka-40402859.

Dutkiewicz, P. (2011). 'Missing in Translation: Re-conceptualizing Russia's Developmental State'. In *Russia: The Challenges of Transformation*, edited by P. Dutkiewicz, D. Trenin. Social Science Research Council and New York University Press.

DW (n.d.). 'Fact Check: Fake News Thrives Amid Russia-Ukraine War'. Available at: https://www.dw.com/en/fact-check-fake-news-thrives-amid-russia-ukraine-war/a-61477502. Last Updated 12 May 2022. Accessed 19 July 2022.

Dylevsky, I. N., Komov, S. A., Korotkov, S. V., Rodionov, S. N., Polyakova, T. A., Fedorov, A. V. (2008). 'К Вопросу о Международно-Правовой Квалификации Информационных Операций' ['On the Issue of International Legal Qualification of Information Operations']. *Voennaya Mysl'* 2 (February): 2–10.

Dzhelaukhov, X. (1966). 'Нанесение Глубоких Ударов' ['Delivering Deep Blows']. *Voennaya Mysl'* 2 (February): 33–41.

Eitelhuber, N. (2009). 'The Russian Bear: Russian Strategic Culture and What It Implies for the West.' *Connections* 9(1): 1–28.

Ermakov, S. (1970). 'Военно-Промышленный Комплекс США Готовит Новую Мировую Войну' ['The US Military-Industrial Complex is Preparing a New World War']. *Voennaya Mysl'* 5 (May): 86–96.

Ermarth, F. W. (2006). *Russian Strategic Culture: Past, Present, and ... In Transition?* Prepared for Defense Threat Reduction Agency, Advanced Systems and Concepts Offce (October). Available at: https://irp.fas.org/agency/dod/dtra/russia.pdf.

Erokhin, I. V. (1991). 'О Разработке Концепции Военной Реформы' ['On the Development of the Concept of Military Reform']. *Voennaya Mysl'* 11–12 (December): 36–45.

Evangelista, M. (1988). *Innovation and the Arms Race: How the United States and Soviet Union Develop New Military Technologies*. Ithaca, NY: Cornell University Press.

Evsyukov, A. V., Khryapin, A. L. (2020). 'Роль Новых Систем Стратегических Вооружений в Обеспечении Стратегического Сдерживания' ['The Role of New Strategic Weapons Systems in Providing Strategic Deterrence']. *Voennaya Mysl'* 12 (December): 26–30.

Eyffinger, A. (2007). 'A Highly Critical Moment: Role and Record of the 1907 Hague Peace Conference'. *Netherlands International Law Review* 54: 197–228.

Fabian, S. (2019). 'The Russian Hybrid Warfare Strategy – Neither Russian Nor Strategy'. *Defense & Security Analysis* 35(3): 308–325.

Fadeev, A. S., Nichipor, V. I. (2019). 'Военные Конфликты Современности, Перспективы Развития Способов Их Ведения. Прямые и Непрямые Действия в Вооруженных Конфликтах XXI Века' ['Modern Military Conflicts, Prospects for the Development of Ways to Conduct Them. Direct and Indirect Actions in Armed Conflicts of the XXI Century']. *Voennaya Mysl'* 9 (September): 33–41.

Fadeev, R. A. (1867). 'Вооруженные Силы России' ['Russian Armed Forces']. *Russkiy Vestnik [Russian Bulletin]* 23–27 (May): 61–107.

Faletsky, A. N. (1890). 'Бой Четвертого Рода Оружия' ['Fight of the Fourth Kind of Weapon']. *Voennyi Sbornik* 1 (January): 52–69.

Fedorov, V. G. (1904). *Вооружение Русской Армии в Крымскую Кампанию [Armament of the Russian Army in the Crimean Campaign]*. Published for the 50th anniversary of the Crimean Campaign. St Petersburg: Printing house of S. N. Tsepov.

Fedorov, V. G. (1911). *Вооружение Русской Армии за XIX Столетие [Armament of the Russian Army in the 19th Century]*. Printed by order of the Main Artillery Directorate.

Fedorov, Yu. E. (2002). 'США и Европа в Меняющемся Мире: Конфликт или Взаимодополняемость Стратегических Культур?' ['The USA and Europe in a Changing World: Conflict or Complementarity of Strategic Cultures?']. *Yevropeyskaya Bezopasnost': Sobytiya, Otsenki, Prognozy [European Security: Events, Assessments, Forecasts]* 6: 7–11.

Feinstein, S. G., Pirro, E. B. (2021). 'Testing the World Order: Strategic Realism in Russian Foreign Affairs'. *International Politics* 58: 817–834.

Fenenko, A. V. (2012). 'Фактор Тактического Ядерного Оружия в Мировой Политике' ['The Factor of Tactical Nuclear Weapons in World Politics']. *Vestnik Moskovskogo Universiteta [Bulletin of Moscow University]* 25(2): 35–61.

Filippov, V. F. (1984). 'О Техническом Перевооружении и Организационной Перестройке Соединений Сухопутных Войск США' ['On the Technical Re-equipment and Organizational Restructuring of the Formations of the US Ground Forces']. *Voennaya Mysl'* 4 (April): 62–68.

Fitzsimonds, J. R., van Tol, J. M. (1994). 'Revolutions in Military Affairs'. *Joint Force Quarterly* 4: 24–31.

Flynn, G. (1989/2021). 'Doctrine, Images, and the East-West Military Relationship,' 1–26. In *Soviet Military Doctrine and Western Policy*, edited by G. Flynn, Vol. 49. First published 1989. Reissued 2021. New York: Routledge.

FPI [Advanced Research Foundation] (n.d.). 'О Фонде' ['About the Fund']. Available at: https://fpi.gov.ru/about/. Accessed 20 July 2022.

Galeotti, M. (2020). 'The Gerasimov Doctrine.' *Berlin Policy Journal* (April 28). Available at: https://cutt.ly/vHUUktd.

Galkin, D. V., Kolyandra, P. A., Stepanov, A. V. (2021). 'Состояние и Перспективы Использования Искусственного Интеллекта в Военном Деле' ['The State and Prospects for the Use of Artificial Intelligence in Military Affairs']. *Voennaya Mysl'* 1 (January): 113–124.

Gareev, M. A. (1992). 'Вопросы Военной Доктрины и Строительства Вооруженных Сил Российской Федерации' ['Issues of Military Doctrine and the Development of the Armed Forces of the Russian Federation']. *Voennaya Mysl'*, Special Issue (July): 38–41.

Gareev, M. A. (1993). 'О Некоторых Общих Положениях Военной Доктрины и Военной Стратегии' ['On Some General Provisions of Military Doctrine and Military Strategy']. *Voennaya Mysl'*, Special Issue (February): 38–40.

Gareev, M. A. (2008). 'Стратегическое Сдерживание: Проблемы и Решения' ['Strategic Deterrence: Problems and Solutions']. *Krasnaya Zvezda [Red Star]* (October 8).

Gaydunko, Yu. A., Makarova, S. P. (2019). 'К Вопросу о Роли и Месте России в Современном Мире' ['On the Question of the Role and Place of Russia in the Modern World']. *Voennaya Mysl'* 4 (April): 6–14.

Gerasimov, V. V. (2013a). 'Основные Тенденции Развития Форм и Способов Применения ВС, Актуальные Задачи Военной Науки по Их Совершенствованию' ['The Main Trends in the Development of Forms and Methods of Use of the Armed Forces, The Urgent Tasks of Military Science to Improve Them']. Report at the General Meeting of the Academy of Military Sciences. *Voyenno-Promyshlennyy Kur'yer* 8, No. 476 (February 27).

Gerasimov, V. V. (2013b). 'Ценность Науки в Предвидении. Новые Вызовы Требуют Переосмыслить Формы и Способы Ведения Боевых Действий' ['The Value of Science is in Foresight. New Challenges Require Rethinking the Forms and Methods of Warfare']. *Voyenno-Promyshlennyy Kur'yer* (February 26). Available at: https://vpk-news.ru /articles/14632.

Giles, K. (2015). *Russia's Hybrid Warfare: A Success in Propaganda*. Working Papers on Security Policy (January). Berlin: Federal Academy for Security Policy.

Giles, K., Boulegue, M. (2019). 'Russia's A2/AD Capabilities: Real and Imagined.' *Parameters* 49(1–2): 21–36.

Gladkov, D. I. (1989). 'О Понятии "Высокоточное Оружие"' ['On the Concept of "Precision Weapons"']. *Voennaya Mysl'* 8 (August): 38–43.

Glebovich, V. G. (1991). 'Противоспутниковое Оружие в Военной Стратегии США' ['Anti-Satellite Weapons in US Military Strategy']. *Voennaya Mysl'* 10 (October): 68–75.

Glikman, E. (2022). 'Своих Не Бросаем?' ['Do We Leave Ours?']. *Novaya Gazeta [New Newspaper]*. March 22. Available at: https://novayagazeta.ru/articles/2022/03/22 /svoikh-ne-brosaem.

Glinoetsky, N. (1859). 'Военное Обозрение' ['Military Review']. *Voennyi Sbornik* 2 (February): 749–760.

Glinoetsky, N. (1868). 'Иностранное Военное Обозрение' ['Foreign Military Review']. *Voennyi Sbornik* 61: 59–84.

Gobarev V. M. (1999). 'Soviet Policy Toward China: Developing Nuclear Weapons 1949–1969'. *The Journal of Slavic Military Studies* 12(4): 1–53.

Goldblat, J. (2002). *Arms Control : The New Guide to Negotiations and Agreements*. 2nd edition. London: SAGE Publications.

Goldman, E. O., Andres, R. B. (1999). 'Systemic Effects of Military Innovation and Diffusion'. *Security Studies* 8(4): 79–125.

Goncharov, A. M., Ryabov, S. V. (2021). 'Искусственный Интеллект Как Основное Направление Развития Робототехнических Комплексов' ['Artificial Intelligence as the Main Direction in the Development of Robotic Systems']. *Voennaya Mysl'* 6 (June): 65–70.

Gorbunov, V. N., Bogdanov, S. A. (2009). 'О Характере Вооруженной Борьбы в XXI Веке' ['On the Nature of Armed Struggle in the 21st Century']. *Voennaya Mysl'* 3 (March): 2–15.

Graf, F. (1861). 'Оружейные Заводы в России' ['Arms Factories in Russia']. *Voennyi Sbornik* 21: 365–394.

Gray, C. S. (1981a). 'National Style in Strategy: The American Example'. *International Security* 6(2): 21–47.

Gray, C. S. (1981b). *Nuclear Strategy and National Style*, Vol. I. Final Report for Period February 1, 1980 – July 31, 1981. New York: Hudson Institute. Prepared for the Defense Nuclear Agency in Washington. Contract No. DNA 001-80-C-0121.

Gray, C. S. (1999). 'Strategic Culture as Context: The First Generation of Theory Strikes Back'. *Review of International Studies* 25(1): 49–69.

Gray, C. S. (2006). *Recognizing and Understanding Revolutionary Change in Warfare: The Sovereignty of Context*. Carlisle Barracks: Strategic Studies Institute.

Guzzini, S. (2005). 'The Concept of Power: A Constructivist Analysis'. *Millennium: Journal of International Studies* 33(3): 495–521.

Gwertzman, B. (1985). 'U.S. Says Soviet [Union] Violates ABM Treaty'. *The New York Times* (February 2). Available at: https://www.nytimes.com/1985/02/02/world/us-says-soviet-violates-abm-treaty.html.

Harrison, M. (2000). 'New Postwar Branches (1): Rocketry'. In *The Soviet Defence-Industry Complex from Stalin to Khrushchev*, edited by J. Barber, M. Harrison. London: Macmillan Press.

Hashim, A. S. (1998). 'The Revolution in Military Affairs Outside the West'. *Journal of International Affairs* 51(2): 431–445.

Hearing (1980). 'Status of the MX Missile System'. Hearing before the Committee on Armed Forces, House of Representatives, Ninety-Sixth Congress, 2nd Session (May 1). Washington: US Government Printing Office. Available at: https://cutt.ly/9HTeEp6.

Higgins, A. P. (1909/2010). *The Hague Peace Conferences: And Other International Conferences Concerning the Laws and Usages of War – Texts of Conventions with Commentaries*. New York: Cosimo Classics. First Published 1909. Reissued 2010.

Horowitz, M. (2010). *The Diffusion of Military Power: Causes and Consequences for International Politics*. Princeton: Princeton University Press.

Hundley, R. O. (1999). *Past Revolutions, Future Transformations: What Can the History of Revolutions in Military Affairs Tell Us About Transforming the U.S. Military?* Santa Monica: RAND.

Hynek, N., Solovyeva, A. (2020). *The Logic of Humanitarian Arms Control and Disarmament: A Power-Analytical Approach*. London: Rowman and Littlefield.

Hynek, N., Solovyeva, A. (2022). *Militarizing Artificial Intelligence: Theory, Technology, and Regulation*. New York: Routledge.

Igumnova, L. (2011). 'Russia's Strategic Culture Between American and European Worldviews'. *Journal of Slavic Military Studies* 24: 253–273.

Ilnitsky, A. M. (2021). 'Ментальная Война России' ['The Mental War of Russia'], *Voennaya Mysl'* 8: 19–33.

Ilyin, S. (1967). 'Идеологические Аспекты Революции в Военном Деле' ['Ideological Aspects of the Revolution in Military Affairs']. *Voennaya Mysl'* 10 (October): 41–52.

Interfax (2021a). '"Рособоронэкспорт" Продал за Рубеж Подводные Лодки с Ракетами "Калибр"' ['"Rosoboronexport" Has Sold Submarines with "Kalibr" Missiles Abroad']. August 25. Available at: https://www.interfax.ru/russia/786374.

Interfax (2021b). 'Танк "Армата" Не Пойдет на Экспорт, Пока Его Не Получит Российская Армия' ['The Armata Tank Will Not Be Exported Until the Russian Army Receives It']. August 24. Available at: https://www.interfax.ru/russia/786175.

Interfax (2022a). 'Принят Закон о Спецмерах в Экономике при Силовых Операциях за Пределами РФ' ['A Law on Special Measures in the Economy During Military

Operations Outside the Russian Federation Was Adopted']. July 6. Available at: https://www.interfax.ru/russia/850794.

Interfax (2022b). 'Путин Подписал Закон об Отмене Возрастного Предела для Контрактников' ['Putin Signed the Law on the Abolition of the Age Limit for Contract Workers']. May 28. Available at: https://www.interfax.ru/russia/843442.

Interfax (2022c). 'Путин Призвал Помочь Тем, Кто Хочет Поехать в Донбасс Добровольцем' ['Putin Urged to Help Those Who Want to Go to the Donbass as a Volunteer']. March 11. Available at: https://www.interfax.ru/russia/827570.

Interfax (2022d). 'Путин Сообщил Россиянам о Начале Военной Операции на Украине. Текст.' ['Putin Informed the Russians About the Start of a Military Operation in Ukraine. Text.']. February 24. Available at: https://www.interfax.ru/russia/824020.

Ionov, A. N. (1992). 'Некоторые Уроки Маленькой Войны' ['Some Lessons of a Small War']. *Voennaya Mysl'* 3 (March): 79–80.

Ivanov, A., Naumenko, I., Pavlov, M. (1971). *Ракетно-Ядерное Оружие и Его Поражающее Действие [Nuclear-Rocket Weapons and Their Damage Effect]*. Moscow: Voenizdat.

Ivanov, K. (1962). 'Изменения в Военной Политике и Стратегии США' ['Changes in US Military Policy and Strategy']. *Voennaya Mysl'* 7 (July): 46–56.

Ivanov, O. (2007). 'Американская Стратегическая Культура' ['American Strategic Culture']. *Obozrevatel' [Observer]* 204 (1): 87–97.

Ivanov, S. (1969). 'Советская Военная Доктрина и Стратегия' ['Soviet Military Doctrine and Strategy']. *Voennaya Mysl'* 5 (May): 39–50.

Ivasik, V. A., Pis'yaukov, A. S., Khryapin, A. L. (1999). 'Ядерное Оружие и Военная Безопасность России' ['Nuclear Weapons and Russia's Military Security']. *Voennaya Mysl'* 4 (August): 71–73.

Ivory, D., Ismay, J., Lu, D., Hernandez, M. Queen, C. S., Ruderman, J., White, K., Higgins, L., Wong, B. G. (2022). 'What Hundreds of Photos of Weapons Reveal About Russia's Brutal War Strategy'. *The New York Times*. June 19. Available at: https://www.nytimes.com/interactive/2022/06/19/world/europe/ukraine-munitions-war-crimes.html.

Ivshina, O. (2022). 'Груз 200: Что Известно о Потерях Российской Армии в Украине к Началу Июля' ['Cargo 200: What is Known about the Losses of the Russian Army in Ukraine by the Beginning of July']. BBC News. July 8. Available at: https://www.bbc.com/russian/features-62087305.

Izvestia (2018). 'Средства ПВО Объединят Искусственным Интеллектом' ['Air Defense Systems Will Be United by Artificial Intelligence']. May 2. Available at: https://iz.ru/733333/aleksandr-kruglov-aleksei-ramm-evgenii-dmitriev/sredstva-pvo-obediniat-iskusstvennym-intellektom.

Izvestia (2022). 'Сирийские Добровольцы Объяснили Мотивы Принять Участие в Спецоперации РФ' ['Syrian Volunteers Explained Motives to Take Part in Russian Special Operation']. March 14. Available at: https://iz.ru/1304584/2022-03-14/siriiskie-dobrovoltcy-obiasnili-motivy-priniat-uchastie-v-spetcoperatcii-rf.

Johnson, Ch. (1999). 'The Developmental State: Odyssey of a Concept'. In *The Developmental State*, edited by M. Woo-Cumings. Ithaca–New York: Cornell University Press.

Johnston, A. I. (1995a). *Cultural Realism: Strategic Culture and Grand Strategy in Chinese History*. Princeton, New Jersey: Princeton University Press.

Johnston, A. I. (1995b). 'Thinking about Strategic Culture'. *International Security* 19(4): 32–64.

Jones, D. R. (1990). 'Soviet Strategic Culture', 35–49. In *Strategic Power: USA/USSR*, edited by C. G. Jacobsen. London: St Martin's Press.

Jones, S. G. (2022). *Russia's Ill-Fated Invasion of Ukraine: Lessons in Modern Warfare*. Center for Strategic and International Studies. June 1. Available at: https://csis-website-prod.s3

.amazonaws.com/s3fs-public/publication/220601_Jones_Russia%27s_Ill-Fated _Invasion_0.pdf?Ggqjb.JsRbJzr_wlu5jrVT_Xe3AW3jur.

Kalinovsky, O. N. (2001). '"Информационная Война" – Это Война?' ['Is the "Information War" a War?']. *Voennaya Mysl'* 1 (February): 57–59.

Karpovich, B. (1952). 'Характерные Черты Военной Идеологии Империализма' ['Characteristic Features of the Military Ideology of Imperialism']. *Voennaya Mysl'* 1 (January): 47–62.

Kashirina, T. V. (2011). 'Создание Правовой Базы Переговорного Процесса Между СССР и США по Ограничению Стратегических Вооружений в 1969–1972 Годах' ['Creation of a Legal Basis for the Negotiation Process Between the USSR and the USA on the Limitation of Strategic Arms in 1969–1972']. *Ekonomika. Nalogi. Pravo* [*Economy. Taxes. Law*] 4: 124–129.

Keefer, S. (2014). '"Explosive Missals": International Law, Technology, and Security in Nineteenth-Century Disarmament Conferences.' *War in History* 21(4): 445–464.

Khaneneva, V. (2022). 'Путин Рассказал о Формировании Украины' ['Putin Spoke About the Formation of Ukraine']. *Gazeta.ru.* June 17. Available at: https://www.gazeta.ru /politics/news/2022/06/17/17954804.shtml.

Khlopov, V. (1950). 'О Характере Военной Доктрины Американского Империализма'. ['On the Nature of the Military Doctrine of American Imperialism'] *Voennaya Mysl'* 6 (June): 67–78.

Khomutov, A. V. (2021). 'О Противодействии Противнику в Условиях Ведения Им "Многосферных Операций"' ['On Countering the Enemy in the Context of His "Multi-Sphere Operations"']. *Voennaya Mysl'* 5 (May): 27–41.

Khryapin, A. L., Kalinkin, D. A., Matvichuk, V. V. (2015). 'Стратегическое Сдерживание в Условиях Создания США Глобальной Системы ПРО и Средств Глобального Удара' ['Strategic Deterrence in the Context of the US Creation of a Global Missile Defence System and the Means of Global Strike']. *Voennaya Mysl'* 1 (January): 18–22.

Kim, E. M. (1993). 'Contradictions and Limits of a Developmental State: With Illustrations from the South Korean Case'. *Social Problems* 40(2): 228–249.

Kirby, P. (2022a). 'Why Has Russia Invaded Ukraine and What Does Putin Want?' BBC News (May 9). Available at: https://www.bbc.com/news/world-europe-56720589.

Kirby, P. (2022b). 'Russia Claims First Use of Hypersonic Kinzhal Missile in Ukraine'. BBC News (March 19). Available at: https://www.bbc.com/news/world-europe-60806151.

Kirilenko, G. V., Trenin, D. V. (1992). 'Формула Безопасности: От Паритета к Стратегической Стабильности' ['Security Formula: From Parity to Strategic Stability']. *Voennaya Mysl'* 8–9 (August): 15–19.

Kirillov, V. V., Kryuchkov, Yu. N. (2008). 'Влияние Войн на Развитие и Международное Значение России в Мире' ['The Influence of Wars on the Development and International Significance of Russia in the World']. *Voennaya Mysl'* 2 (February): 10–21.

Kiselev, V. A., Vorobyev, I. N. (2015). 'Гибридные Операции как Новый Вид Военного Противоборства' ['Hybrid Operations as a New Type of Military Confrontation']. *Voennaya Mysl'* 5: 41–48.

Klein, B. S. (1988). 'Hegemony and Strategic Culture: American Power Projection and Alliance Defence Politics.' *Review of International Studies* 14(2): 133–148.

Klein, B. S. (1989). 'The Textual Strategies of the Military: Or, Have You Read Any Good Defense Manuals Lately?' In *International/Intertextual Relations: Postmodern Readirigs of World Politics*, edited by J. Der Derian, M. J. Shapiro. Lexington, Mass.: Lexington Books.

Knápek, J., Efmertová, M., Mikeš, J. (2011). 'Nuclear Energy in Czechoslovakia: An Outline and Description of Its Development and Trends'. *Annales Historiques De L'électricité* 9 (December): 59–80.

Kofman, M., Fink, A., Gorenburg D., Chesnut M., Edmonds J., Waller, J. (2021) *Russian Military Strategy: Core Tenets and Operational Concepts*. CNA (August). Available at: https://www.cna.org/archive/CNA_Files/pdf/russian-military-strategy-core-tenets-and-operational-concepts.pdf.

Kokoshin, A. A. (2002). 'Асимметричный Ответ. Он Всегда Найдется у России для Предотвращения Угроз Государству' ['Asymmetric Response. Russia Will Always Have It to Prevent Threats to the State']. Interview with A. A. Kokoshin in the newspaper *Trud* [*Labour*]: February 27. Conducted by Yuri Stroganov. Available at: http://viperson.ru/articles/asimmetrichnyy-otvet-on-vsegda-naydetsya-u-rossii-dlya-predotvrascheniya-ugroz-gosudarstvu.

Kokoshin, A. A. (2009). 'Революция в Военном Деле и Проблемы Создания Современных Вооруженных Сил России' ['The Revolution in Military Affairs and Problems of Creating the Modern Armed Forces of Russia']. *Vestnik Moskovskogo Universiteta* 25(1): 46–62.

Kokoshin, A. A., Baluevsky, Yu. N., Potapov V. Ya. (2015). 'Влияние Новейших Тенденций в Развитии Технологий и Средств Вооруженной Борьбы на Военное Искусство' ['The Impact of the Latest Trends in the Development of Technologies and Means of Armed Struggle on Military Art']. *Vestnik Moskovskogo Universiteta* 25(4): 3–22.

Konopatov, S. N., Yudin, V. V. (2001). 'Традиционный Смысл Понятия "Война" Устарел' [The Traditional Meaning of the Concept of "War" is Outdated']. *Voennaya Mysl'*, No. 1 (February): 53–57.

Korneychuk, V. (1962). 'Обеспечение Защиты Войск от Средств Массового Поражения' ['Ensuring the Protection of Troops from Weapons of Mass Destruction']. *Voennaya Mysl'* 3 (March): 43–51.

Kornienko, A., Korolev, V. (1967). 'Экономические Аспекты Советской Военной Доктрины' ['Economic Aspects of the Soviet Military Doctrine']. *Voennaya Mysl'* 7 (July): 28–37.

Korobeinikov, M., Shabaev, G., Sokolov V. (1967). 'Морально-Психологическая Подготовка Советских Воинов в Современных Условиях' ['Moral and Psychological Training of Soviet Soldiers in Modern Conditions']. *Voennaya Mysl'* 5 (May): 44–55.

Korotchenko, E. G. (1986). 'К Вопросу о Защите Войск от Высокоточного Оружия в Операциях' ['On the Issue of Protecting Troops from High-Precision Weapons in Operations']. *Voennaya Mysl'* 1 (January): 19–25.

Korotchenko, E. G. (1991). 'Современная Военно-Политическая Обстановка и Проблемы Военного Искусства' ['The Modern Military-Political Situation and Problems of Military Art']. *Voennaya Mysl'* 8 (August): 19–23.

Korovushin, V. V. (1990). 'Некоторые Актуальные Проблемы Военной Стратегии' ['Some Actual Problems of Military Strategy']. *Voennaya Mysl'* 12 (December): 27–33.

Kotkin, S. (2016). 'Russia's Perpetual Geopolitics: Putin Returns to the Historical Pattern'. *Foreign Affairs* (May).

Koyanovich, A. (1959). 'Strategic Defence' ['Стратегическая Оборона']. *Voennaya Mysl'* 12 (December): 30–39.

Koziratsky, Yu. L., Budnikov, S. A., Skopin, D. V. (2010). 'Об Упреждающем Применении Средств Радиоэлектронной Борьбы' ['On the Pre-emptive Use of Electronic Warfare']. *Voennaya Mysl'* 2 (February): 52–57.

Kozlov, S. (1959). 'Действительно Ли Пересматриваются Основы Военной Стратегии США?' ['Are the Foundations of US Military Strategy Being Revised?']. *Voennaya Mysl'* 1 (January): 65–76.

Krasilshchikov, V. A. (2003). 'Азиатские "Тигры" и Россия: Страшен ли Бюрократический Капитализм?' ['Asian "Tigers" and Russia: Is Bureaucratic Capitalism Scary?'] *Mir Rossii [The World of Russia]* 4: 3–43.

Krasnov, A. B. (1999). 'Авиация в Югославском Конфликте' ['Aviation in the Yugoslav Conflict']. *Voennaya Mysl'* 5 (October): 71–74.

Krause, K. (1992). *Arms and the State: Patterns of Military Production and Trade.* Cambridge: Cambridge University Press.

Kreidin, S. V. (1999). 'Глобальное и Региональное Ядерное Сдерживание: К Системе Принципов и Критериев' ['Global and Regional Nuclear Deterrence: Towards a System of Principles and Criteria']. *Voennaya Mysl'* 4 (August): 73–80.

Krepinevich, A. F. (1994). 'Cavalry to Computer: The Pattern of Military Revolutions'. *The National Interest* 37: 30–42.

Krylov, N. (1967). 'Ракетно-Ядерный Щит Советского Государства' ['Nuclear-Missile Shield of the Soviet State']. *Voennaya Mysl'* 11 (November): 15–23.

Kryshtanovskaya, O., White, S. (1996). 'From Soviet Nomenklatura to Russian Elite'. *Europe-Asia Studies* 48(5): 711–733.

Kulakov, V. (1964). 'Вопросы Военно-Технического Превосходства' ['Issues of Military-Technical Superiority']. *Voennaya Mysl'* 1 (January): 12–23.

Kuptsov, I. M. (2011). 'Борьба с Гиперзвуковыми Летательными Аппаратами (ГЗЛА): Новая Задача и Требования к Системе Воздушно-Космической Обороны (ВКО)' [Combating Hypersonic Aircraft ([Russian abbreviation:] GZLA): A New Task and Requirements for the Aerospace Defence System ([Russian abbreviation:] VKO)]. *Voennaya Mysl'* 1 (January): 10–17.

Lagovsky, A. (1970). 'Экономика Вооруженных Сил' ['Economics of the Armed Forces']. *Voennaya Mysl'* 1 (January): 59–67.

Lalu, P. (2021). 'The Fighting Power of Russia's Armed Forces'. Chapter 10, 289–346. In *Putin's Russia: Economy, Defence and Foreign Policy*, edited by S. Rosefielde. Singapore: World Scientific Publishing.

Lamont, C., Boduszynski, M. P. (2020). *Research Methods in Politics and International Relations.* London: SAGE Publications.

Larsen, J. A. (2002). 'An Introduction to Arms Control'. Chapter 1, 1–15. In *Arms Control. Cooperative Security in a Changing Environment*, edited by J. A. Larsen. Boulder: Lynne Rienner Publishers.

Lastochkin, Yu. I. (2015). 'Роль и Место Радиоэлектронной Борьбы в Современных и Будущих Боевых Действиях' ['The Role and Place of Electronic Warfare in Modern and Future Combat Operations']. *Voennaya Mysl'* 12 (December): 14–19.

Law, W.-W. (2009). 'The Developmental State, Social Change, and Education'. Vol. 22. In *International Handbook of Comparative Education*, edited by R. Cowen, A. M. Kazamias. Springer.

Leer, G. (1861a). 'Влияние Нарезного Оружия на Современное Состояние Тактики' ['The Influence of Rifles on the Modern State of Tactics']. *Voennyi Sbornik* 3 (March): 27–42.

Leer, G. (1861b). 'Влияние Нарезного Оружия на Современное Состояние Тактики' ['The Influence of Rifles on the Modern State of Tactics']. *Voennyi Sbornik* 7 (July) 55–78.

Leer, G. (1861c). 'Влияние Нарезного Оружия на Современное Состояние Тактики' ['The Influence of Rifles on the Modern State of Tactics']. *Voennyi Sbornik* 4 (April): 297–316.

Leer, G. (1861d). 'Влияние Нарезного Оружия на Современное Состояние Тактики' ['The Influence of Rifles on the Modern State of Tactics']. *Voennyi Sbornik* 19: 33–60.

Leer, G. (1863). 'Значение Критической Военной Истории в Изучении Стратегии и Тактики' ['The Significance of Critical Military History in the Study of Strategy and Tactics']. *Voennyi Sbornik* 31: 57–92.

Leer, G. (1894). *Метод Военных Наук* [*The Method of Military Sciences*]. St Petersburg.

Lenta (2022a). 'Техника Специальной Операции: Какое Оружие Используют Российские Военные на Украине?' ['Special Operation Vehicles: What Weapons Does the Russian Military Use in Ukraine?']. March 25. Available at: https://lenta.ru/articles/2022/03/25/weapon/.

Lenta (2022b). 'Путин Назвал Две Составляющие Гарантий Безопасности России' ['Putin Named Two Components of Russia's Security Guarantees']. June 17. Available at: https://lenta.ru/news/2022/06/17/armiyaiflot/.

Leonidov, L. V., Viktorov, V. P. (1986). 'Вероятные Способы Развязывания и Ведения Обычной Войны' ['Probable Ways of Unleashing and Waging a Conventional War']. *Voennaya Mysl'* 1 (January): 74–80.

Levadov, L. V. (1985). 'Итоги Оперативной Подготовки Объединенных Вооруженных Сил НАТО в 1984 Году' ['The Results of the Operational Training of the Joint Armed Forces of NATO in 1984']. *Voennaya Mysl'* 3 (March): 64–72.

Levshin, V. I., Nedelin, A. V., Sosnovsky, M. E. (1999). 'О Применении Ядерного Оружия для Деэскалации Военных Действий' ['On the Use of Nuclear Weapons to De-escalate Hostilities']. *Voennaya Mysl'* 3 (June): 34–37.

Lomov, N. (1963). 'Советская Военная Доктрина' ['Soviet Military Doctrine']. *Voennaya Mysl'* 1 (January): 14–30.

Lotareva, A., Ivshina, O. (2022). '"Вышел за Хлебом – Оказался под Мариуполем." Как Устроена Принудительная Мобилизация в Армии Непризнанных ДНР и ЛНР' ['"I Went Out for Bread – I Ended Up Near Mariupol." How Forced Mobilization Works in the Army of the Unrecognized DNR and LNR']. BBC News. May 18. Available at: https://www.bbc.com/russian/features-61480788.

Lynch, A. C. (2001). 'The Realism of Russia's Foreign Policy'. *Europe-Asia Studies* 53(1): 7–31.

Lyubin, M. D. (2009). 'К Вопросу об Истории Развития и Перспективах Радиоэлектронной Борьбы' ['On the Issue of the History of the Development and Prospects for Electronic Warfare']. *Voennaya Mysl'* 3 (March): 64–75.

MacFarquhar, N. (2022). '"Coffins Are Already Coming": The Toll of Russia's Chaotic Draft'. *The New York Times*. October 16. Available at: https://www.nytimes.com/2022/10/16/world/europe/russia-draft-ukraine.html.

Maksheev, O. (1890a). 'Железные Дороги в Военном Отношении' ['Railways in Military Terms']. *Voennyi Sbornik* 11 (November): 30–58.

Maksheev, O. (1890b). 'Железные Дороги в Военном Отношении' ['Railways in Military Terms']. *Voennyi Sbornik* 12 (December): 241–284.

Manachinsky, A. Ya., Chumak, V. N., Pronkin, E. K. (1992). 'Операция "Буря в Пустыне": Итоги и Последствия' ['Operation "Desert Storm": Results and Consequences']. *Voennaya Mysl'*, No. 1 (January): 88–92.

Martens, F. (1900). 'Гаагская Конференция Мира: Культурно-Исторический Очерк' ['Hague Peace Conference: Cultural-Historical Essay']. *Vestnik Evropy* 2 (March): 5–28. Available at: https://www.prlib.ru/item/323534, p.24–25.

Marudin, P. (1962). 'Малогабаритное Ядерное Оружие и Его Использование' ['Small-Sized Nuclear Weapons and Their Use']. *Voennaya Mysl'* 3 (March): 64–70.

Maslennikov, O. V., Aliev, F. K., Vassenkov, A. V., Tlyashev, O. M. (2020). 'Интеллектуализация – Важная Составляющая Цифровизации Вооруженных Сил Российской Федерации' ['Intellectualization is an Important Component of the Digitalization of the Armed Forces of the Russian Federation']. *Voennaya Mysl'* 7 (July): 67–76.

Maslennikov, O. V., Kurochkin, V. P., Aliev, F. K., Tlyashev, O. M. (2019). 'Об Информатизации Вооруженных Сил Российской Федерации' ['On Informatization of the Armed Forces of the Russian Federation']. *Voennaya Mysl'* 12 (December): 57–67.

McDermott, R. (2009). 'Russia's Armed Forces: The Power of Illusion'. *Russie.Nei.Visions* 37. Ifri: Russia/NIS Center (March). Available at: https://www.ifri.org/sites/default/files /atoms/files/ifrirussianmilitarypowermcdermottengmars09.pdf.

Medem, N. (1859). 'Несколько Слов о Конной Артиллерии Вообще и о Русской в Особенности' ['A Few Words About Horse Artillery in General and About Russian Artillery in Particular']. *Voennyi Sbornik* 2 (February): 407–432.

Mediazona (2022). *Кто Гибнет на Войне с Украиной. Исследование 'Медиазоны'* [*Who Dies in the War with Ukraine. Research by 'Mediazona'*]. April 25. Available at: https://zona.media /article/2022/04/25/bodycount.

Meduza (2022). *Грубо Говоря, Мы Начали Войну… Расследование 'Медузы' о Наемниках на Войне в Украине* [*Roughly Speaking, We Started a War… 'Meduza's' Investigation into Merce-naries in the War in Ukraine*]. July 13. Available at: https://meduza.io/feature/2022/07/13 /grubo-govorya-my-nachali-voynu.

Mikhailyonok O. M. (2012). 'Стратегическая Культура как Системообразующий Фактор Общественно-Политического Согласия' ['Strategic Culture as a System-Form-ing Factor of Socio-Political Consent'], 125–141. In *Россия Реформирующаяся* [*Reforming Russia*], edited by M. K. Gorshkov. Yearbook, Vol. 11. Moscow: New Chronograph.

Mikhalev, Yu. A., Zvoshchik, E. V. (2018). 'Значение Доктрины Монро в Формировании Американской Стратегической Культуры' ['The Significance of the Monroe Doctrine in the Formation of American Strategic Culture']. *Vestnik Moskovskogo Gosudarstvennogo Lingvisticheskogo Universiteta* [*Bulletin of the Moscow State Linguistic University*] 794(1): 52–59.

Milaeva, O. V., Siushkin, A. E. (2012). 'Сравнительный Анализ Стратегической Культуры США и Евросоюза (На Материалах Стратегий Безопасности 2002–2010 Годов)' ['Comparative Analysis of the Strategic Culture of the United States and the European Union (Based on the Security Strategies of 2002–2010)']. *Izvestiya Vysshikh Uchebnykh Zavedeniy* [*News of Higher Educational Institutions*] 23(3): 19–28.

Milenin, O. V., Sinikov, A. A. (2019). 'О Роли Авиации Воздушно-Космических Сил в Современной Войне. Беспилотные Летательные Аппараты Как Тенденция Развития Военной Авиации' ['On the Role of Aviation of the Aerospace Forces in Modern Warfare. Unmanned Aerial Vehicles as a Trend in the Development of Military Aviation']. *Voennaya Mysl'* 11 (November): 50–57.

Milioukov, P. N. (1911). *Вооруженный Мир и Ограничение Вооружений* [*Armed Peace and Arms Limitation*]. St Petersburg Peace Society. Vol. 1. St Petersburg: Printing house of B. M. Wolf.

Milko, A. (1961). 'Цена Гонки Вооружений' ['The Price of the Arms Race']. *Voennaya Mysl'* 5 (May): 50–61.

MoD [Ministry of Defence] (n.d.). 'Структура и Реализация Инновационной Деятельности' ['Structure and Implementation of Innovation Activities']. Available at: https://mil.ru/mission/innovacia/struct.htm. Accessed 5 July 2022.

MoD [Ministry of Defence] (2020). 'Военный Инновационный Технополис "Эра" создан в соответствии с Указом Президента Российской Федерации от 25 июня 2018 г. № 364' ['Military Innovative Technopolis "Era" was created in accordance with the Decree of the President of the Russian Federation dated 25 June 2018, no. 364']. March 5. Available at: https://mil.ru/era/about.htm.

Molotov, V. M. (1945). 'Доклад В. М. Молотова на Торжественном Заседании Московского Совета 6 Ноября 1945 Года' ['Report by V. M. Molotov at the Solemn Meet-ing of the Moscow Soviet on November 6, 1945']. *Voennaya Mysl'* 10–11 (November): 5–17.

Monin, M. (1953). 'Атомный Империализм' ['Atomic Imperialism']. *Voennaya Mysl'* 8 (August): 90–95.

Morgan, P. M. (2000). 'The Impact of the Revolution in Military Affairs'. *Journal of Strategic Studies* 23(1): 132–162.

Morgan, P. M. (2012). 'Elements of a General Theory of Arms Control'. Chapter 3, 15–40. In *Arms Control: History, Theory, and Policy*, edited by R. E. Williams, P. R. Viotti, Vol. 1: Foundations of Arms Control. Oxford: Praeger.

Moskalenko, K. (1969). 'Постоянная Боевая Готовность – Категория Стратегическая' ['Permanent Combat Readiness – A Strategic Category']. *Voennaya Mysl'* 1 (January): 14–20.

Movsesyan, L. (2022). 'Путин Заявил о Готовности Использовать "Все Имеющиеся Средства" для Защиты России' ['Putin Announced His Readiness to Use "All Available Means" to Protect Russia']. *RTVI.* September 21. Available at: https://rtvi.com/news/putin-zayavil-o-gotovnosti-ispolzovat-vse-imeyushhiesya-sredstva-dlya-zashhity-rossii/.

Murray, W. (1997). 'Thinking about Revolutions in Military Affairs'. *Joint Force Quarterly* 16: 69–76.

Murray, W., Knox, M. G. (2001a). 'Thinking about Revolutions in Warfare'. Chapter 1, 1–14. In *The Dynamics of Military Revolution, 1300–2050*, edited by M. G. Knox, W. Murray. Cambridge: Cambridge University Press.

Murray, W., Knox, M. G. (2001b). 'Conclusion and The Future Behind Us'. Chapter 10, 175–194. In *The Dynamics of Military Revolution, 1300–2050*, edited by M. G. Knox, W. Murray. Cambridge: Cambridge University Press.

N. D. N. [anonymized] (1861a). 'Общий Обзор Преобразований по Части Устройства Вооруженных Сил России с 1856 по 1860 Год' ['A General Review of the Transformations in the Structure of the Armed Forces of Russia from 1856 to 1860']. *Voennyi Sbornik* 17(1) (January): 3–48.

N. D. N. [anonymized] (1861b). 'Общий Обзор Преобразований по Части Устройства Вооруженных Сил России с 1856 по 1860 Год' ['A General Review of the Transformations in the Structure of the Armed Forces of Russia from 1856 to 1860']. *Voennyi Sbornik* 2 (February): 303–352.

N. L. [anonymized] (1870). 'Картечники и Их Боевое Значение' ['Mitrailleuses and Their Combat Significance']. *Voennyi Sbornik* 11 (November): 139–158.

Naryshkina, O. M. (2017). 'Тернистый Путь к "Глобальному Нулю"' ['The Thorny Path to "Global Zero"']. *Вестник Московского Университета* [*Bulletin of Moscow University*] 25(3): 67–88.

National Defence (2021). 'Россия Провела Успешные Испытания Противоспутниковой Системы' ['Russia Successfully Tests Anti-Satellite System'] 11 (November).

Nefedov, S. (2010). *История России: Факторный Анализ* [*History of Russia: Factoriography*]. Vol. 2: 'От Окончания Смуты до Февральской Революции' ['From the End of the Troubles to the February Revolution']. Moscow: The Territory of the Future.

Nepobedimy, S. P., Prokofiev, V. F. (2006). 'Некоторые Взгляды на Роль Российского Оружия в Эпоху Современных Вызовов' ['Some Views on the Role of Russian Weapons in the Age of Modern Challenges']. *Voennaya Mysl'* 6 (June): 71–74.

Neumann, I. B. (2008). 'Russia as a Great Power, 1815–2007'. *Journal of International Relations and Development* 11: 128–151.

Nikitin, S., Baranov S. (1968). 'Революция в Военном Деле и Мероприятия КПСС по Повышению Боевой Мощи Вооруженных Сил' ['The Revolution in Military Affairs and the Measures of the CPSU to Increase the Combat Power of the Armed Forces']. *Voennaya Mysl'* 6 (June): 3–14.

Nikolaev, Yu. A. (1992). 'Военно-Техническая Политика России на Современном Этапе' ['Military-Technical Policy of Russia at the Present Stage']. *Voennaya Mysl'*, Special Issue (July): 29–34.

Nikolsky, V. (1954). 'Управляемые Снаряды и Беспилотные Средства Нападения Вооруженных Сил США' ['Guided Missiles and Unmanned Means of Attack of the US Armed Forces']. *Voennaya Mysl'* 7 (July): 84–95.

Novozhilova, E. O. (2011). 'Войны Настоящего и Будущего' ['Wars of the Present and Future']. *Voennaya Mysl'* 2 (February): 3–12.

NV (2022). 'Из-за HIMARSов в РФ – Паника. Никто в Мире Больше Не Купит Российских Противоракетных Систем – Военный Эксперт' ['Because of HIMARS, in the Russian Federation – [There Is] Panic. Nobody in the World Will Buy Russian Anti-Missile Systems Anymore – Military Expert']. July 12. Available at: https://nv.ua/ukraine/events/rossiya-bolshe-ne-prodast-svoi-s-300-i-s-400-potomu-chto-oni-ne-unichtozhayut-rakety-s-himars-ekspert-novosti-50255972.html.

Oganisyan, L. D. (2017). 'Стратегические Культуры США и ЕС в Средиземноморской Политике' ['Strategic Cultures of the USA and the EU in Mediterranean Policy']. *Sovremennaya Yevropa [Contemporary Europe]* 75(3): 47–54.

Ogarkov, N. V. (1985). *История Учит Бдительности [History Teaches Vigilance]*. Moscow: Voenizdat.

Oleynikov, P. V. (2000). 'German Scientists in the Soviet Atomic Project'. *The Non-Proliferation Review* 7(2): 1–30.

Olshevsky, V. (1890). 'По Поводу Употребления Артилерии в Малых Отрядах' ['On the Use of Artillery in Small Detachments']. *Voennyi Sbornik* 1 (January): 113–117.

Orlov, V. (2021). '"Армата" Пошла в Войска: Т-14 Может Стать Основой Будущего Беспилотного Танка' ['"Armata" Was Supplied to the Troops: T-14 Can Become the Basis of a Future Unmanned Tank']. *Voyenno-Promyshlennyy Kur'yer* (December 13). Available at: https://vpk-news.ru/articles/65070.

Ostapov [Colonel Ostapov] (1890). 'Из Записок Участника Войны 1877–1878 Годов' ['From the Notes of a Participant in the War of 1877–1878']. *Voennyi Sbornik* 5 (May) 180–201.

Owen, T. C. (1985). 'The Russian Industrial Society and Tsarist Economic Policy, 1867–1905'. *The Journal of Economic History* 45(3): 587–606.

Paliy, A. I. (1991). 'Борьба с Системами Боевого Управления в Операциях Вооруженных Сил НАТО' ['Combat Control Systems in the Operations of the NATO Armed Forces']. *Voennaya Mysl'* 4 (April): 70–76.

Panaeva, A. Ya. (1986). *Воспоминания [Memoirs]*. Moscow: Pravda.

Paulsen, R. A. (1994). *The Role of US Nuclear Weapons in the Post-Cold War Era*. Alabama: Air University Press.

Pavlov, D. A., Belsky, A. N., Klimenko, O. V. (2015). 'Актуальные Вопросы Обеспечения Военной Безопасности Российской Федерации' ['Topical Issues of Ensuring the Military Security of the Russian Federation']. *Voennaya Mysl'* 1 (January): 3–10.

Payne, K. (2018). 'Artificial Intelligence: A Revolution in Strategic Affairs?' *Survival* 60(5): 7–32.

Pechorkin, V. (1962). 'О Предвидении в Советской Военной Науке' ['On Foresight in Soviet Military Science']. *Voennaya Mysl'* 12 (December): 22–33.

Pechorov, S. L. (1992). 'Ненаступательная Оборона: Выход из Тупика?' ['Non-Offensive Defence: A Way Out of the Impasse?']. *Voennaya Mysl'* 3 (March): 12–18.

Pechurov, S. L. (1997). 'Революция в Военном Деле: Взгляд с Запада' ['Revolution in Military Affairs: A View from the West']. *Voennaya Mysl'* 4 (August): 73–80.

Petrakov, A. (1871). 'О Практической Стрельбе в Полевой Артиллерии' ['On Practical Shooting in Field Artillery']. *Artilleriyskiy Zhurnal [Artillery Magazine]* 4.

Pfetsch, F. R., Rohloff, C. (2000). *National and International Conflicts, 1945–1995: New Empirical and Theoretical Approaches*. London: Routledge.

Philips, N., Hardy, C. (2002). *Discourse Analysis: Investigating Process of Social Construction*. Qualitative Research Methods Series, Vol. 50. London: SAGE Publications.

Pintner, W. M. (1984). 'The Burden of Defense in Imperial Russia, 1725–1914'. *The Russian Review* 43(3): 231–259.

Pipes, R. (1977). 'Why the Soviet Union Thinks It Could Fight and Win a Nuclear War'. *Commentary* 64 (July): 21–34.

Pipes, R. (1993). *Russia under the Bolshevik Regime*. New York: Alfred A. Knopf.

Podberezkin, A. I. (1989). 'Войны, Военные Конфликты – Не Инструмент Рациональной Политики в Современных Условиях' ['Wars, Military Conflicts are Not Instruments of Rational Politics in Modern Conditions']. *Voennaya Mysl'* 3 (March): 52–58.

Podymov, V. (2018). 'Ударная Военная "Пятилетка": Итоги Военного Строительства ВС РФ за Период 2012–17 Годов' ['Striking Military "Five-Year Plan": Results of the Military Development of the Armed Forces of the Russian Federation for the Period 2012–17']. *Obozreniye Armii i Flota [Review of the Army and Navy]* 1 (February): 30–39.

Polegaev, V. I., Alferov, V. V. (2015). 'О Неядерном Сдерживании, Его Роли и Месте в Системе Стратегического Сдерживания' ['On Non-Nuclear Deterrence, Its Role and Place in the System of Strategic Deterrence']. *Voennaya Mysl'* 7 (July): 3–10.

Politsyn, A. V. (1992). 'Взгляд на Войну Новой Эпохи' ['A Look at the War of a New Era']. *Voennaya Mysl'* 3 (March): 69–70.

Poloskov, S. (1958). 'Научное Значение Искусственных Спутников Земли' ['The Scientific Importance of Artificial Earth Satellites']. *Voennaya Mysl'* 1 (January): 31–40.

Poltorak, A. (1950). 'Американский Империализм – Злостный Нарушитель Законов и Обычаев Войны' ['American Imperialism – A Malicious Violator of the Laws and Customs of War']. *Voennaya Mysl'* 12 (December): 35–52.

Polyakova, A. (2018). 'Weapons of the Weak: Russia and AI-Driven Asymmetric Warfare'. *Brookings* (November 15). Available at: https://www.brookings.edu/research/weapons -of-the-weak-russia-and-ai-driven-asymmetric-warfare/.

Ponomarev, S. A., Poddubny, V. V., Polegaev, V. I. (2019). 'Критерии и Показатели Неядерного Сдерживания: Военный Аспект' ['Criteria and Indicators of Non-Nuclear Deterrence: A Military Aspect']. *Voennaya Mysl'* 11 (November): 97–100.

Povaliy, M. (1967). 'Развитие Советской Военной Стратегии' ['Development of the Soviet Military Strategy']. *Voennaya Mysl'* 2 (February): 63–76.

Povaliy, M. (1973). 'Некоторые Вопросы Развития Военного Искусства в Послевоенный Период' ['Some Questions on the Development of Military Art in the Post-War Period']. *Voennaya Mysl'* 1 (January): 54–65.

Pozharov, A. I. (1990). 'Военно-Экономические Аспекты Ориентации Оборонного Строительства на Качественные Параметры' ['Military-Economic Aspects of the Orientation of Defence Construction to Qualitative Parameters']. *Voennaya Mysl'* 10 (October): 39–45.

Pravda [no author] (1946). 'В Комиссии По Контролю Над Атомной Энергией' ['On the Commission for the Control of Atomic Energy']. 146 (10228): June 21.

Primgazeta [Primorskaya Gazeta] (2016). 'Дмитрий Рогозин Отметил Успехи Приморья в Авиа- и Судостроении' ['Dmitry Rogozin Noted the Success of Primorye in Aircraft- and Shipbuilding']. June 24. Available at: https://primgazeta.ru/news/dmitry -rogozin-noted-the-success-of-primorye-in-aircraft-and-shipbuilding.

Provorov, K. (1972). 'Ракетно-Космические Средства Нападения и Проблемы Борьбы с Ним' ['Rocket-Space Means of Assault and Problems of Combating It']. *Voennaya Mysl'* 5 (May): 92–96.

Pustogarov, V. V. (2000). 'Our Martens: F. F. Martens, International Lawyer and Architect of Peace,' edited and translated by W. E. Butler. The Hague: Kluwer Law International.

Puzenkin, I. V., Mikhailov, V. V. (2015). 'Роль Информационно-Психологических Средств в Обеспечении Обороноспособности Государства' ['The Role of Information and Psychological Means in Ensuring the Defence Capability of the State']. *Voennaya Mysl'* 7 (July): 11–15.

Ramazanov, Zh. Sh. (2008). 'Азиатская Модель Как Вторая Модель Рынка' ['The Asian Model as the Second Market Model']. *Izvestiya Tomskogo Politekhnicheskogo Universiteta [Bulletin of the Tomsk Polytechnic University]* 312(6): 68–71.

Raska, M. (2016). *Military Innovation in Small States: Creating a Reverse Asymmetry.* New York: Routledge.

Report (1879). Отчет Главного Комитета по Устройству и Образованию Войск с Октября 1874 Года по Октябрь 1878 Года [Report of the Main Committee on the Organization and Formation of Troops from October 1874 to October 1878]. St Petersburg.

Reporter [Репортёр] (2020). 'Заявлено о Потере Одного Танка Т-14 "Армата" в Сирии' ['One T-14 "Armata" Tank Reported to Be Lost in Syria']. April 30. Available at: https://topcor.ru/14417-zajavleno-o-potere-odnogo-tanka-t-14-armata-v-sirii.html.

Reuters (2020). 'Russia Releases Secret Footage of 1961 "Tsar Bomba" Hydrogen Blast'. August 28. Available at: https://www.reuters.com/article/us-russia-nuclear-tsar-bomba-idUSKBN25O1U9.

Reuters (2022). 'Russia Says Destroyed Large Depot with Western Weapons in Ukraine, Interfax Reports'. June 12. Available at: https://www.reuters.com/world/europe/russia-says-destroyed-large-depot-with-western-weapons-ukraine-ifx-2022-06-12/.

Reznichenko, V. (1972). 'Характерные Черты и Способы Ведения Наступления' ['Characteristic Features and Methods of Conducting an Offensive']. *Voennaya Mysl'* 1 (January): 52–60.

RG [*Rossiyskaya Gazeta*] (2014). 'Путин: События в Крыму Показали Новые Возможности ВС России' ['Putin: Events in Crimea Showed New Capabilities of the Russian Armed Forces']. March 28. Available at: https://rg.ru/2014/03/28/vozmozhnosti-anons.html.

RIA FAN [Federal News Agency] (2017). 'ВКС РФ в Сирии Реализовали Принцип "Одна Цель – Одна Бомба"' ['Russian Aerospace Forces in Syria Implemented the Principle of "One Target – One Bomb"']. November 7. Available at: https://riafan.ru/994185-vks-rf-v-sirii-realizovali-princip-odna-cel-odna-bomba.

RIA Novosti (2022). 'Кадыров Анонсировал Отправку на Украину Новых Подразделений из Чечни' ['Kadyrov Announced the Departure of New Units from Chechnya to Ukraine']. March 21. Available at: https://ria.ru/20220321/kadyrov-1779303376.html.

Rodkin, S. (1963). 'Контрудары в Современных Операциях' ['Counterattacks in Modern Operations']. *Voennaya Mysl'* 2 (February): 48–51.

Roger, Z. G. (1978/1979). 'The Economics of Arms Control'. *International Security* 3(3) (Winter 1978–1979): 94–125.

Rogers, C. J. (2000). '"Military Revolutions" and "Revolutions in Military Affairs": A Historian's Perspective'. Chapter 2, 21–36. In *Toward a Revolution in Military Affairs?*, edited by T. Gongora, H. von Riekhoff. *Defense and Security at the Dawn of the Twenty-First Century.* Westport: Greenwood Press.

Romanchuk, A. V., Dulnev, P. A., Orlyansky, V. I. (2020). 'Изменения Характера Вооруженной Борьбы По Опыту Военных Конфликтов Начала XXI Века' ['Changes in the Nature of Armed Struggle Based on the Experience of Military Conflicts at the Beginning of the 21st Century']. *Voennaya Mysl'* 4 (April): 66–81.

Romanov, V. V., Chigak, V. P. (1991). 'О Применении Космических Средств в Районе Персидского Залива' ['On the Use of Space Assets in the Persian Gulf Region']. *Voennaya Mysl'* 3 (March): 76–80.

Rose, G. (1998). 'Neoclassical Realism and Theories of Foreign Policy'. *World Politics* 51(1): 144–172.

Rudyuk, V. K. (1991). 'О Двух Подходах к Развитию Противовоздушной Обороны' ['On Two Approaches to the Development of Air Defence']. *Voennaya Mysl'* 11–12 (December): 61–65.

Rybachenok, I. S. (2005). *Россия и Первая Конференция Мира 1899 Года в Гааге* [*Russia and the First Peace Conference of 1899 in The Hague*]. Moscow.

Rykhtik, M. I. (2003). 'Стратегическая Культура и Новая Концепция Национальной Безопасности США' ['Strategic Culture and a New Concept of US National Security]. *Vestnik Nizhegorodskogo Gosudarstvennogo Universiteta im. N. I. Lobachevskogo* [*Bulletin of the Nizhny Novgorod State University named by N. I. Lobachevsky*] 1: 203–219.

Saifetdinov, H. I. (2014). 'Информационное Противоборство в Военной Сфере' ['Information Confrontation in the Military Sphere']. *Voennaya Mysl'* 7 (July): 38–41.

Sankaran, J. (2022). 'Russia's Anti-Satellite Weapons: An Asymmetric Response to U.S. Aerospace Superiority'. *Arms Control Association* (March). Available at: https://www.armscontrol.org/act/2022-03/features/russias-anti-satellite-weapons-asymmetric-response-us-aerospace-superiority.

Satterfield, G. (2010). 'Revolution in Military Affairs (RMA)', 261–267. In *The Military-Industrial Complex and American Society*, edited by S. M. Pavelec. Santa Barbara, California: ABC Clio.

Schelling T. C., Halperin, M. H. (1961/1985). *Strategy and Arms Control*. Washington: Pergamon-Brassey's. Originally published 1961. Reissued 1985.

Schmemann, S. (1993). 'Russia Drops Pledge of No First Use of Atom Arms'. *The New York Times* (November 4). Available at: https://www.nytimes.com/1993/11/04/world/russia-drops-pledge-of-no-first-use-of-atom-arms.html.

Schmitt, E., Gibbons-Neff, T., Ismay, J. (2022). 'As Russia Runs Low on Drones, Iran Plans to Step In, U.S. Officials Say'. *The New York Times*. July 17. Available at: https://www.nytimes.com/2022/07/17/us/politics/drones-ukraine-russia-iran.html.

Scott, H. F. (1992). 'Soviet Military Doctrine in the Nuclear Age'. In *Soviet Military Doctrine from Lenin to Gorbachev: 1915–1991*, edited by W. C. Frank, P. S. Gillette. Greenwood Press.

Scoville, H. (1976). 'A Different Approach to Arms Control – Reciprocal Unilateral Restraint'. Chapter 9, 170–175. In *Arms Control and Technological Innovation*, edited by D. Carlton, C. Schaerf. New York: John Wiley&Sons.

Sedin, L. (1962). 'Быть Начеку, Держать Порох Сухим!' ['Be Alert, Keep the Gunpowder Dry!']. *Voennaya Mysl'* 12 (December): 16–21.

Selivanov, V. V., Ilyin, Yu. D. (2019). 'Методические Основы Формирования Асимметричных Ответов в Военно-Техническом Противоборстве с Высокотехнологичным Противником' ['Methodological Foundations for the Formation of Asymmetric Responses in Military-Technical Confrontation with a High-Tech Enemy']. *Voennaya Mysl'* 2 (February): 5–14.

Selivanov, V. V., Ilyin, Yu. D. (2020a). 'О Комплексировании Средств и Способов Подготовки Асимметричных Ответов при Обеспечении Военной Безопасности'

['On the Integration of Means and Methods for Preparing Asymmetric Responses While Ensuring Military Security']. *Voennaya Mysl'* 1 (January): 48–60.

Selivanov, V. V., Ilyin, Yu. D. (2020b). 'Методика Комплексной Подготовки Асимметричных Ответов при Программно-Целевом Планировании Развития Вооружения' ['Methodology for the Integrated Preparation of Asymmetric Responses in Program-Target Planning for the Development of Weapons']. *Voennaya Mysl'* 2 (February): 53–58.

Sharafutdinova, G. (2011). *Political Consequences of Crony Capitalism inside Russia*. Notre Dame: University of Notre Dame Press.

Shavrov, I. (1975). 'Мировая Ядерная Война – Главная Опасность для Человечества' ['World Nuclear War is the Main Danger to Mankind']. *Voennaya Mysl'* 6 (June): 11–22.

Shevchenko, V. (2023). 'Ukraine War: Russia Goes Back to Prisons to Feed Its War Machine'. BBC News. October 26. Available at: https://www.bbc.com/news/world-europe-67175566.

Shishkin, N. K. (1990). 'Борьба за Огневое Превосходство: Проблемы и Пути Решения' ['The Struggle for Fire Superiority: Problems and Solutions']. *Voennaya Mysl'* 10 (October): 18–22.

Shoaib, A. (2022). 'Ukraine's Drones Are Becoming Increasingly Ineffective as Russia Ramps Up Its Electronic Warfare and Air Defenses'. *Insider*. July 3. Available at: https://www.businessinsider.com/drones-russia-ukraine-war-electronic-warfare-2022-7.

Shoumikhin, A. (2009). 'Change and Continuity in Russian Arms Control'. *Comparative Strategy* 28: 140–153.

Shoumikhin, A. (2011). 'Nuclear Weapons in Russian Strategy and Doctrine'. In *Russian Nuclear Weapons: Past, Present, and Future*, edited by S. J. Blank. Strategic Studies Institute Book.

Shtrick, S. (1968). ['Окружение и Уничтожение Противника при Ведении Боевых Действий Без Применения Ядерного Оружия' ['Encirclement and Destruction of the Enemy in the Conduct of Hostilities Without the Use of Nuclear Weapons']. *Voennaya Mysl'*, 1 (January): 58–66.

Simonov, N. (2000). 'New Postwar Branches (2): The Nuclear Industry'. In *The Soviet Defence-Industry Complex from Stalin to Khrushchev*, edited by J. Barber, M. Harrison. London: Macmillan Press.

Sinyatkin, D. A., Bozhkov, A. Yu., Gorchakov, M. A. (2018). 'Создание Многофункциональных Беспилотных Летательных Аппаратов: Пути Решения Проблемных Вопросов' ['Creation of Multifunctional Unmanned Aerial Vehicles: Ways of Solving Problematic Issues']. *Voennaya Mysl'* 10 (October): 86–91.

SIPRI [Stockholm International Peace Research Institute] (2018). *Trends in International Arms Transfers*. Fact Sheet (March). Available at: https://www.sipri.org/sites/default/files /2018-03/fssipri_at2017_0.pdf.

Sitnov, A. P., Rakhmanov, A. L. (1999). 'Основа Системного Развития Вооружения и Военной Техники России' ['The Basis for the Systemic Development of Weapons and Military Equipment in Russia']. *Voennaya Mysl'* 5 (October): 2–5.

Sizov, Yu. G., Skokov, A. L. (1992). 'Значение Высокоточного Оружия в Современной Войне' ['The Importance of Precision Weapons in Modern Warfare']. *Voennaya Mysl'* 12 (December): 37–42.

Skovorodkin, M. (1963). 'О Влиянии Ракетного Оружия на Военное Искусство' ['On the Influence of Rocket Weapons on Military Art']. *Voennaya Mysl'* 5 (May): 14–26.

Slipchenko, V. I. (1999). *Война Будущего. Шестое Поколение.* [*War of the Future. The Sixth Generation.*]. Moscow: Московский Общественный Научный Фонд [Moscow Non-Governmental Science Foundation].

Sloan, E. (2002). *The Revolution in Military Affairs: Implications for Canada and NATO*. Montreal: McGill-Queen's University Press.

Slonimsky, L. Z. (1898). 'Вооруженный Мир и Проекты Разоружения' ['Armed Peace and Disarmament Projects']. *Vestnik Evropy* [*Bulletin of Europe*] 5: 778–792.

Snegovaya, M., Petrov, K. (2022). 'Long Soviet Shadows: The Nomenklatura Ties of Putin Elites'. *Post-Soviet Affairs* 38(4): 329–348.

Snyder, J. (1977). *The Soviet Strategic Culture: Implications for Limited Nuclear Operations.* No. R-2154-AF. Santa Monica: RAND Corporation (September).

Snyder J. (1994). 'Russian Backwardness and the Future of Europe'. *Daedalus* 123(2): 179–201.

Sokirko, V. (2022a). 'Американские HIMARS Станут Первой Целью для России на Украине' ['American HIMARS Will Be the First Target for Russia in Ukraine']. *Gazeta.ru.* June 1. Available at: https://m.gazeta.ru/army/2022/06/01/14934296.shtml.

Sokirko, V. (2022b). 'Рецепт Против Американских HIMARS на Украине Есть. Это "Торнадо-С"' ['There Is a Recipe Against American HIMARS in Ukraine. This is "Tornado-S"']. *Gazeta.ru.* July 13. Available at: https://www.gazeta.ru/army/2022/07/13/15117332.shtml?updated.

Sokolovsky, V. D. (ed.) (1963). *Военная Стратегия* [*Military Strategy*]. 2nd edition. Moscow: Voenizdat.

Sokov, N. (2021). 'US-Soviet/Russian Cooperation on Article VI of the NPT', 187–233. In: Bidgood, S., Potter, W.C. (eds) *End of an Era: The United States, Russia, and Nuclear Non-proliferation.* Monterey: James Martin Center for Nonproliferation Studies, Middlebury Institute of International Studies (August).

Spegele, B. (2022). 'Chinese Firms Are Selling Russia Goods Its Military Needs to Keep Fighting in Ukraine'. *The Wall Street Journal.* July 15. Available at: https://www.wsj.com/articles/chinese-firms-are-selling-russia-goods-its-military-needs-to-keep-fighting-in-ukraine-11657877403.

Stalin, I. V. (1946/1997). 'Ответы на Вопросы, Заданные Московским Корреспондентом "Сандей Таймс" А. Вертом, Полученные 17 сентября 1946 года' ['Answers to Questions Put by the Moscow Correspondent of *The Sunday Times* A. Werth, Received on September 17, 1946']. Source: Stalin, I. V. (1997) *Essays*, Vol. 16, 37–39. Moscow: Writer.

Stepshin, M. P., Anikonov, A. N. (2021). 'Развитие Вооружения, Военной и Специальной Техники и Их Влияние на Характер Будущих Войн' ['Development of Weapons, Military and Special Equipment and Their Influence on the Nature of Future Wars']. *Voennaya Mysl'* 12 (December): 35–43.

Sterlin, A. E., Protasov, A. A., Kreidin, S. V. (2019). 'Современные Трансформации Концепций и Силовых Инструментов Стратегического Сдерживания' ['Modern Transformations of the Concepts and Power Tools of Strategic Deterrence']. *Voennaya Mysl'* 8 (August): 7–17.

Sviridova, A. (2019). 'Векторы Развития Военной Стратегии' ['Vectors of the Development of Military Strategy']. *Krasnaya Zvezda* (March 4). Available at: http://redstar.ru/vektory-razvitiya-voennoj-strategii/.

Szakonyi, D. (2020). *Russia as a Failed Developmental State: Economic Policy and Predation under Sanctions.* Stanford: Freeman Spogli Institute for International Studies (September). Available at: https://fsi-live.s3.us-west-1.amazonaws.com/s3fs-public/memo_4_-_szakonyi.pdf.

Sistema.com (2022). 'Ad-Hoc Notice'. May 4. Available at: https://sistema.com/press/pressreleases/ad-hoc-notice_3.

TASS (2021a). 'Шойгу Заявил, что Государственные Испытания Гиперзвуковой Ракеты "Циркон" Завершаются' ['Shoigu Said that State Tests of the "Zircon" Hypersonic Missile are Being Completed']. December 21. Available at: https://tass.ru/armiya-i-opk/13258039.

TASS (2021b). 'Доля Призывников в Российской Армии Сократилась Примерно до 30%. Остальные Места Укомплектованы Военнослужащими по Контракту' ['The Share of Conscripts in the Russian Army Has Fallen to About 30%. The Rest of the Places are Staffed by Military Personnel Under Contract']. March 15. Available at: https://tass.ru/armiya-i-opk/10903667?utm_source=google.com&utm_medium=organic&utm_campaign=google.com&utm_referrer=google.com.

TASS (2022). 'Partial Mobilization Applies to Reservists with Military Experience, Specialty'. September 21. Available at: https://tass.com/defense/1511049?utm_source=google.com&utm_medium=organic&utm_campaign=google.com&utm_referrer=google.com.

Thompson, M. J. (2011). 'Military Revolutions and Revolutions in Military Affairs: Accurate Descriptions of Change or Intellectual Constructs?' *Strata* 3: 82–108.

Tikhomirov, A. V., Bykov, A. A. (1978). 'Крылатые Ракеты – Новый Вид Стратегического Оружия' ['Cruise Missiles – A New Type of Strategic Weapon']. *Voennaya Mysl'* 12 (December): 77–85.

Toffler, A., Toffler, H. (1993). *War and Anti-War: Making Sense of Today's Global Chaos*. New York: Warner Books.

Tolchenov, M. (1949). 'Американская Печать о Характере Будущей Войны' ['American Press about the Nature of the Future War']. *Voennaya Mysl'* 6 (June): 68–79.

Tolshmyakov, V. I., Orlova, T. V. (2020). 'Военно-Политические Аспекты Обеспечения Военной Безопасности Российской Федерации' ['Military-Political Aspects of Ensuring the Military Security of the Russian Federation']. *Voennaya Mysl'* 11: 33–40.

Tolstyakov, O. (1964). 'Гражданская Оборона в Ракетно-Ядерной Войне' ['Civil Defence in a Nuclear-Rocket War']. *Voennaya Mysl'* 1 (January): 34–42.

Tonkikh, F. P. (1985). 'Соотношение Человека и Техники в Войне' ['The Ratio of Man and Technology in War']. *Voennaya Mysl'* 3 (March): 57–63.

Tretyak, I. M. (1990). 'Оборонная Достаточность и Противовоздушная Оборона' ['Defence Sufficiency and Air Defence']. *Voennaya Mysl'* 12 (December): 2–11.

Trofimov, B. (1970). 'Баллистические Ракеты с Многозаряднготи Головными Частями MIRV и Принципы Их Боевого Применения' ['Ballistic missiles With Multiply Charged warheads (MIRV) and the Principles of Their Combat Use']. *Voennaya Mysl'* 11 (November): 81–84.

Tsygankov, A. P. (2022). *Russian Realism: Defending 'Derzhava' in International Relations*. New York: Routledge.

Tyushkevich, S. (1969). 'Методология Соотношения Сил в Войне' ['Methodology of the Correlation of Forces in War']. *Voennaya Mysl'* 6 (June): 26–37.

Ustinov, D. F. (1982). *Служим Родине, Делу Коммунизма* [*We Serve the Motherland, the Cause of Communism*]. Moscow: Voenizdat.

Vagts, D. F. (2000). 'The Hague Conventions and Arms Control'. *The American Journal of International Law* 94(1): 31–41.

Vakhrushev, V. A. (1999). 'Локальные Войны и Вооруженные Конфликты: Характер и Влияние на Военное Искусство' ['Local Wars and Armed Conflicts: The Nature and Influence on Military Art']. *Voennaya Mysl'* 4 (August): 20–28.

van Creveld, M. (1991). *Technology and War: From 2000 B.C. to the Present*. New York: Free Press.

Vannovsky, P. (1861). 'Несколько Слов об Обучении в Войсках Стрельбе в Цель' ['A Few Words on Target Shooting Training of the Troops']. *Voennyi Sbornik* 2 (February): 445–456.

Varfolomeeva, A. (2018). 'Signaling Strength: Russia's Real Syria Success is Electronic Warfare Against the US'. *The Defense Post* (May 1). Available at: https://www.thedefensepost.com/2018/05/01/russia-syria-electronic-warfare/.

Vasiliev, I. (1974). 'Scientific-Technical Progress and the Development of Military Affairs' ['Научно-Технический Прогресс и Развитие Военного Дела']. *Voennaya Mysl'* 2 (February): 90–94.

Verbruggen, M. (2019). 'The Role of Civilian Innovation in the Development of Lethal Autonomous Weapon Systems'. *Global Policy* 10(3): 338–342.

Vesti.ru [Вести.ru] (2015). 'Демонстрация Возможностей: Чем и Из Чего Россия Ударила по ИГИЛ с Каспийского Моря' ['Demonstration of Capabilities: With What and from What Did Russia Hit ISIS From the Caspian Sea']. October 7. Available at: https://www.vesti.ru/article/1745906.

Vestnik Evropy [no author] (1898). 'Иностранное Обозрение' ['Foreign Review']. 5: 380–394.

Vestnik Evropy [no author] (1899a). 'Иностранное Обозрение' ['Foreign Review']. 1: 807–816.

Vestnik Evropy [no author] (1899b). 'Иностранное Обозрение' ['Foreign Review']. 3 (June): 798–810.

Vestnik Evropy [no author] (1899c). 'Иностранное Обозрение' ['Foreign Review']. 5 (September): 368–380.

Vetrov, Yu. K. (1984). 'Высокоточное Оружие и Развитие Тактики Ударной Авиации' ['Precision Weapons and the Development of Strike Aviation Tactics']. *Voennaya Mysl'* 2 (February): 46–55.

Vetrov, Yu. K. (1985). 'Высокоточное Оружие и Развитие Тактики Истребительной Авиации' ['Precision Weapons and the Development of Fighter Aviation Tactics']. *Voennaya Mysl'* 6 (June): 25–34.

Vishnevsky, E., Golomb, Z. (1970). 'Военные Действия Без Применения Ядерного Оружия' ['Military Action Without the Use of Nuclear Weapons']. *Voennaya Mysl'* 2 (February): 62–70.

Voennaya Mysl' [no author] (1951). 'Ответ Товарища И. В. Сталина Корреспонденту "Правды" Насчет Атомного Оружия' ['Answer of Comrade I. V. Stalin to the "Pravda" Correspondent About Atomic Weapons']. 10 (October): 3–4.

Voennaya Mysl' [no author] (1969). 'Военная Стратегия – Основной Элемент Военной Науки и Военного Искусства' ['Military Strategy is the Main Element of Military Science and Military Art']. 11 (November): 56–63.

Voennaya Mysl' [no author] (1971). 'Советская Военная Наука – Важный Фактор Оборонного Могущества Страны' ['Soviet Military Science is an Important Factor of the Country's Defence Power']. 2 (February): 3–15.

Voennaya Mysl' [no author] (1990a). 'О Военной Доктрине СССР (Проект)' ['On the Military Doctrine of the USSR (Project)']. Special Issue (June): 24–31.

Voennaya Mysl' [no author] (1990b). 'Концепция Военной Реформы (Проект)' ['Military Reform Concept (Draft)']. Special Issue (June): 3–23.

Voennaya Mysl' [no author] (1990c). 'Военная Реформа: Опыт, Проблемы, Перспективы' ['Military Reform: Experience, Problems, Perspectives']. 4 (April): 30–41.

Voennaya Mysl' [no author] (1992). 'Основы Военной Доктрины России (Проект)' ['Fundamentals of the Russian Military Doctrine (Draft)']. Special Issue (May): 3–9.

Voennyi Sbornik [no author] (1863). 'Русское Военное Обозрение' ['Russian Military Review']. 34: 515–570.

Voennyi Sbornik [no author] (1868). 'Русское Военное Обозрение' ['Russian Military Review']. 7 (July): 37–61.

Von der Hoven, A. (1883). 'Новейшие Усовершенствования Ручного Огнестрельного Оружия' ['Recent Improvements in Hand Firearms']. *Voennyi Sbornik* 6 (June): 252–271.

Von-Vocht [partially anonymized] (1890). 'Новое Вооружение и Влияние Его на Боевые Действия Пехоты' ['New Armaments and Their Influence on Infantry Combat']. *Voennyi Sbornik* 10: 258–282.

Vorobyev, I. N. (1984a). 'Новое Оружие – Новая Тактика' ['New Weapons – New Tactics']. *Voennaya Mysl'* 2 (February): 34–45.

Vorobyev, I. N. (1984b). 'Новое Оружие – Новая Тактика' ['New Weapons – New Tactics']. *Voennaya Mysl'* 6 (June): 47–59.

Vorobyev, I. N. (1992). 'Уроки Войны в Зоне Персидского Залива' ['Lessons of the War in the Persian Gulf Zone']. *Voennaya Mysl'* 4–5 (May): 67–74.

Vorobyev, I. N., Kiselev, V. A. (2006a). 'Стратегия Непрямых Действий в Новом Облике' ['The Strategy of Indirect Actions in a New Look']. *Voennaya Mysl'* 9 (September): 2–10.

Vorobyev, I. N., Kiselev, V. A. (2006b). 'Высокоточное Сражение' ['High-Precision Combat']. *Voennaya Mysl'* 11 (November): 15–22.

Vorobyev, I.N., Kiselev, V. A. (2011). 'От Современной Тактики к Тактике Сетецентрических Действий' ['From Modern Tactics to the Tactics of Network-Centric Actions']. *Voennaya Mysl'* 8 (August): 19–27.

Walt, S. M. (1987). *The Origins of Alliances*. Ithaca, New York: Cornell University Press.

Walt, S. M. (2018). 'The World Wants You to Think Like a Realist'. *Foreign Policy*. May 30. Available at: https://foreignpolicy.com/2018/05/30/the-world-wants-you-to-think-like-a-realist/.

Waltz, K. N. (1979). *Theory of International Politics*. Reading, MA: Addison-Wesley.

Weiss, L. (2000). 'Developmental States in Transition: Adapting, Dismantling, Innovating, Not "Normalizing"'. *The Pacific Review* 13(1): 21–55.

Wendt, A. (1998). 'On Constitution and Causation in International Relations'. *Review of International Studies* 24(5): 101–118.

Williams, I. (2017/2018). 'The Russia – NATO A2/AD Environment.' *Missile Threat*. Center for Strategic and International Studies. Published January 3, 2017. Modified November 29, 2018. Available at: https://missilethreat.csis.org/russia-nato-a2ad-environment/.

Witteried, P. F. (1972). 'A Strategy of Flexible Response'. *Parameters* 2(1): 2–16. Carlisle, PA: US Army War College. No. 17013–5238.

Wolfe, B. D. (1967). 'Backwardness and Industrialization in Russian History and Thought'. *Slavic Review* 26(2): 177–203.

Woo-Cumings, M. (1999). 'Introduction: Chalmers Johnson and the Politics of Nationalism and Development'. In *The Developmental State*, edited by M. Woo-Cumings. Ithaca, New York: Cornell University Press.

Woolf, A. F. (2022). *Russia's Nuclear Weapons: Doctrine, Forces, and Modernization*. Congressional Research Service, No. R45861 (April). Available at: https://sgp.fas.org/crs/nuke/R45861.pdf.

Yakovlev, V. N. (ed.) (1999). *Ракетный Щит Отечества* [*Missile Shield of the Fatherland*]. Moscow: The Central Publishing and Printing Complex of Strategic Rocket Forces (Russian abbreviation: ЦИПК РВСН).

Zaionchkovsky, P. A. (1952). *Военные Реформы 1860–1870 Годов в России* [*Military Reforms of 1860–1870 in Russia*]. Moscow: Moscow University Press.

Zaionchkovsky, P. A. (1973). *Самодержавие и Русская Армия на Рубеже XIX–XX Столетий 1881–1903* [*Autocracy and the Russian Army at the Turn of the XIX–XX Centuries 1881–1903*]. Moscow: Издательство Мысль [Publishing House Mysl].

Zakharov, A. N. (1991). 'Тенденции Развития Вооруженной Борьбы' ['Trends in the Development of Armed Struggle']. *Voennaya Mysl'* 11–12 (December): 9–15.

Zakharov, A. N. (1999). 'Операция "Лис Пустыни": Развитие Стратегии и Оперативного Искусства' ['Operation "Desert Fox": The Development of Strategy and Operational Art']. *Voennaya Mysl'* 5 (October): 67–70.

Zaretsky, B. L. (2015). 'Воздушно-Космическая Безопасность России' ['Aerospace Security of Russia']. *Voennaya Mysl'* 9 (September): 23–28.

Zeddeler, L. (1876). 'Влияние Оружия, Заряжающегося с Казны, на Огонь, Бой и Боевую Подготовку Пехоты' ['The Effect of Breech-Loading Weapons on Fire, Combat, and Infantry Training']. *Voennyi Sbornik* 1 (January): 59–90.

Zeddeler, L. (1878). 'Несколько Практических Выводов из Нашей Последней Войны' ['Some Practical Conclusions from Our Last War']. *Voennyi Sbornik* 5 (May): 65–78.

Zeman, Z. A. B. (2000). 'Czech Uranium and Stalin's Bomb'. *Historian* 67: 11–17.

Zemskov, V. (1969a). 'Характерные Особенности Современных Войн и Возможные Способы Их Ведения' ['Characteristic Features of Modern Wars and Possible Methods of Their Conduct']. *Voennaya Mysl'* 7 (July): 20–27.

Zemskov, V. (1969b). 'Войны Современной Эпохи' ['Wars of the Modern Age']. *Voennaya Mysl'* 5 (May): 51–62.

Zevin, L. (2008). 'Может ли Россия Стать "Евроазиатским Тигром"'? ['Can Russia Become a "Eurasian Tiger"'?] Review on Alexandrov (2007). *Vostok [East]* 3: 156–162.

Zgirovskaya, E. (2016). '"Перекуем Мечи на Томографы": Предприятия Оборонки Займутся Производством Медицинской Техники' ['"Let's Forge Swords for Tomographs": Defence Industry Enterprises Will Be Engaged in the Production of Medical Equipment']. *Gazeta.ru.* July 1. Available at: https://www.gazeta.ru/army/2016/07/01/8352941 .shtml?updated.

Zheltikov, I., Polyakov, N. (1966). 'К Вопросу о Роли Человека и Техники в Войне' ['On the Question of the Role of Man and Technology in War']. *Voennaya Mysl'* 11 (November): 53–60.

Zhuravlev, A. A. (1990). 'О Воздушно-Наземной Операции' ['On the Air-Land Operation']. *Voennaya Mysl'* 6 (June): 78–80.

Zimmerman, A. (1859). 'Заметки о Крымской Войне' ['Notes on the Crimean War']. *Voennyi Sbornik* 4 (April): 379–453.

Zysk, K. (2021a). 'Defence Innovation and the 4th Industrial Revolution in Russia.' *Journal of Strategic Studies* 44(4): 543–571.

Zysk, K. (2021b). 'Military R&D, Innovation and Breakthrough Technologies'. In *Advanced Military Technology in Russia Capabilities and Implications*, edited by S. Bendett, M. Boulègue, R. Connolly, M. Konaev, P. Podvig, K. Zysk. Chatham House (September). Available at: https://www.chathamhouse.org/sites/default/files/2021-09/2021-09-23-advanced -military-technology-in-russia-bendett-et-al.pdf.

1tv.ru (2022). 'Добровольцы Перед Отправкой в Донбасс Тренируются на Базе Спецназа в Чеченской Республике' ['Volunteers Train at the Base of Special Forces in the Chechen Republic Before Being Sent to Donbass']. June 19. Available at: https://www.1tv .ru/news/2022-06-19/431512-dobrovoltsy_pered_otpravkoy_v_donbass_treniruyutsya _na_baze_spetsnaza_v_chechenskoy_respublike.

List of Interviews[24]

Interview no. 1
Name: **Graeme P. Herd**
Affiliation: George C. Marshall European Center for Security Studies
Venue: Zoom
Date: 12 January 2022
Time (Prague): 12:00–13:12

Interview no. 2
Name: **Nikolai Sokov**
Affiliation: James Martin Center for Nonproliferation Studies & Vienna Center for Disarmament and Non-Proliferation
Venue: Zoom
Date: 13 January 2022
Time (Prague): 10:00–11:18

Interview no. 3
Name: **Simon Miles**
Affiliation: Duke University
Venue: Zoom
Date: 17 January 2022
Time (Prague): 19:00–19:57

Interview no. 4
Name: **Stephen Blank**
Affiliation: Foreign Policy Research Institute
Venue: Skype
Date: 17 January 2022
Time (Prague): 21:30–22:15

---

24 All interviewees gave their voluntary consent to be cited in this work.

Interview no. 5
Name: **Samuel Bendett**
Affiliation: CNA
Venue: Zoom
Date: 19 January 2022
Time (Prague): 14:30–14:57

Interview no. 6
Name: **Iver B. Neumann**
Affiliation: Fridtjof Nansen Institute
Venue: Zoom
Date: 19 January 2022
Time (Prague): 19:00–19:27

Interview no. 7
Name: **Mark Galeotti**
Affiliation: UCL School of Slavonic and East European Studies,
    Royal United Services Institute (RUSI) & Mayak Intelligence
Venue: Zoom
Date: 26 January 2022
Time (Prague): 15:00–15:35

Interview no. 8
Name: **Dmitry Gorenburg**
Affiliation: CNA
Venue: Zoom
Date: 31 January 2022
Time (Prague): 15:00–15:20

Interview no. 9[25]
Name: **Vasily A. Veselov**
Affiliation: Moscow State University
Venue: Zoom
Date: 03 February 2022
Time (Prague): 14:00–15:05

Interview no. 10
Name: **Scott Keefer**
Affiliation: Bournemouth University
Venue: Zoom
Date: 23 February 2022
Time (Prague): 13:00–13:20

---

25 This conversation was not originally conducted in an interview format. It was a professional consultation as part of the author's remote internship pursued at that moment at Moscow State University. Having agreed to be cited in this text afterwards, Vasily A. Veselov is listed as an interviewee for consistency.